Roxanne Wheeler

Seasons of a Woman's Life

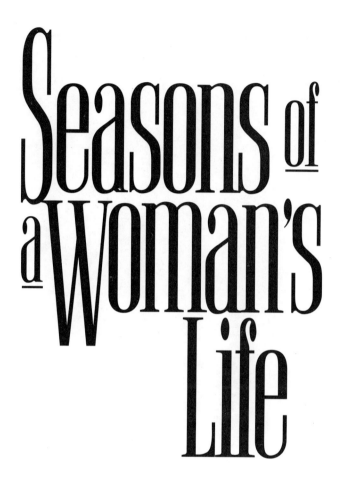

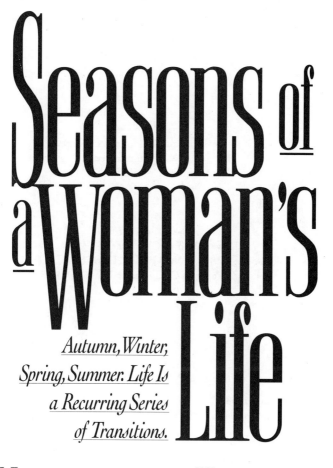

Seasons of a Woman's Life

Autumn, Winter, Spring, Summer. Life Is a Recurring Series of Transitions.

NORMAJEAN HINDERS

BROADMAN
& HOLMAN
PUBLISHERS

Nashville, Tennessee

4261-42
0-8054-6142-6
Dewey Decimal Classification: 305.4
Subject Heading: WOMEN/CHRISTIAN LIFE
Library of Congress Card Catalog Number: 94-3359

Library of Congress Cataloging-in-Publication Data

Hinders, Normajean., 1943–
    Seasons of a woman's life/ by Normajean Hinders
        p. cm.
    ISBN 0-8054-6142-6
    1. Women—Psychology. 2. Life change events. 3. Women—Religious
life. I. Title.
HQ1206.H52   1994
155.6'33—dc20   94-3359
                                                  CIP

All personal stories in this book are used by permission. Names have been changed to protect confidentiality.

*In loving memory of and deepest
gratitude to my
parents,
Fred and Lois Berger*

Contents

Acknowledgments   *ix*

Introduction   *1*

Part I   Transitions

Chapter One   For Everything There Is a Season   9
Chapter Two   A Season of Growth   17
Chapter Three   A Season of Change   29
Chapter Four   A Time for Every Purpose   37

Part II   The Winter Woman

Chapter Five   A Season of Loss   51
Chapter Six   A Season of Grief   65
Chapter Seven   The Winter of Life   81

Part III   The Spring Woman

Chapter Eight   The Nature of New Beginnings   97
Chapter Nine   The Freedom of Forgiveness   107
Chapter Ten   A Season of Awakenings   121

Part IV   The Summer Woman

Chapter Eleven   A Season of Balance   141
Chapter Twelve   A Season of Expression   157
Chapter Thirteen   Reflections of Worth   167

Part V   The Autumn Woman

Chapter Fourteen   As the Years Turn   185
Chapter Fifteen   Be Still and Know   201
Chapter Sixteen   A Season of Harvest   215

Epilogue   *229*

Notes   *233*

Acknowledgments

❧

A writer friend of mine told me writing a book and giving birth to a baby are similar events. However, a book keeps you up before its birth; a child afterwards. I wish to thank numerous mid-wives who labored with me in bringing this book to life.

To my husband, Duane:

My deepest appreciation to you for your unflagging confidence, love, and encouragement throughout this entire adventure. Without your moral support, your faith in me when I had little in myself, and your incredible assistance on the computer, I could not have accomplished this task.

To my daughter, Gretchen:

Thank you for your love and support with drawing the grief-recovery wheel and for your willingness to listen while I figured out my thoughts throughout this project. Blessings to you in all of your seasons.

To my son, Todd:

For your willingness to eat frozen dinners, empty the dishwasher, and help with meals which freed me to write, and for your love and confidence, I am very appreciative. Thank you!

To Sharon, Bonnie, and Jon:

For praying, reading manuscript variations, and challenging me always to keep moving and growing, thank you.

To Edie and Bob Munger and Joan and Bud Dermody:

I greatly appreciate your provision of a safe haven for me when I needed a place to retreat to research and write.

To Vicki:

Thank you for believing in this project and for your gentle teaching.

To my Covenant group, other friends and family who supported me in prayer, walks, talks and other acts of encouragement,

I couldn't have done it without your support and love, Thank you!

To all of you who bravely shared your stories with me and have been willing to share them in the pages of this book, I am most grateful.

Introduction

꽃

When I renew I stand on an ocean beach, wind whipping through my hair, eyes transfixed on the repetitive cycle of crashing wave and circling gull. The salted air whips up sand that stings, and I pull my hat lower over my face and tighten my jacket. But the hypnotic effect of the rolling wave on the cold, rugged northern California coast speaks to me of change.

How like our lives is the unrelenting wave. One minute the wave gains strength and crashes with a mighty roar against rock formation and shore. The next it sloshes inertly into soggen sand only to be replaced moments later by another cycle of turbulence ending in another moment's calm before the remaining water is sucked back to sea.

This book is the result of many conversations with women of all ages who have struggled with the transitions of their lives. Many of them wondered why their lives seemed always to be in flux. Some women were grieving the loss of a marriage that ended in divorce or of a mate by death. Other lives were in upheaval due to job loss and change and major moves. Others were grieving the death of a child, multiple changes in their lives, or the loss of their own innocence to abuse in childhood. Many asked, "What's a normal passage?" or "Why is it taking me so long to get through this? Or, "What do I do once I'm through this time of grieving?"

In 1991 I spoke at a conference in Honolulu, Hawaii, for Hawaiian Island Ministries. One of my topics was entitled "Women in Transition." In my research, I discovered a whole body of literature that confirmed what the women I had met were experiencing. Women's lives do not flow in predictable, calm passages. Rather it is common for a woman's life to be filled with change. For many women life is a succession of waves flowing and crashing one upon the other. Some women barely notice the changing tides and waves; others are continually caught in the swirling foam and turbulence of change.

The women at the Honolulu conference not only wanted suggestions for going through each transition, but they also wanted to know what to do on the other side of one. They wanted to go beyond the crisis mentality. They wanted to discover how to dream their own dreams and find ways of implementing them.

As a result of this initial conference and several others that followed, I realized to see how the seasonal metaphor is an appropriate picture of how we women develop our adult identity. As you read this book you will discover that in each season of your life you have tasks to perform. When you accomplish them, your sense of personal identity and value will deepen.

When you are plunged into times of transition and the upheaval of change, you are a winter women. The winter woman is a woman who is grieving, who sees life in shades of black, and who has more questions than answers. When you stop running from the pain of your loss and actively grieve, you are ready to enter into spring.

Spring is a season of new beginnings. To enter fully into spring, you must face your fears and learn the process of forgiveness. As a spring woman you learn to dream and you discover what makes your heart sing. It is a season of joy, excitement, and seed planting.

The summer woman is a woman of balance and self-confidence. She knows her limitations and her abilities. As summer is a season of first harvest, so you will harvest the dream which you planted in spring. You discover the mirrors that have reflected your worth, and you discover your own voice.

Once you discover your value and heal from the sorrows you experience in the winters of your life, you have a responsibility to give back to the broader community. The autumn woman is a giving woman. In autumn you recognize the needs beyond the walls of your personal world, and you explore ways to give as you formulate a new dream or broaden the old. But you also learn that your being is more important than your doing. You learn to renew your personal spirit by sitting quietly before God.

A woman in all of her seasons searches for meaning in her life. She searches for and discovers that life has a spiritual dimension as well as temporal. She also discovers a Comforter in her grieving, an Ally and Partner in her dreaming, an accurate Mirror in measuring her self worth, and an Encourager in her giving. You can be this woman.

Many of the principles in this book are not exclusively for women. Many concerns we face as women are human concerns that impact men as well. My desire is for you to grasp a vision of all that God intended you to be. Each season is but one out of four; women are not meant to dwell in any one forever. My hope is that you will find a vision and joy in all the seasons of your lives.

Part I

Transitions

There is an appointed time for everything. And
there is a time for every event under heaven.

Ecclesiastes 3:1

Chapter One

For Everything There Is a Season

⚜

A block from our suburban home is a five-acre farm. In late spring the vegetable stand opens and sells freshly picked strawberries. As summer approaches the fare increases to apricots, lettuce, onions, beans, and locally grown fruits. As spring melds into summer, the succulent white corn ripens for sale. Toward summer's end, the large sunflowers are cut down, and the corn stalks are tied and lie propped against the stand. In October the front lot becomes a pumpkin patch replete with a train, a petting zoo, and a crawl through jack-o-lantern. By Thanksgiving weekend, lights and a flocking shed replace corn and pumpkins, and the fresh aroma of pine and fir Christmas trees fills the air.

For several days twice a year—once in late autumn before winter deepens and again in early spring before planting—I am awakened early by the sound of tractors plowing the fields. The tractor's large disc knives cut deep into the soil, churning the dry matter deeply into the earth. The land lies fallow until early spring when the rototiller turns the ground, breaking up hard clods, exposing the dirt to light, and preparing the soil to receive seed.

What a model this process is for our lives. No sooner than I think my garden is planted and growing nicely, the weather shifts, a new season begins to form, and the old must pass away so something new can be planted. In nature the new grows out of the old. When the old decom-

7

poses it becomes the nutrients for the next crop the following year. Although we embrace the changing of the seasons, we often resist the natural forces of change and growth that occur in our own lives.

Forces of Change

In the past twenty-five years the roles of women in our culture have been in transition. We struggle to discover the balance between career and family, between satisfying our own individual needs and serving the needs of others, and between what others say we should be and who we know, at least in our heads if not our hearts, God created us to be.

Changing Lives

In addition to the cultural shifts and transitions, we all have personal journeys of change and passages that bring us joy and sorrow. The seasons we journey through are as unique as we are and as timeless and universal as our mother's journey before us.

Women develop their identity in the world differently from men. Because there has been so little research on a woman's adult life cycle, we have accepted the male model that life will flow in predictable linear steps from career goal to career goal to retirement and death. Women, we are now discovering, actually move through their adult lives in cycles—in grand sweeping rolls of equilibrium and disequilibrium, of stability and instability.

We need only to examine our biological cycle to find evidence of this. When a young girl is eleven to fourteen, she begins her period, and from then until menopause, her life moves in a biological and emotional cycle. For a couple of weeks life is "normal." For a week to ten days, she gains weight and feels intensified emotions, followed by a week of menstruation. As she ages, her body registers the ongoing changes and challenges of time as her hormones prepare her for menopause.

Not only are our biological clocks programmed to teach us that change is part of life, but so is our basic emotional and psychological nature. As responders, relaters, and nurturers, our lives are affected by those around us. Listening to my two children when they were teenagers gave me a glimpse into the differences between men and women. My daughter and her friends discussed people, relationships, and feelings. My son and his friends devoured sports statistics and movie trivia. Movie trivia does not create interpersonal crises. Shifts in close friendships do.

For a woman life is a series of changes and transitions, of ill-timed events, of crises and the resolving of them, of changing seasons and the resisting of them. For a mother, life is dictated by her children, their illnesses and activities; her husband; and her own needs. The single woman struggles with singleness, to participate in the dating world, to accept singleness, to set goals on marriage or career. Our roles of daughter, sibling, friend, neighbor, and concerned citizen thrust us into turbulent water in which we cannot always swim.

Changing World

Furthermore, the world has become smaller. Maybe it is a myth that women of an earlier generation felt more in control of their lives, but nonetheless, we accept their roles as valid. When a woman saw a need, she pursued a course of action . . . a pie for the new family down the street, a casserole for the neighbor who had experienced a death in her family, an afternoon chat with a friend. Life ebbed and flowed in smaller, more manageable circles.

Our nature has not changed with the advent of more technology, with our entry into the work force or with global awareness of crises. Our heart still yearns to meet needs, to relate meaningfully and productively. But, as our circle of awareness increases, our capacity to juggle competing demands decreases.

Today's news carries reports of famine in Africa, nuclear threat in Korea, and pleas for help from Russia. Closer to home, we encounter the homeless man on the street asking to work for food and see behind him a young woman and infant huddled in the doorway. As we watch the changes in the former Soviet Union, we wonder, Who is our enemy now? We are grieved by the wars of independence in Yugoslavia, Moldavia, Armenia/Azerbaijan. Anne Morrow Lindbergh in *The Gift from the Sea* addressed the dilemma:

> The world is rumbling and erupting in ever-widening circles around us. The tensions, conflicts and sufferings even in the outermost circle touch us all, reverberate in all of us . . . Modern communication loads us with more problems than the human frame can carry. My life cannot implement in action the demands of all the people to whom my heart responds.

Our grandmothers, and even our mothers, lived in a circle small enough to let them implement in action most of the impulses of their hearts and minds. We were brought up in a tradition that has now become impossible, for we have extended our circle through space and time.[1]

So not only are our own lives changing, but indeed we ride the tide of other lives in other places. How do we learn to care for what we can, to rejoice in what we have when others are less fortunate, and give beyond ourselves without being in despair that we cannot change everything? We must guard against the dilemma of despair or emotional numbing. Emotional numbing occurs when our system shuts down and we no longer see the need around us. We thus walk by the homeless and not even see them, let alone have a feeling about them or for them.

For most of us no texts or tutors explain the way of women in times of change and transition. If only I had known that life is a series of rolling waves and not a linear progression of change, maybe I would not have wasted so much energy as a younger woman wondering what was wrong because my life wasn't moving in predictable patterns. For indeed, it appears that life is made up of transitions: of times of waiting and doing, of cycles of confusion and stability. For me the challenge becomes how to inhabit the moment, and how to actively accept that this moment has poignancy and that pain, discomfort, disequilibrium can be my tutor.

Is it possible that we have misunderstood the basic nature of things? The industrial revolution introduced us to a mechanized view of humanity. Raw material is gathered, and then sent to a factory where a product is produced, packaged, and sent to market. The product is used, wears out, and is thrown away. Subtly the value we place on others and ourselves has shifted to doing rather than being. When the individual has ceased producing or outlived her usefulness, the company or the family releases her from work.

A Common Journey

I spoke recently at a seminar where women of all ethnic, age and cultural backgrounds shared their common struggle with change. They spoke of major moves, loss of friendship, the aging process, uncertain futures, single parent struggles, mid-life evaluations. Each story demonstrated that a woman is deeply impacted by not only the vicissitudes of life, but by her own internal yearnings and desires and by the changes and upheavals occurring in the lives of others. Each story is unique and in a profound way reflective of a woman's adult journey.

Loss of Friendship. Malia spoke first. Gesturing to the young woman sitting next to her, she said, "We're like soul sisters. We grew up together here in Hawaii and had our first babies at the same time. Now Beth is moving to the mainland with her military husband. She's leaving a month before my baby is due. We are both sad, but we'll make the best of it."

Mid-life Transitions. Another woman spoke: "My last child went away to college a year ago, and I decided to go back to college and find an "identity." It was my mid-life crisis. But in the middle of it, my husband decided to have his own mid-life crisis, sold his business and now wants to go back to the mainland. We don't know where we are going. So I'm really in transition. I'm a military wife, so I'm used to having my roots pulled. But when Uncle Sam moved us, we could be angry at the powers that be. Now I'm just angry."

A noted pastor's wife from the Mainland spoke next. "I'm fifty-three years old and I grew up believing that the best thing I could do was help everyone else do their thing and be the best they could be. And now my children are doing fine by themselves and I help my husband a lot. But I'm surrounded by women who are getting degrees and doing things. I'm not sure I want to do that, but something says I should. I'm not sure it's me or what's going on around me."

Single Parenting. Chris is a young mom in her mid-thirties: "I'm a new single mother and I have to work now. I've been working all along part time, but now it's all on my shoulders. I have two boys, seven and nine. Even though I know the Lord is there, the reality is really tough."

Entering Adulthood. "I've been sheltered in the school system. You have a set schedule, you know. You come home, do your homework and go to sleep. I just finished school and now I'm having to face adult life . . . ." Twenty-one-year-old Kalina just graduated from the University.

Mieko summed up the theme of our sharing by saying: "I'm in my own personal transition. I'm noticing that the changes in other people's lives bring change in mine. I have just retired and had hoped to travel and do things I haven't had time for. But I have a parent who is ill. Her needs and demands affect my lifestyle and choices.

A Model for Adulthood

I remember that, in my twenties, I believed adult life would go smoothly in a predictable, logical unfolding of happy events. I believed adults had power and control over the circumstances of their lives. And, if by chance all did not go well, there was undoubtedly something wrong with that adult. I would just have to learn what the key was and do it right. When I became an "adult" I was ill prepared for the changes, and the struggles life brought. Somehow the child in me believed that being grown up meant being equipped to handle life—whatever that meant.

In fact, I remember as a young teenager arguing that we did not have to know sorrow in order to grow and be wise. I hated the thought that growth could primarily come out of pain, that peace and wisdom could follow chaos and suffering. Somehow I had not seen the stories of pain and sorrow, the honesty of struggle in the Bible.

Two years after my high school graduation, the world exploded. We barely averted nuclear war in the Soviet Missile crisis; President Kennedy was assassinated; Vietnam, with all of its horror and pain erupted nightly in our living rooms; and far away places became household words associated with pain and death: Bay of Tonking, Ho Chi Min Trail, Saigon. The leader of a peaceful resistance—the kind I believed was all that was necessary—was assassinated. Then, within seven years of my junior year in college, seven precious family members died including both of my parents, my grandmother, and my husband's mother and his second set of parents, an aunt and uncle. Neither my life nor the world at large was moving in predictable patterns of enlightened bliss. I began to realize that life was made up of transitions, of times of waiting, as well as of arrivals, of periods of chaos and periods of calm.

During these years a rock group popularized a wonderful passage of scripture that so beautifully describes a more accurate picture of reality than I had been willing to accept.

> There is an appointed time for everything. And there is a time for every event under heaven—
> A time to give birth, and a time to die;
> A time to plant, and a time to uproot what is planted.
> A time to kill, and a time to heal;
> A time to tear down, and a time to build up.
> A time to weep, and a time to laugh;
> A time to mourn, and a time to dance.
> A time to throw stones, and a time to gather stones;
> A time to embrace, and a time to shun embracing.
> A time to search, and a time to give up as lost;
> A time to keep, and a time to throw away.

A time to tear apart, and a time to sew together;
A time to be silent, and a time to speak.
A time to love, and a time to hate.
A time for war, and a time for peace.   (Eccles. 3;1–8)

As a young woman I would have chosen to have only the positives of those couplets. Now, I have seen the blessing and the power of the Lord more profoundly in the darker, less chosen parts. Joni Eareckson Tada says it this way in *A Step Further*:

> When you think about it, a lot of us would never have thought about God in the first place had He not used some problems to get our attention. "God whispers to us in our pleasures, speaks in our consciences, but shouts in our pains: it is His megaphone to rouse a deaf world." . . . And so God mercifully puts pain and suffering in front of us as "blockades on the road to Hell." [2]

In fact, life is made up of all these parts. We have only to look to nature and the progression of life which follows the seasons to see that joy follows sorrow as surely as spring follows winter. Spring's newness is followed by summer's richness—soft breezes, long established days, bright sun and rapid growth. The deepening hues of Eastern maples and scurrying of squirrels remind us that winter is sure to come and we must prepare. We begin life in spring, grow strong in summer, put our wisdom to practice in autumn, and prepare for the unwinding of our days and death in the winter of our lives.

As we look at a woman's adult life, we need a model on which to place life's events. Sometimes having a road map, a visual model to hang the journey on, can be helpful. The seasons metaphor is just such a map. As we explore the developmental seasons and the accompanying spiritual qualities of each season, we will be able to appreciate the rich tapestry of a woman's life.

The Winter Woman

As we look at the seasons it seems fitting to begin with winter. We view winter as a time of death, decay, slumber, and grieving. In nature the days shorten and the vibrant colors of autumn turn rapidly to dark gray. Snow falls; plants are dormant. Trees drop their leaves and the animal world sleeps and withdraws. It is a season of resting and waiting.

A pruned hedge, rose bush, or tree lies silently building up strength and nutrients for spring growth.

The woman in the season of winter is one who is grieving. She has experienced loss, change, death, despair, helplessness, hopelessness, anger, the depression from loss. She faces a season of endings.

We may face many winters in our lives. The woman in her eighties and nineties faces her last winter. As in every season, she can navigate this one knowing deeply that even in this season there is a purpose in accepting the changes in her body, her productivity, and her relationships. The woman who runs from this season ends up bitter, depressed, and unfulfilled.

A woman in winter is one who

- understands the nature of grief.
- understands that grief is a process.
- prepares for her chronological winter season.

The Spring Woman

Spring creeps in under cover of lingering winter clouds and storms. When the skies clear, we are surprised by the brilliant yellows of blooming daffodils, forsythia, and acacia. Barren trees become dappled in misty greens. Fields are tilled, fertilized, and seeded for summer harvest. As the weeks pass, spring unfolds in waves of color and bird song.

In the spring of a woman's life, she finds joy and excitement in new beginnings. She embraces new ideas and new opportunities. A spring woman chooses life, lets go of sorrow, and embraces hope.

Thus, the tasks of the spring woman are these:

- To move out of winter into spring. She says goodbye to the old and welcomes the new by embracing the child of the past instead of ignoring her, letting go of fear, and actively forgiving.
- To formulate a dream by learning the power of praying and dreaming, by seeking the support, friendship and encouragement of others; and by choosing a season of spiritual beginnings.

The Summer Woman

Summer is a time of first fruits and early harvests. Summer storms don't last long and are followed by the warmth of the sun. The summer season is characterized by commitment, by flowering and richness, by personhood. It is a time when we deepen who we are, what we want, where we are going and with whom. It's a time of deepening friendships, renewing our spiritual commitment. It's an active time. We are at once independent and interdependent, individuated and connected. We have a deep sense of ourselves with an accurate perception of our strengths and weaknesses. We value ourselves and are nurtured by the value others have of us. Balance is a key word. But the journey is a difficult one. We must successfully pass through winter and spring to be a summer woman. Her main task is to develop her ego strength.

The summer woman demonstrates ego strength when she

- weathers transitions, reevaluates her dreams, and celebrates her choices.
- finds emotional balance.
- finds her own unique voice.
- discovers the mirrors that define her.

The Autumn Woman

When we look at the colors of autumn, we see a dramatic shift from the hazy, diffused hues of summer. The dry dusty days explode into the sharp, crisp hues of autumn. Words that come to mind for fall are vibrancy, boldness, texture, and strength. The days may be warm, but the nights may turn chill and crisp. The final harvest is brought in and what has been sown is reaped.

The autumn woman is one who is committed to the broader community. It is a season of giving back, of faith that what she accomplishes has meaning. She begins to see the purpose for the winters, summers, and springs of her life and the purpose in former sufferings and in her own personal journey. Like the wisdom of Hebrews 12, she has been through the refiner's fire; she has been disciplined and she yields in autumn the "peaceful fruit of righteousness" (Hebrews 12:11).

Many of us may think of years here. The autumn woman is one who has been through winter, but she is not necessarily an old woman.

The autumn woman is one who

- understands the process of growth.
- learns power and peace through personal discipline.
- gives out of her storehouse of harvested produce for the benefit of others. She acts for the common good not in self-interest.

Reflection

Throughout our journey in this book, you will have an opportunity to record your own ideas, feelings and memories. The questions are designed as springboards for your evaluation of your seasons as a woman. As you read through each description, you may have identified where you are or at least recognized similarities to former seasons in your life. In your journal, identify the season that best characterizes your life. Be as specific as you can concerning the circumstances of your life at this particular season.

Chapter Two

A Season of Growth

※

One of my favorite places for personal renewal is on the northern California coast. Jagged cliffs plunge hundreds of feet to meet the unrelenting onslaught of pounding surf. Over the centuries, wind, storm, earthquake, and churning wave have carved their influence on the surface of the earth. Likewise the experiences of our lives and our response to them cut, groove, and shape our character.

Each season lived, each transition successfully navigated, etches into our being something that makes us unique. All the experiences of our lives—the joys and sorrows, our perceptions of life events, the words spoken to and about us—weave together in a tapestry we call self. All that makes me uniquely me as distinct from you is self. And what we learn determines to a great extent our ability or inability to cope with stress, to be intimate with those we love, and embrace life.

How we go through each season—and the transitions into and out of them—is determined in great measure by what we learned or did not learn as children. The goal of early life is to teach us skills to master each stage of life that follows. But if our earliest experiences do not teach us adequately, we learn adaptive measures that may or may not serve us well. The child raised by an alcoholic learns to watch for any sign of her parent's temper. She learns to predict moods and behavior by subtle changes in a facial expression or tone of voice. She learns when to prepare for pain. As an adult she may still view the world with a practiced eye, scanning friends and family for warning signs. She may wear herself out trying desperately to keep the peace and ward off tension before it arises because of the fear she learned as a child. The past impacts her present.

The Value of Knowing Yourself

A woman who has a sense of self is able to articulate her own feelings and opinions. She is able to distinguish what she thinks and feels from what others in her life think and feel. Over the years I have discovered that women devalue themselves when they take on the values of others around them, and have a difficult time making choices, of dreaming their own dreams, without feeling guilty or selfish. Or, out of fear, they expect others to fulfill their dreams.

Mary never finished college and throughout her adult life hid this fact from friends and colleagues alike. Education was highly prized in her family, but when she had failed a course, she dropped out, too humiliated to continue. As an adult she pushed her children and her husband to succeed where she had not.

Often when we do not make healthy choices, we suffer and those we love suffer. Someone with an unclear sense of self may blame others for her lack of well being. "If only my husband (best friend, parents, children) would change, then I would be happy and contented, and life would go well for me." On the other hand, someone who has a clear sense of self might say, "If I'm going to be happy, what do I need to choose or change? What are my options?"

Kathy came to me distraught. When her children reached school age, she had returned to the work force as a kindergarten teacher. When I met her she was sharing a room with a veteran teacher whose materials were all over the room. Kathy had struggled all year with how to establish her space and her identity. She also faced a schedule that took her away from her family for longer hours.

"Kathy," I asked, "if you could choose to have your work schedule and classroom arrangement any way you would want, what would you choose?"

"Oh, nothing I say really counts at that school anyway. I know I couldn't possibly have what I want."

I responded: "Do you know what you want if you could?"

She protested again, "I don't want to make waves and create a crisis. This woman is just too powerful. I've always known how to do what's expected of me, I'm just frustrated. It's not fair."

After I asked her a third time, acknowledging that it is hard to communicate what one wants, she finally told me this: "What I'd really like is my own room so that I can create the atmosphere of calm and order I feel is vital for learning." She went on to elaborate other legitimate details and desires—unexpressed because she believed that she had no control over the circumstances of her life. With a bit more probing, she was able to admit how angry she was at this co-teacher, and how deprived she felt because no one acknowledged her value, competence, and success with her students and their parents. Then she changed her tone. "But I feel guilty saying I'm angry with her. I have a job and have good students. I shouldn't feel this way. I should be grateful for what I have."

But Kathy did not feel grateful. She felt frustration, anger, helplessness, and inadequacy.

Kathy, however, was willing to risk change. First, she began to investigate what was and was not possible regarding the schedule for the following year and what rooms were available. Once she had gathered her data, she approached her principal and laid before her the pros and cons of the present situation. She also told her boss that she had found a room and asked how she could go about claiming it for herself for the fall.

Compromise followed. She successfully negotiated her own classroom and a more equitable schedule. In time, the guilt left as she began to acknowledge that she not only had the ability to think and feel, but had the ability to be heard by others for effective negotiation.

The Origin of Self

Which has more impact in the development of a child's personality—heredity or environment? The most commonly accepted view is that a combination of heredity, environment, and the individual's perceptions of her environment, and experiences creates the self.

Most mothers will tell you that each child demonstrates his or her unique self even before birth. My son was an incredibly quiet womb child. After he was born he turned into a whirlwind. He did everything early and did not sleep through the night until he was teenager. Our daughter, on the other hand, was a very active womb child, poking and prodding. But she entered the world calmly, sleeping for long periods of time. When she awoke, she would make a single cry as if to say, "If it's not inconvenient, I would like to be fed." Children bring to life a set of predispositions of character on which heredity and environment write their script.

Developmental Tasks

In his book *Identity, Youth and Crisis* Erik Erikson, [1] a developmental psychologist, has delineated certain stages of human personality formation. Each of these stages poses challenges and tasks that must be accomplished in order for the child to grow into a well-balanced human being. If the task is not learned, then the individual must meet the challenge at some future point in life—adolescence, mid-life or during another emotionally challenging and vulnerable time.

If we look again at Ecclesiastes 3 we recognize the principle that God has ordered seasons to occur in a certain order. The reverse is therefore also true. If events occur out of normal sequence, and our life tasks are not accomplished, there is confusion and disorder.

Childhood

In the first year of life we learn basic trust. In a deep way the child believes, "Mother will come to hold me, feed me, change me. I will not be abandoned. I am cared for and nurtured, therefore I am wanted and valued." The child develops a sense of predictability about life and so has the view, "Because life has gone well for me in the past, no matter what struggles I face, it will continue to go well for me." When nurtured and held close, the baby learns to open her spirit, to bond deeply with another human being.

However, a child who lives in turmoil, who is not responded to with affection and nurture, will develop a sense of distrust about the world. The child will act tentatively, apprehensively, and cautiously about trusting herself to be competent or others to be safe.

Any time during childhood a child's sense of equilibrium can be shattered by trauma and loss. The death of a sibling or parent; moving from place to place; physical, sexual, emotional abuse; extreme sibling rejection and teasing; or rejections by peers and teachers can all erode the basic quality of trust developed by a child in this first year of life.

As a child grows, she learns to be part of a family, and also to be a separate person. We call this process *individuation*: "I am not you and you are not me. I am my own self." The second stage of life falls between eighteen months to three years and is called the stage of *autonomy*. "I'll do it myself!" and "No!" characterize the language of this age. A baby who has developed trust can then risk saying no to the very person who she must rely on for sustenance. This stage marks the beginning of personhood where the child sees herself as separate from Mom. We are likely to call a two year old rebellious, selfish, or "terrible," but actually this is a vital stage for the development of ongoing trust. "My mommy can handle my independence. She will not cease to love me if I am who am" is an important message for the child to believe.

At the same time, a child feels increasingly secure to express herself when the parent assumes the task of enforcing boundaries or limits for the child. A parent might say, "You have every right not to like what I've asked you to do, but you must do what I ask you to do. If you don't, here is what will happen." The child's "no!" is not an anti-mom or anti-parent expression, but rather an active statement of "Here I am and there you are."

However, if during these years, the child is humiliated and harshly criticized for independent moves, the child develops the opposite of autonomy which is *shame and doubt*.

The third stage of development of personhood occurs between three and five years and is called *initiative*. A four-year-old girl demonstrates this independent step of personhood dramatically. She may become bossy and self-assured; she knows everything. She knows how to do everything and she is quite willing and ready to show everyone how. She becomes more aware of her daddy's presence and involvement in her life and actively seeks his attention.

However, if this passage is not encouraged and understood, *guilt* results. The child's antics and actions of self-expression can be squashed with harsh words and excessive discipline. The child's internal message then becomes, "There must be something wrong with me. Everyone is unhappy with me." The message is more than, "I've done a bad thing." The message is, "I am a bad child."

The fourth stage of childhood covers ages five to twelve and is called the age of *industry*. Its opposite development is *inferiority*. Were we encouraged to try new things? Were we praised and affirmed for new beginnings? Were we encouraged to dream and find ways to put our dreams into reality? Or were we shamed and belittled and ignored? Were our brothers encouraged in areas we would have loved to have succeeded?

Children in these middle childhood years show rather than tell their feelings about what is going on in their lives. Cheryl's parents were divorced when she was three. She had done fairly well in kindergarten, but in first grade her mother remarried and enrolled Cheryl by her new name in her old school. When her mother would become angry or frustrated, she would take her feelings out on Cheryl by pulling her by her hair and throwing dishes. Cheryl's grades and classroom behavior began to decline. She picked fights and prided herself in being able to beat up the boys. She would laugh when disciplined. What had happened? When a child acts out, changes her behavior dramatically, or behaves too perfectly during these years, she likely hides pain beneath the surface. Instead of having a solid sense of productivity and industry, the child develops an inferiority that shows itself as acting out, withdrawal, or perfectionistic behavior. Cheryl was acting out the emotional and physical abuse occurring at home but could not or would not betray the one on whom she had to rely for nurturance and care.

As adults we soon reap what we missed. By looking at these stages of development we can discern where we skipped our sequential task and begin the process of recovering what was lost. Why is that important? one might ask. Wherever lies have been believed in our past, wherever wounding has gone ungrieved, freedom is blocked. If a young sapling is planted in fertile soil in a protected area, and exposed to light and water, the tree grows strong and firm. But if a boulder is thrown against the sapling and its surroundings block the sun, the young tree has to bend and reach to find light and sustenance. Likewise, our souls become bent and damaged by the boulders in our own lives. By being bent, we expend much more energy coping with life's struggles than if we were growing without boulder damage.

Adolescence

In the teen years the adolescent reactivates all of the above stages and again tries to develop what has not been accomplished before. During the teen years all that has gone before bears fruit. Erikson describes the task of this period as a search for *identity*. If the tools and tasks learned in earlier stages have not been adequately learned, or the circumstances of the teen environment is overly stressful, *identity confusion* is the result.

During the early stages of adolescence, the divergency between males and females becomes more dramatic. Until puberty there is a wider acceptance of girls in general play. Women who have had brothers and played sports often report that a dramatic shift occurred when their bodies began to change and menses started. In the early stages of adolescence young girls report still being eager to be part of the gang, to be treated as a peer.

A young woman's sense of self is also affected by whether her faither accepts or rejects his daughter's emerging womanhood. Caroline reports: "I was very close to my Daddy when I was a child. I remember dancing with him around the living room or having his approval when I showed off a new dress. But after age ten when I developed breasts, my father withdrew from the hugs that were so common in earlier years. When I was twelve I had been given a new full slip. I thought I looked beautiful in it. I rushed out hoping Daddy might notice me. He did, but not in the way that I had hoped. He acknowledged me with a look of disgust and ordered me "to get some clothes on." I was crushed! I had been his tomboy but in those pre-teen years I felt him pulling away. I felt ugly and dirty. I needed to know that he still loved me. The messages from then on from my mother were directed at my body, how I looked like a whore. I was an innocent child and had no idea for many years what they were talking about. All I knew was that I had lost my father and I didn't know why."

Many fathers become uncomfortable with their daughters during adolescence due to their own inabilities and weaknesses, not because there is anything wrong with the daughter's behavior. Contrast Caroline's father's response with Karen's. "My father treated all of us kids with respect. When my brother would tease us, Dad would defend the girls and would tell him when he had gone too far. When Mom told him I had started my period (I was thirteen), I remember he sent me a rose with these words: 'Dear Karen, you are beginning the journey of womanhood. I love you, I am proud of you and I am glad you are my daughter. Love, Dad.'" Many a father treats this time of development with benign neglect, failing to realize the vital role he plays in affirming the feminine in his daughter.

The Adult Life Cycle

Erikson generalizes for women his experiences with a male research population and his own personal experiences as a male. More recent research indicates that the adult life cycle for women is very different from men. The traditional male cycle is to leave school, decide on a profession, seek employment which he may change once or twice in his work lifetime, and retire. A man traditionally adds marriage in his twenties, but his main goal in life is his career.

Relational Identity. A woman on the other hand has relational goals. Her primary task during and after formal schooling is coupling. Traditionally she has viewed work or career as filler for a private life of husband and children. In fact, women often delay gaining an adult identity apart from the roles they have until after coupling. A man goes for his own personal career goals before and during marriage.

Women traditionally have developed their sense of identity by being someone's daughter, wife, mother. A woman's worth is often identified with her roles rather than with her person. Thus when her roles shift and change, she struggles for a sense of balance and direction and self. My mother always wrote her name "Mrs. Frederick J. Berger," and it was a crisis of identity after my father's death to sign her name "Lois Berger." Women in my generation, on the other hand, insisted on carrying their own name into marriage, hyphenated it, or went by their first name. Throughout the seventies and eighties, a woman wanted to be identified not just as someone's wife, but as an individual in her own right. How do women affirm the unique qualities we have as individuals, pursue our own dreams, and affirm our abilities, and at the same time value deeply our relationships with others? As we explore the summer woman, we will examine more fully the paradox of individuality and interdependence.

We must also remember that, unlike her male counterpart's, a woman's identity does not develop in lock-step stages, and, as Iris Sanquilliano in her book *In Her Time* expresses, "not in a rigid, predictable progression of conflicts, identity, mastery and autonomy, but rather in great surges of billowing change, unexpected, unpredictable off time events which forever change the course of a woman's life." She goes on to say, "If an event is predictable, it's unlikely to be experienced as a crisis, and if it isn't experienced as a crisis, it is unlikely to 'shock' women into growing."[2] And it is precisely in those moments of transition, of unexpected crises or adventure that we begin to acknowledge our abilities, our sensibilities—in essence, our identity, our selfhood.

Journey to Individuation. Individuation is the journey of becoming a separate individual who makes choices. When a young girl is valued for what she thinks and is shown respect, she has greater freedom to stay connected with her family. If she feels unable to express questions in the areas of politics, religion, social issues, or family problems and is led to feel guilty or shameful, she may give up her journey for individuation out of fear of losing the closeness with family. Or she may openly rebel and move further away from the family values in order to say once again, "There you are and here I am. I am different from you. See me as me and not as a reflection of you."

For young men, the journey of individuation leads them, as it did the prodigal son, away from home. In order to find himself, he had to face the consequences of his own behavior. He had to realize that he needed to rebond and become part of his family once again. Rebonding and interdependence occurs for the male in our culture after leaving home. In many cultures, the young man is called out from the world of women and made to go through certain rituals to become a man. The bar mitzvah in Jewish tradition carries with it the rite of passage into manhood. A woman's rite of passage from girlhood to womanhood is starting her period. She does not leave the world of women to become a woman; instead, she is drawn into a new relationship with men.

Women for the most part do not strive to be independent to define themselves. Young women, more so than young men, depend on others for self-definition and affirmation, and they are adept at anticipating other people's demands and needs. One widely cited 1970s study[3] reported girls, when doing poorly on exams in school or when confronted with an error, would turn inward, blame themselves, and say, "What's wrong with me?" Young men, on the other hand, generally blamed the test, the teacher, or circumstances, but would not turn the failure or loss inward.

The important quality we see in the model of female development is interdependence: relational, contextual, and personal. In fact, more women than men find their identity in their interpersonal relationships. Jean Baker Miller, a noted researcher on women, says it this way, "One central feature is that women stay with, build on and develop in a context of attachment and affiliation with others. Indeed, women's sense of self becomes very much organized around being able to make and then to maintain affiliations and relationships. Eventually, for many women, the threat of disruption of an affiliation is perceived as not just a loss of a relationship, but as something closer to a total loss of self."[4] She prefers to live with others in a mutually satisfying arrangement than live alone and she prefers an exchange of ideas that leads to consensus in decision-making where everyone benefits.

Image Isn't Everything. The image of the business woman in male-style suits using male business skills may have helped them gain credibility in the market place, but she lost a core sense of being female. In recent years, a woman's corporate style and dress now reflect characteristics more consistent with a woman's way of being in the world. She may wear softer colors and more flowing garments. She may lead by consensus management characterized by inclusion rather than exclusion. In the 1970s and 1980s, writings about and for women emphasized that women's intellectual capacities were equal to and the same as men. In the later 1980s and 1990s, research affirms that women, though equally competent intellectually, are different in their approach to intellectual functioning, and these differences are positive, not indications of weakness.

Even though most of us do not ride the crest of cultural change or adopt every new view that emerges, nonetheless, we are influenced by a national perspective of women. The stay-at-home mom struggles with whether she is doing the right thing, and the working mom struggles with exhaustion over her dual roles. We women need to learn what is wisest, what is needful in our own experience and come to terms with a personal vision rather than yielding to cultural shifts.

Although we may generalize about basic characteristics of women, we may find encouragement that there is much to celebrate in the way a woman develops her sense of value. Women are all unique—with different roles, different goals, different dreams, and different stories to tell.

The Spiritual Life

We are not only mind (thought and emotions) and body, but we are also spirit. Our spirit is the part of our being that resonates with beauty, shows compassion to the wounded, lamblasts evil, and reaches upward for a relationship with the Creator. Through our personal spirit God the Father teaches us, communicates with us and when we are hurt as children, taught lies about our character, and choose to act in destructive ways, our personal spirit darkens. When our personal spirit is nurtured through communion with God, worship, and exposure to beauty our whole being flourishes. Paul Tournier, the imminent Swiss psychiatrist, points out that it is artificial to view humankind as living in two worlds, but one. We have both a natural and a supernatural existence:

As a part of nature, man is subject to its forces and its laws. But he is distinct from the animal in that God has created him 'in his image,' that is, a spiritual as well as a natural being. He belongs to two worlds at the same time, the natural and the supernatural, even though he may not yet have become aware of this through faith. This is what confers upon him an eternal mystery. This is what explains how he may appear so self-contradictory, how the best and the worst are inextricably mixed together in us. [5]

A Woman's Sense of Self

As I conclude this section, let me summarize what I am saying about a woman's sense of self.

- All that makes me uniquely me as distinct from you is self.
- The more able I am to value my own thoughts and feelings, the more able I am to care for you.
- A woman who has a sense of self is able to articulate her own feelings and opinions. She is able to discern what she thinks and feels from what others in her life think and feel.
- A woman with a sense of self has the ability to be heard by others and negotiate effectively.
- She acknowledges that her human nature and her spiritual nature are interwoven threads in the same tapestry.

Reflection

As you conclude this chapter, consider the following questions. You may wish to start with just one or you may wish to spend a few moments jotting down your initial response to several.

1. How are girls and women valued in your family? What messages were given to you about your value as you were growing up? How were you treated in comparison to brothers, male cousins, or friends by grandparents, parents, siblings, friends, or the church?

2. Today, on a scale from one to ten with ten being highest, how would you rank your personal sense of value?

3. What good and/or traumatic events happened to you or occurred in your family that you think are important? In what stage of development does each memory fall?

Chapter Three

A Season of Change

❧

I lived for some time in Hawaii. There, you have to look closely to notice the transitions between seasons. In other parts of the country, the seasons change dramatically. In California, where I live now, spring begins in early February when a riot of yellow acacia splashes across the landscape. Plump buds appear on the trees. The grays and browns of winter are replaced by the yellows and new greens of sprouting trees and the pink and white blush of blossoms. Whether the transition is dramatic or subtle, there is a time of change, an unfolding from one season to another.

Our lives follow the same pattern. As a child I was fascinated by circus performers who did aerial tricks high above the tent floor. On one side a swing would be released while the performer swung from the opposite side. The two swings would go back and forth until, at exactly the right moment, the performer would release her grip and reach for the oncoming swing or the arms of her partner. From the moment she left the stand until she arrived safely on the opposite platform, she was committed to change. There was no going back, and the audience held its collective breath until she landed safely on the opposite platform.

However, a transition is not just the pause between letting go of the old and grabbing hold of the new. It is the entire process from crisis or restlessness to instability, through chaos and unfolding into resolution and a new equilibrium.

Change Happens

Sometimes change is created by our own good decisions or bad decisions. At other times change begins with restlessness and a vague notion that something is wrong. The question that comes most commonly to mind is, "What's wrong with me?" And at the same time we may feel challenge and a growing sense of excitement.

When others make decisions that affect our lives, disequilibrium also occurs. If the event is anticipated, such as a child going to kindergarten or leaving home for the first time, the loss is significant, but a new order emerges fairly soon. When the event that triggers the chaos is unanticipated, unasked for, uncontrolled—as when a husband announces he is leaving for another woman or when someone dies—the loss can be traumatic and debilitating. A time of prolonged grieving is legitimate, normal, and expected.

Changes that come randomly are the ones that create the most trauma in an individual's life. In 1989 a major earthquake occurred in northern California, where I live. Those who shared our trauma by television knew more about the unfolding events than we who were in the middle of it. The earthquake tore at well-developed defenses and carefully built belief systems. We discovered that we are not the masters of our own destiny in the ultimate sense. We saw the chaos of a home destroyed; we picked up debris and contacted insurance companies. The internal trauma is harder to see—every creak or rumble sets us on alert for "The Big One."

There are special times when God jostles our complacency and equilibrium. Jokingly we may say to one another, "Don't pray for patience. You'll find yourself in a situation where you will need it." Our spiritual journey, like any other one, is a developmental one. So why does it surprise us that as we draw closer to the living God we are called to change?

Even though we know letting go of the old is a good thing, it is painful grieving old losses, developing new habits, thinking new thoughts. We may ask for more wisdom, patience, understanding, compassion, or filling of the Holy Spirit and at the same time pray, "God, please don't let it hurt." Or we may be like the little two-year-old child who wanted to play with the shiny knives. When her daddy moved them to the far corner of the counter, she cried and cried, not understanding the danger. A beautiful, young client of mine prayed each time she found a special boyfriend, "Lord, let this one be the one." When the relationship would fall apart, she would be angry at God for not answering her prayer. Slowly, as we worked through her family sorrows, she began to see that her choice in men had been very lacking and that God was indeed answering her prayers by removing the: "knives" from her grasp as she refined her choices.

The Cycle of Transition

I had been teaching part time and parenting full time for a number of years when I began to have the deep rumblings of dissatisfaction. It was more than the yearning I had always had to be a full time, non-working-out-of-the-home mom. And it was less intense than burnout, though the symptoms were similar. I would sit with my friend Sharon and complain about the pressure, get angry with the administrative decisions at the high school, and gripe about how tired I was. But I loved the classroom, the subject matter, and especially the students. I loved being kept on my toes by those challenging high school students. However, I could feel the winds of change blowing through my soul. Slowly it became obvious: If I were truly in the place I needed to be, I would not be this restless and dissatisfied. I was beginning a transition cycle. I was moving away from a place of equilibrium and moving into a place of *disequilibrium*, which I later discovered is the first stage in the process of change.

The second stage of a personal transition is *identification*. Even though I understood my dilemma more clearly, I had no clue what I was going to do about it. Over time, I was able to sort out what was legitimate tiredness and what was my restless soul. I needed time to pray and look within for what I desired to do instead of exhausting myself with self doubt and recrimination. All my life I had wanted to get an advanced degree in counseling, but I had never pursued the dream. In fact, I had given it up all together.

When a woman begins to validate her deepest desires, she is developing her personhood and beginningto be all that her Creator intended her to be. Many women with whom I work find personal validation difficult. I may ask a client, "What makes your heart sing?" Or "When you were a little girl, what did you want to do when you grew up?" Many of these women—whether they work within or outside the home, whether they are married or single—have a difficult time stopping long enough to recognize where they have been drawn off track.

Women are often embarrassed or feel inadequate to launch out on their own to make healthy changes in their lives. Often a woman comes into counseling because she is very unhappy and wants her husband, her children, her boyfriend, or parents fixed so that her life will be happier. Even when the husband or children, boyfriend or parents do need to change, we generally discover that depression, anger, and confusion emerge in a woman when she has lost confidence in her own ability to change her life, fulfill her own desires, or dream her own dream.

As I began to dream the dream, I felt freer even though I had made no decision. Although I knew the way ahead could be rocky, I was able to rest, pray, and plan without feeling entraped and hopeless. I could think about going back to school and doing something different.

The Stages of Transition

The process of transition is a vibrant, moving, living structure of billowing waves that continue to crash on the shore, recede and crash again.

Stage 1: Equilibrium is a stable place. It may not be healthy or a forever place, but it is a known place, a familiar place.

Stage 2: Restlessness is that place of inner upheaval, the beginning of rumblings that all is not well. Strange as it may seem, our children and family may first notice a difference. Children may act out and distract us into believing they are the cause rather than the reflectors of our confusion.

Stage 3: Disequilibrium is a feeling of chaos and confusion triggered by internal or external crises.

Stage 4: Equilibrium and Synthesis is a new state of stability and resting. This new state is richer and fuller because it becomes a synthesis of all the decisions and overcoming that have gone before.

The strange thing about transitions is that one decision brings more cycles of change. Transition means leaving the comfortable, the familiar, the stable. It is the passage through which we plunge into chaos and confusion, followed by a new place of stability and a sense of well being. As we see in the chart above, however, stability is always followed by a new disequilibrium–equilibrium cycle.

What many of us fail to recognize about endings—even good ones—is that it is important to say good-bye to the old before fully embracing the new. I did eventually change careers and return to graduate school. On my last day of teaching, my students had a party for me. Even though I was excited about a new adventure, I was sad at leaving wonderful students and saying good-bye to a fifteen-year profession.

Road Signs Along the Way

Today was one of those glorious days that calls me into the hills. The path my husband and I took wound its way through a forested region and ended in a high meadow from which we could see the entire San Francisco Bay area. The climb was steep with numerous switchbacks. How easy it would have been to have forged our way through the trees to the top. However, hanging off the trail were masses of poison oak, that wonderful creation of nature that makes me itch just by passing it. Again, I was reminded that paths are built for a purpose—to keep us safe.

When we take the inner journey, we likewise need reminders to stay on the path. The following suggestions may help you on this inner journey:

1. *Be patient.* Remember that change is a process and that every ending is the fuel for a new beginning. Not everyone will validate our need for going slowly, so we must validate the journey for ourselves.

2. *Be in a support group.* Finding an accepting group of individuals who are also on a journey can be very encouraging.

3. *Keep a journal.* Though many of us are too overwhelmed in the middle of a change to think about writing, keeping a record of our feelings and activities will be a rich experience.

4. *Practice being honest with yourself about feelings and thoughts.* It is important not to censor what you feel. Often times a woman will feel guilty for having negative feelings or for feeling too strongly. We can practice knowing our thoughts by talking out loud to ourselves. You might feel a little odd at first, but it sometimes helps to put into words what is inside your head. If feeling is hard for you, practice by developing your senses. Touch a variety of textures; notice how stores, rooms, or the outdoors smell; and practice asking yourself, How do I feel right now?

5. *Choose someone to trust.* It is vital to have a sounding board, someone you trust who is willing to listen without judgment to you no matter how crazy you may think you sound. I have found it helpful to remind my friend that I don't expect her or him to fix me; I just need to be heard. If I really want feedback, I need to be clear with my friend that I want her opinion even if I choose not to follow it.

Sometimes individuals find professional assistance helpful on this journey.

6. *Spend time alone.* Take some time, if possible, each day to ask the tough questions, to pray, to be still. When we are in turmoil and are confused by what is going on, the following questions are helpful to ask:

- What are the stress points in my life?
- Do I feel warmly or resentful toward the tasks in my life? Or the lack of them?
- What was going on in my life just before I started feeling out of sorts, in turmoil?
- When else have I felt this way? As a child? As a teenager? As an adult?
- What has changed in my life in the past six months? Are the changes by my choice or by another's?
- Has someone else's life shifted and I am reacting to it?

7. *Take time to rest and play.* If we focus too directly for too long on a problem, the solutions elude us. After we do all we can in thinking and processing, it is helpful to step aside for a short while and do something fun and playful. When the journey is one of deep searching and recovery, this part of the process is very important. Many of us feel so responsible that it is hard to give ourselves permission to play or rest. Now, some women use play as a protection from dealing with reality. If you are one, you may have to take this suggestion lightly and work for balance.

8. *Embrace the new.* When we move from disequilibrium to synthesis and equilibrium, we must validate the journey with a celebration. Some women I know reread their journal to get an overview of what they have accomplished. One friend celebrated a successful passage by taking a trip to the Magic Mountain theme park where she rode roller coasters all day long with her family. Another friend goes to lunch with a special friend. When I graduated from grad school, I threw myself a picnic party for all those who had been my emotional and prayer support .

Equilibrium

According to the apostle Paul in the book of Romans, the characteristics of a successful passage are a renewed sense of hope and an infilling of the love of God.

And not only this, but we also exult in our tribulations, knowing that tribulation brings about perseverance; and perseverance, proven character; and proven character, hope; and hope does not disappoint, because the love of God has been poured out within our hearts through the Holy Spirit who was given to us. (Rom. 5:3-5)

What other qualities tell a woman that she has successfully come to the other side and has reached equilibrium?

She will have a sense of relief, a sense of peace deep within. She will see new possibilities and have new ideas. She will have renewed energy. An inner journey of change can be an exhausting experience, like going through labor and delivery of a new baby.

She may also feel a sense of guilt. Some women feel guilty about feeling good when others are not pleased with her journey. It is easy to doubt your progress when others are disgruntled. When women change by choosing what is good in the long run, but brings pain in the short run, they tend to question their choices.

Guilt can take two forms. Sometimes we blame ourselves for things which are another person's responsibility. Sometimes when parents divorce, children blame themselves. When a father or mother is alcoholic, the child feels responsible for the parent's behavior. These are examples of *illegitimate guilt*. Illegitimate guilt fades with time and when a woman validates what God is doing in her life. Legitimate guilt persists. When guilt persists, we must discover what the wrongdoing is, evaluate what is needful, and change what is appropriate. We carry legitimate guilt when we wound someone intentionally or unintentionally, when we go against the moral order, or choose against what God is directing us to do or be.

A Woman in Transition

It is in transitions, that we grow as individuals. Throughout each transition and its successful passage a woman develops a deeper sense of self.

The end result of life's struggles is character development or of the fulfillment of identity. The apostle Paul acknowledges that life will have its tribulations, its sorrows, its pain. It is how we will go through pain that develops our character. We can also read Paul's encouragement another way. If we do not work through our tribulations with perseverance, if we get stuck along the way, we will not develop character in that area, and therefore, we will lose hope. Is it possible that our reluctance to face our fears and to face our pain creates the loss of hope and limits the outpouring of love through the Holy Spirit into our lives?

The woman in transition is a woman who is in confusion and turmoil, who feels restless and out of control. She also understands that life is an ongoing series of restings and upheavals, of changing seasons. She knows that an ending prepares the ground for new growth and new activity, and she knows that ultimately equilibrium, and a new order will replace the old.

Reflection

Record a current or recent transition. Be sure to include your feelings as well as the events.

1. What did you learn about yourself during this time of change?

2. What helped you most in this season?

Chapter Four

A Time for Every Purpose

※

he seasons of a woman's life encompass not only the physical and emotional vicissitudes of life, but also spiritual seasons. Spiritual transitions are those times when God dips down into our lives. If we look, we see His hand changing the chemistry, changing the circumstances, deepening our understanding of things. We may have asked to know more about His faithfulness and He begins by teaching us obedience. In the midst of the transition, it is often hard to see what the big picture is.

The only way I have been able to go through some of the transitions of my life is to see the event through spiritual eyes. I refer to such times as wake-up calls. Such a call occurred when I was a young mother. I was a spring woman in years and season.

Wake-up Calls

As we left the lights of Santa Barbara behind, the highway stretched in inky blackness before us. We were eager to return home to northern California after the usual hectic Christmas visit to family. Our fifteen-month-old son had finally fallen asleep in the back seat, and we were calmly planning our remaining vacation days.

Although traffic was relatively light, six vehicles were traveling close together when the car to our right blasted his horn and suddenly veered off the road. A large, black dog hurdled across the road and collided with our V.W. Squareback. We jolted, lurched, and stopped dead in our lane. The car behind swerved; others raced ahead and around to avoid hitting us. Cars stopped, flashlights bobbed toward us, shouts of "Are they okay?" "Someone get help." "Get that car off the road." "I've got a flare." We were too stunned to act, and some kind people had taken the initiative to move us to safety. "We're okay," we reassured the voices as we crawled from the car. *Thank God*, I thought. *Yes*, I paused, *thank God, we were all right*. But one wrong move, more speed, more anything—I didn't want to think about it.

Unbeknownst to me, this was my wake-up call. I would face a succession of out-of-control days, weeks, months—interruptions to my well-laid plans and desires in the season to follow.

In February the doctor diagnosed pregnancy, not flu, as the cause of my on-going exhaustion. However, we all did get the flu. At our worst, our son cracked his head on the corner of the coffee table and had to have six stitches above his eye. Three weeks later, my husband, a high school teacher, broke his leg in a school fund-raising basketball game. When our friends asked us to do something with them, we began to jokingly respond, "Yes, if we aren't in the emergency room."

By April, the "sleepies" of early pregnancy were passing only to be replaced by impatience and anger. Each week something else occurred. No one event was major, but events I couldn't control persisted. The angrier and less compassionate I became, the more things fell apart. I railed at God, "What are you doing? When are you going to let up? I'm supposed to be enjoying my new home, my young child, and being pregnant!"

I can still hear the words of the Lord clearly in my mind, "No, child, you may not run or walk. If you choose me, you must first learn to sit and then to crawl." My spirit shrieked in rebellion. "No! I want to run; I don't want to sit here in this pain! I want to have it all understood and life back as usual. I want to plan something and have it happen. I don't want to learn patience or accept living one moment at a time!"

But when the washing machine overflowed with dirty diaper water, I gave up. I had been acting like Balaam, who railed against his donkey; the donkey would not go forward when he saw the angel of the Lord with his sword in hand. Balaam beat the donkey to get him to move. But the donkey would not move into harm's way (Num. 22–23). I was beating the air to get circumstances to change, but nothing would.

Finally, one morning, I knew I needed time to think before the day began. In that quiet hour, I was honest with myself and with the Lord. "All right," I screamed inside, "You win! I don't like it, I don't want to grow anymore. I want to be in charge! But I don't want anymore pain! I'll do it Your way!"

However, the training and discipline were not over just because I yielded. Through the rest of the spring we faced more illness and emergencies, disappointments and delays. But the anger and rage at being out of control were gone. I yearned for a quiet moment, a resting place, but instead of rest, I learned to endure. Instead of calm, I learned to laugh at the chaos, and instead of anger, I learned to say, "Lord, I'm planning to do this. Okay?" I learned to accept what came, to let go of the outcome, and find a measure of peace.

As spring melted into summer, the crises came further and further apart. In fact one day I thought I actually heard in my spirit, "You can walk now." I heaved a sigh of relief and whispered a grateful, "Thanks!"

The clouds lifted and summer broke forth not only in season, but in our souls as we were able to plan, rest and play. A training season, a growing season had passed.

In the spring I could not understand the big picture. I knew I was being taught patience and acceptance. I was learning the hard way what the Scriptures say, " 'My ways are not your ways,' says the Lord." I am in awe even now of how He presents life's choices to His children. He has never put the choice to me as a threat or as a demand: "If you don't do this or that, then I'll zap you." It has always been, "If you choose Me; if you want to go My way; if you want Me to use you, here's the plan."

Summer and early fall were precious gifts to us as we prepared for the advent of our daughter in October. But two weeks after her birth, my daddy, who had heart disease, died unexpectedly on the operating table. No one had prepared us for the seriousness of the operation or for the possible risks. God, though, had been preparing me carefully and thoroughly in the spring for this winter experience. For the following ten days I assisted in funeral preparations and cared for my grieving mother, a newborn, and a very active two year old.

If I had not been taught to accept each moment, I could not have handled my loss and the stress with the calm and peace I miraculously had. As a child I had not been taught discipline, only that someone would come and rescue me from the consequences of my behavior. Being angry and being unable to cope with inconvenience did not serve me well. But the Master Gardener rototilled my spirit deeply that spring, teaching me how to be an adult and not a child demanding my own way.

The Backside of the Mountain

Although Moses is obviously not one of the *women* who illustrate God's principles of seasonal change, he does epitomize God's patience and affirmation of our development as individuals, the importance of hearing God's call, of waiting on His timing and trusting in His preparation in the midst of transitions.

The Old Testament Book of Exodus tells the story of Moses, who was born into a slave family when the Hebrew people were being severely persecuted in Egypt. Pharaoh, fearing their numbers, worked them harder, divided them into smaller groups by shipping them to various parts of the country, and ordered their male children killed. However, the more he persecuted them, the more they banded together and thrived. Moses' mother put him in a little ark made of bulrushes, hoping to save his life. Pharaoh's daughter came to the river and discovered the child. Though she knew it was a Hebrew child, Pharaoh's daughter rescued Moses, and she in turn had Moses cared for by his own mother until he was weaned. Later, he was reared as the son of Pharaoh's daughter. During those early years we cannot help but imagine that Moses was told the story of his deliverance.

Forty years later, Moses killed an Egyptian who was brutalizing a Hebrew slave. When it was discovered, Moses fled Egypt to hide in the wilderness. He sought asylum in the household of Jethro in the land of Midian. Although zealous, he missed God's timing, His purpose, and His methods.

Another forty years passed. On the backside of Mt. Horeb in the land of Midian, tending his father-in-law Jethro's sheep, Moses was about to enter into a transitional time in his life. Scripture records it this way:

> And the angel of the Lord appeared to him in a blazing fire from the midst of a bush; and he looked, and behold, the bush was burning with fire, yet the bush was not consumed.
> So Moses said, "I must turn aside now, and see this marvelous sight, why the bush is not burned up."
> When the Lord saw that he turned aside to look, God called to him from the midst of the bush. (Ex. 3:2–4)

As we explore the qualities of change in Moses' life and in the lives of the nation of Israel, we will also see how these qualities are similar to the transitions in our own lives.

God calls us in the midst of our daily pursuits. He gets our attention in the way He knows best, and He gives us clear instructions when we listen. What happened to Moses during those forty years? He must have wondered deeply about his attempt at defending one of his fellow Hebrews. As he tended sheep the waves of remorse, of regret, of shame had to roll over him in mighty surges. He was humiliated, a prince with a price on his head. He became a man without an identity, without a country. Then God found him and Moses responds, "Here I am."

In the desert burning bushes were not unusual. But this day there was no smoke that would indicate consumption; the dryness did not turn to ash. Only when Moses turned to look did the Lord speak. How many other times might God have spoken, but Moses could not have heard. God used something common in Moses' daily experience to tune his heart to His Spirit.

Once God had his attention, He began to speak. The Lord said: "I have surely seen the affliction of My people who are in Egypt, . . . therefore, I will send you to Pharaoh so that you may bring my people, the sons of Israel, out of Egypt" (Ex. 3:7,10).

Moses responds: "Who am I, that I should go to Pharaoh and that I should bring the sons of Israel out of Egypt?" (v. 11).

Interestingly enough, God did not answer Moses' question of adequacy, but rather spoke to His sufficiency: "Certainly I will be with you" (v. 72). Then He proceeded to lay out the plan clearly and explain all Moses needed to know.

There are a couple of aspects to this encounter at the burning bush that are noteworthy:

God had to first get Moses' attention. A burning bush experience is one that does not follow a normal course yet occurs in the middle of our day-to-day life. God tries to reach us in a variety of ways. He reaches us in our pain, in our shame, and in our circumstances. He leads us to ask the tough questions: "What is it You want to do in my life?" "What needs adjusting?" One of my burning bushes is sleeplessness. Reluctantly, when I can not sleep, I get up and begin to journal the anger, the frustration, the tension. Much to my surprise, beneath the anger and tension I discover deep grieving and sorrow. I sit there before the Lord and cry until I am comforted. Although I am a slow learner, the time between pain and resolution has diminished from weeks and months to days as I've practiced paying attention to the burning bushes in my life.

God will speak clearly from the bush what His desire is. Kristin is a lovely professional woman in her thirties who had a clear list of qualities she wanted in her husband. She met the man of her dreams. He is kind, witty, bright, loving, and yet she is in turmoil. In his mid-thirties he is starting a new profession and is not financially secure. She is panicked. Her dream didn't include financial struggle. "Haven't I struggled enough with a dad who used money to control us kids?" she confided in me one day. "Dad invites us out to dinner and expects us to pay for him! And when we don't give the right gifts in a timely manner he tells us his wife thinks we're cheap. I can't remember the last time he sent me a gift. I'm thirty-eight, for Pete's sake. I should be free of financial tensions!"

As we talked she revealed that just that week the sermon in her church was on God as provider. God drew her attention to her burning bush by underscoring the pain in her life around finances. He spoke clearly that she, not the man in her life, had a problem which needed addressing and healing. The burning bush of financial tension drew Kristin to ask herself some tough questions about her values, her desires, and her wounding in the area of finances.

In our own lives we will recognize a burning bush by several possible symptoms:

- God gets our attention through repeated pain in specific areas of our lives. We may experience the loss of friends or success or freedom. We may face financial difficulties in unexpected ways. We may have repeated fights with those we love. None of our plans may succeed, or we may experience free-floating anger or sorrow.
- We will feel hemmed in on all sides. We will feel paralyzed, out of control, unable to make clear decisions.
- We will gently feel the pressure on our souls to stop and ask "What is going on?"

Transitions challenge us to face our fears and admit our inadequacies. Fear is a strange beast. When it roars in the corridors of our minds we respond in a variety of ways. We may run in terror or withdraw deeply into our souls; we may stand frozen, too paralyzed to move, or we may fight back with false bravado while raging within at our weakness to quell the inner terror. The apostle Paul aptly addresses the nature of fear when he states, "God did not give us a spirit of fear , but of love, power and a sound mind" (2 Tim. 1:7). When we operate out of fear, we are alienated from those we love, we become powerless and helpless; and our thinking becomes unclear, tentative, and confused.

When life begins to change, the fear beast roars. He attacks us at at least three of our weakest points:

Fear of Humiliation. If we are going to choose to grow through times of stress and transition, we must face our fears and our inadequacies. Moses had to deal with his fear before he could move forward. Moses was afraid of being discounted, of being humiliated. His thoughts were probably these: "Who will believe me? So, if they ask who sent me, what should I say?"

He knew if he had an answer to the *who,* the *what* of the plan would follow. He wanted reassurance that he went with adequate authority.

His self-doubt was strong. Forty years previously he had begun a battle without the authority or the power and had failed. God clearly and fully explained to Moses his authority:

> Thus you shall say to the sons of Israel: the Lord, the God of your fathers, the God of Abraham, the God of Isaac, and the God of Jacob, has sent me to you. This is My name forever. (Ex. 3:15).

God reassured Moses that he would be listened to; *"And they will pay heed to what you say."* Likewise when we address our fears honestly before the Father, He patiently draws our attention to truth about His character and His ways in our life.

Fear of Rejection. Moses also had to face his fear of rejection. He asked, *"What if they will not believe me or listen to what I say. For they may say, 'the Lord has not appeared to you'"* (Ex. 4:1).

Moses was very much aware of his inadequacy. In fact, he argued every angle with God to get out of going back to Egypt. And God listened to all of Moses' excuses. But Moses did not get off the hook. Finally, Moses gave up and gave in.

Fear of annihilation. Moses also had to face his past. Moses would return to Egypt knowing there was a death warrant on his head. He was able to face this fear knowing he went by the hand of a greater authority than Pharoah. I wonder if Moses saw how uniquely he was prepared for the mission to follow. He was trained not only in the ways of the Egyptian court, but he was taught as a child the ways of God. He had the knowledge of the system and the awareness of court protocol, a sense of law, culture and language, but he had a vision beyond bondage. And, he had learned the wilderness well in forty years. He was comfortable under the stars and with the way of the land of the desert. His transition places were learning places and preparing places.

In order to reassure Moses that He was powerful, God commanded Moses to use his staff, a common shepherd's tool, "to perform the signs" (Ex 4:17). What had been common was now consecrated and set aside for a new purpose. God took Moses' training as an Egyptian and the staff, a reminder of his years in the wilderness, to work deliverance for his people. As hard as it may be to grasp, God does indeed weave all the threads of our lives together for a purpose. And, if we are willing to move, He will not leave us on the backside of the mountain.

In the midst of our own pursuits, there is a call on our lives. The dream is implanted. But often instead of embracing the new, we see the future through our fear and our past. Like Moses we only see our inadequacies and our weakness of character. Like Moses, we have a hard time believing that who we are and what we have done can have any purpose.

When we acknowledge circumstances to be of crisis proportions— when our attention is grabbed, and we choose to act—then change happens and growth occurs. Moses engaged God in discussion around the details of this mission. To be fully used, Moses had to face his fears. And, in order for Moses to let go of his fear he needed to be

- honest with God about his fear.
- reassured that God had a plan.
- assured he would not fail again.

Our lives are intricately balanced. One member of a family changes and everyone is affected. Newton, in his third law, stated it this way: "For every action there's an equal and opposite reaction somewhere in the universe." Balance must be achieved, but in the process of achieving that balance disequilibrium occurs.

Once Moses entered Egypt, conditions worsened before deliverance took place. Moses approached Pharaoh on behalf of the children of Israel with a request to leave to worship their God in the wilderness. But such a request made Pharaoh's heart harden toward them, and he demanded the same output with fewer resources (Ex. 5:5–21). As Moses negotiated, the people's suffering intensified. Moses continued to hold up the hope and the promise of rescue, but "they did not listen to Moses on account of their despondency and cruel bondage" (Ex. 6:9). He in turn, in anger and frustration, returned repeatedly to the Lord to make sure he had his instructions straight.

If the Israelites had not experienced the pain of Egypt they would not have left. Consider the nature of frogs. Because they are cold blooded creatures, they adapt to the temperature of their environment. If you put a frog in a kettle of boiling water, the frog jumps out. But if you put the frog in cold water and slowly turn up the heat, the frog cooks to death.

The Israelites, like the cold water frog, kept adapting to the pain of slavery. They cried for help, but they had so adopted a slave mentality that they could not envision freedom. When they cried out for God's intervention, they just wanted the pain to stop They would have been satisfied with peaceful coexistence and serving in Egypt. God envisioned freedom and rulership. Because of their victimization, they had no vision.

If they were to inherit freedom and lay claim to the land of their inheritance promised to their ancestors, they needed to experience the pain that would untie the cord of bondage of second class status and the willingness to let go of the familiar. Unless experiences are viewed as crises and the pain of staying is greater than the pain of changing, we tend not to change. They had to hate the cause of their pain enough that they were willing to leave.

Yet even after they left Egypt, they were furious with Moses for taking them into the wilderness. They quickly forgot the pain and the disease of Egypt. They were sure they would die in the desert. Growing up and out of a victim mentality is challenging and difficult. Life in the wilderness demanded trusting in God for their sustenance, learning how to govern and rule themselves, and embracing a victor instead of a victim mentality. God got them out of Egypt and then He had to get Egypt out of them.

Victimization. Likewise we may accept unhealthy relationships; stressful, exhausting work conditions; or destructive behavior from family, boss, and friends because it is familiar. We may pretend that we are noble in putting up with pain, but more often than not we put up because we have learned coping mechanisms that work. We feel helpless because our knowledge of options is limited.

What would some of these qualities of victim mentality look like?

A person who has a victim mentality believes:

- "Life will never go well for me."
- "Nothing I do will ever improve my status."
- "If I try, life will only get worse."

- "Unless the power structure changes or someone rescues me, I will not be okay."
- "If I don't succeed, it's not my fault."
- "I have to work harder than anyone else just to stay even."

Melissa was raised in a Christian home where godly principles were taught and modeled by her father. However, his father had been an alcoholic, and Melissa's mother was also an alcoholic who hid her chemical dependency behind physical illness. Her father did not protect his children from the excesses of their mother. Melissa learned to be the "perfect" daughter to help stabilize the craziness. Her sister, who was thirteen months younger, accepted the role of the "bad" daughter. Her overt rebellion and drinking were her attempts at saying, "Won't someone please notice something terrible is happening in my family." Ultimately she too became an alcoholic.

Melissa married at eighteen to escape home. Her husband was a successful professional who was very giving and kind when all was going well, but who acted out his anger. He had been raised in a violent home. Throughout Melissa's adult life, crises and catastrophes followed her. Her husband criticized and belittled her thoughts, ideas, and dreams. Then when their daughter was seven and son two, her husband died of cancer. Her cry was always, "Why does God keep giving me this pain?"

After several unsuccessful relationships, she finally began to ask herself the tough questions: "Why *do* bad things happen to me? What do I have to do about changing these patterns?" Rather than continuing to blame God, she started looking for truth. She began to examine the messages of her belief system, as well as her denial and the impact of her mother's alcoholism. She could see that she created chaos in her own life by the choices she made. She was drawn to people who would continue to wound her, and she continued in patterns that perpetuated a victim stance.

Primary versus secondary pain. The chaos Melissa experienced in her adult life was *secondary pain.* We create secondary pain when we continue the denial of that original childhood pain. We believe, "If I feel the pain of being abandoned by my parent (mistreated, abused, yelled at by those I love), I will die." This is *primary pain.* We either run from (flight) the painful situation or become aggressors (fight) trying to get the pain to stop.

When we stop running, we can begin to look at our *primary pain,* feel the losses of childhood, recognize the impact of those experiences on our adult life, and begin to change our behavior. When we do, we can see the advantages of facing primary pain.

- Secondary pain begins to abate.
- We become aware that we create crises with those we love and move toward changing the pattern.
- We practice acting by choice rather than "off the cuff."
- We learn to feel appropriate feelings. We can direct anger where anger is due and loving feelings where they are due.
- We direct our energies toward the source of our pain rather than punishing others or internalizing the pain and becoming depressed.

God's call is to wake us up. If we cannot see the big picture yet, we are to yell for help as the children of Israel did. He may answer with a burning bush. He may lead us to a Moses to hold out the hope when we cannot see the way. The Israelites first had to loathe their pain and see its destruction. Second, they had to be delivered out of the abusive environment in order to heal and have perspective. Third, they would develop over time an ability to trust God in Moses' leadership. Finally, they were strong enough, and certain enough of their own faith to begin inhabiting their own lands, towns, and homes. They had to be led out of Egypt (slavery) in order to be brought into their promised land (freedom).

We don't know exactly how long the series of plagues took before Pharaoh relented and let the people go. But we do know the people wandered in the wilderness for forty years as they prepared for their new identity as a nation. They lived and died, loved and hated, acted obediently and rebelled defiantly until they were able to envision a new identity. The transition almost became their way of life. Then one day, in the midst of daily pursuits, God spoke: "You have stayed long enough at this mountain. Turn and set your journey, go in and possess the land" (Deut. 1:6b,8a).

Like Moses, we are often awakened to new possibilites and new directions by a divine wake-up call. Such a call leads us into a transition time, a time in the wilderness of grieving, healing and growth. The journey into the past to understand the messages we received as children and to heal from the pain experienced, does not leave us wandering in a wilderness, but rather frees us to turn and set our journey, to inhabit new territory, to become victors instead of victims.

Once we understand that transitions are part of the fabric of life, we are more able to accept rather than resist change. The issue is not so much whether we will encounter a burning bush or a wilderness experience, but rather how we will go through it when it comes. In the next chapter we will explore strategies for growing through the grieving process as we explore the season of winter.

Reflection

Your personal time is a chance to honestly evaluate your readiness to change. You may find examining your attitudes and fears a painful experience, so begin cautiously.

1. List several experiences in your life that could be burning bush wake-up calls. Record not just the event, but also record the feelings you were experiencing at the time.

2. What fears do you need to face? In what ways have your fear messages limited your life and choices?

3. What would you call your Egypt experience, where you feel stuck and unable to make good choices for changing your own experience?

4. Do you have a victor or victim mentality? Write down any of the traits under victimization that may fit your current or past experiences.

Part II

The Winter Woman

❧

Weeping may last for the night, but a shout of joy comes in the morning.

(Ps. 30:5)

CHAPTER FIVE

A Season of Loss

O*nce the Christmas trees are sold,* the lights are taken down, and the sales shed is boarded up, the field on the corner sits silent and abandoned. Winter! A season of death and decay, of slumber, of storm and stress, of grief. In nature the days shorten, the vibrant colors of autumn turn to dark grey. Rains pelt the earth and snow blankets the colder regions. Trees are barren. Animals and birds withdraw and slumber. A pruned hedge, rose bush, or tree stands silently building up strength and nutrients for spring growth.

A Time to Grieve

The winter woman is a grieving woman. She has experienced loss, death, despair. She sees only the wilderness and never the promised land. She faces a season of endings. The woman who is full of years is also a winter woman. She is a woman facing her last season. However, as we will see, she may be a spring or summer woman in how she lives out her days. Her task is to confront her mortality and choose how she will make her final winter journey.

Questions permeate this season in a woman's life. Why do I have to suffer? Why is this happening to me? Her sorrow extends beyond annoyances or temporary interruption in her daily pursuits. She is catapulted into turmoil. A winter season is characterized by intense, physical symptoms of pain, crashing disruptions of normal life, and unrelenting emotional disorientation.

The Power of Loss

By its very nature a winter season is unpredictable and out of our control. At times we feel "normal," actively involved in daily pursuits. At other times we are overwhelmed with tears, sorrow, and bone-crushing pain. Sorrow becomes an unbidden stalker, a dragon consuming us in one moment with the fire of grief; then he waits, fire contained, now docile and still but ever present, readying himself for another attack.

Transitions and changes that occur out of season create inner storm and stress. We may prepare ourselves for the death of an elderly relative or friend—but when we are in our twenties and our parents appear young to us, we do not anticipate their deaths. I was not prepared for my father's death. No one understood. There were no comrades to empathize with my loss. Within two years my mother also died. Knowing my friends were sharing their children's growing years with grandparents only made my loss deeper.

Winter Tasks

Even though we may not understand or see what lies ahead, there are tasks to perform. If we do not learn from our winter season, we will remain bitter, reliving the past rather than embracing the present and preparing for the future. If we do not successfully accomplish the tasks of other winter seasons, we will look back in our final winter season and ask, "Has my life meant anything?" The chapters to follow explore the tasks of a winter season.

A woman in winter is one who

- understands the nature of grief.
- understands that grief is a process.
- prepares for her chronological winter season.

The Nature of Grieving

Even as we acknowledge the power of winter storms—the power of our losses—we often minimize their importance in our own lives. Often a woman will come to me and complain of depression, loss of interest in life, and/or a generalized anger. She asks, "What's wrong with me?" I usually respond, "What was going on in your life just before this heaviness and loss of interest in life occurred?" In surprise, her response is usually this: "Do you think what happened two weeks, (six months, three years ago), could have anything to do with this?"

Inevitably, a major loss preceded the change in emotional well-being. Then she may say, "But I cried at the time my friend (parent, child, spouse, neighbor) died and grieved for several months, but I should be over that by now. No one wants to be around a crybaby." Or, "I have so much to be grateful for, I shouldn't be moping around in self pity." When we overreact to current life changes or are overcome by feelings we cannot explain, we must ask, "Is it possible this is impacted by an earlier loss I don't want to face?"

Timing

A winter season must be lived through. One cannot go faster or slower than what the healing of time brings. The passage through the stages of grieving, some experts say, takes at least one year. In fact, feelings of the loss may linger on into other seasons.

The time it takes to grieve will vary with each individual. There will be moments, long after our active grieving season has ended, when the defenses are down and we are hit by a wave of memory. Tears well up in our eyes; our throats constrict. Memories and yearning for the past well up from deep within. As each of my children graduated from high school, I wished my parents could have been there, proudly watching their grandchildren march to "Pomp and Circumstance."

Learned Attitudes Toward Grieving

Cultural traditions impact our ability to grieve. The media admired Jacqueline Kennedy because she sat poised and dry-eyed during her husband's funeral. A woman is considered strong when she is controlled, weak if she shows emotion.

Our own ethnic and cultural background gives a model for grieving. Recently a local Jewish oncologist's fourteen-year-old son was killed in a mountaineering accident. During the temple services the family wept. At the reception after the service, friends spoke of the family's loss. For a week the family opened their home to the community and their temple friends for a period of active mourning. Either the rabbi or the cantor was with them each night. Friends came to talk, to cry, to share stories. The mother was surrounded by love and nurture and hugs and support. There was an open acknowledgement that grief lasts and loved ones are worthy to be remembered.

The ancients dealt with death more directly. The aged died at home. Families lived near each other and grieved together. In the story of Lazarus, ritual mourners came to Mary and Martha's house to assist them grieve. Mourning was given a proper, open place in the cultural fabric.

Family rules also impact our attitudes toward grieving. What messages does your family give when someone is in pain? Do you remember as a small child how your sorrow was acknowledged or how others dealt with their losses? One way of remembering is by asking yourself, "What do I do now when I'm hurting? What do I tell myself? Am I compassionate with myself or harsh? Accepting or critical?

Did your family give you permission to cry and express your feelings? If so you learned, "When I cry, I will be comforted." In that comfort you were able to go on to enjoy the good times of life and to successfully go through seasons of sorrow. Other families may say in behavior or words, "Don't be a crybaby," or "What will people think?"

Did your family have a don't-talk-rule for family pain? If a child breaks the rule, she feels shame at betraying the family.

Did your family shield you from the experience of death and dying? Parents forget that children have ideas and feelings and can understand when a caring adult explains clearly what is going on. If you were excluded, you may have questioned your value to the family. When Mildred was ten, her nearest and dearest grandmother died. The day of the funeral preparations, service and family gathering, Mildred was whisked away to a neighbor's house for the day and night. No one explained why she was going or what was going on. She was the only sibling of four not in attendance. Abandonment, isolation, helplessness, loss of value were all feelings Mildred experienced. "What's the matter with me that I can't be at home?" she wondered. We must assist our children to join in the family grieving and give them freedom to ask questions.

Faces of Grief

People who are uncomfortable with pain usually follow the don't-feel, don't-cry, don't-grieve, don't-show-emotion rules. We may be afraid that if we start to cry, we won't be able to stop. Others have learned to deny their own pain. Sometimes we may feel helpless when we are with someone who is grieving. We want to fix the other person because of our own discomfort. When my mother died, my good friend and neighbor sent me a card with a big happy face on it. On the inside it said, "Have a Happy Day." She could not face the reality of the pain of death.

Some of us may have a fear of being morbid, of focusing too much on death. Therefore we run from it. Or we may be afraid of our own mortality and would prefer to pretend temporal life is eternal? We may spiritualize our grief: "Scripture says death is swallowed up in victory. I just want to focus on being victorious." As Christians we may become very confused, wanting to acknowledge the power and presence of God and somehow feeling, "If I show my anger, sorrow, pain I'm somehow not demonstrating my faith." The second beatitude says, "Blessed are those who mourn, for they shall be comforted" (Matt. 5:4). Is it possible that if we do not mourn our losses and face our fears that we limit the power of the Holy Spirit to comfort us, and therefore we are left feeling more deeply alone?

Ungrieved Losses

Divorce, chronic illness, the death of a spouse, the death of a child, the loss of one's own or a spouse's job are easily recognized losses in a woman's life. However, we also experience unrecognized losses: acknowledged, hidden, minimized. Ungrieved, these losses resurface powerfully in other ways as it did for Gail.

Recently Gail and her family decided to move. She had lived within twenty minutes of her childhood home her entire life. Once the papers were signed and she prepared to move, she fell apart. She doubted the wisdom of the move, grieved the loss of her home, which she had not liked in the first place, and spent most days in tears. She was touching a buried grief.

When she was thirteen, her seventeen-year-old brother had been responsible for a fatal car accident in which he and others were killed. The grief plunged her mother into a mental and emotional collapse from which she has not emerged. Not only did Gail lose her brother, but also she lost her mother's presence in her life. Her father went with her to buy her prom dress and did the cooking and caretaking of the family. Her brother had become very rebellious just prior to his death. During this period, she and her family had moved into a new home. Beneath the loss of her current home was a deep fear that something terrible would happen to her current family if they were to move.

In Gail's family of origin, the brother was never mentioned, never talked about. No one acknowledged the loss. In order to protect herself and to survive, Gail plunged herself into working hard academically and being as active as she could away from home. As an adult she over-extended herself to prove to everyone she was tough and could endure anything. By working extended hours on the computer she damaged her wrists and she returned to work prematurely after illness. She could face anything, except the pain of her brother's death and the loss of her mother's involvement in her life. "I couldn't believe," she reports, "that it wasn't our current move that was the tragedy. But now I know this current sorrow is for my brother and what I lost when he died."

Delayed grief and grief not fully acknowledged impacts the power with which we experience successive change and loss.

Defense Mechanisms

Children do not have the ability to handle severe pain directly without help. Hence, a child does what she needs to do in order to survive. Our defense mechanisms protect us. Denial is one form of defense. When someone is unable to face the reality of a present or past situation, we say that that person is in denial. Sometimes denial can be self imposed and decided consciously: "I will not hurt; I will not remember." But more commonly denial is an unconscious response to intense pain and the inability to resolve the grief in a satisfactory manner. An adult wounded as a child may glorify the abusing parent as the best parent in the world, recreate his or her childhood as the happiest childhood, and say she was raised in the best family. In reality Dad came home drunk, yelled at the children, and sent terror into the hearts of each of them. But the child denied in order to survive.

Another protection system is dissociation. A person who dissociates splits off from all of the reality of a situation or part of it. A woman may remember the incidents of sexual abuse by a significant family member, but not feel the physical or emotional memories. Or she may react strongly in sexual situations, feeling the terror of the abuse, but not have a concrete memory of the details. We have three kinds of memories: picture memories, body memories, and feeling memories. The wounded individual, in other words, may have amnesia for any part or for the whole of past painful events. Thus when she is faced with a situation that triggers her subconscious memory of her hidden pain, she may act to protect that tender spot.

If we learn to deny the experience of pain, we take that habit into adulthood. When we are faced with situations with our own children, spouse, friends, or relationships at work, we may act inappropriately for what is occurring in the present. The winter woman may experience deeper pain because of past pain and because she has developed coping mechanisms that do not aid her in her adult crises.

Why is this relevant? Current national statistics indicate that one in four women have been sexually abused. The primary abuser is generally a trusted family member: father, brother, uncle, cousin and, in some cases, even a mother. Therefore, if we have not been abused ourselves, someone we love probably has been. It is crucial that we understand the nature of violation and how to heal or how to be agents of support to those needing healing. When we fail to understand or we discount the pain of others, we undermine rather than enhance the healing journey.

Symptoms of Hidden Pain

Any trauma perceived as shame or pain and not dealt with influences our well being. When we have hidden pain, we may react in several ways:

- over-react to situations in our lives. Minor inconveniences take on the character of a major disaster. If our kindergartner is slow at learning her letters, we're convinced she'll never go to college.
- limit our involvement in life out of fear. But we may say "that's just the way I am. I've always been afraid of _____." We avoid new

situations, closed in places, meeting new people, starting new projects, and, in extreme situations, leaving our homes.

- develop personality traits that hide the pain and cover our fear. We may become controlling, overly enthusiastic, overly opinionated and judgmental, aggressive and demanding, or passive and retiring. Instead of taking responsibility for our own actions, we may blame the government, our children, our spouses, or God for any situation not to our liking.
- ignore or minimize pain symptoms in our own children because recognizing similar pain in them would force us to act differently from our parents and may touch our hidden, forgotten sorrow.
- marry or be attracted to partners or friends who recreate what we are familiar with or who keep the messages of our lack of worth alive.

Emily never felt valued as a female child. She knew deep inside that her father wanted her to be a boy and was disappointed with a third daughter. She spent her childhood proving her worth to her father. She chose male friends who were bright and capable, but she never believed she was worthy to marry them. In fact, she had a succession of male partners who were alcoholic and needy. "They made me feel I was worth something. With them I could be in control and strong. With a man of quality I'm afraid I would feel unworthy and of no value. I would not be in control." But with each relationship the winds of winter and sorrow kept blowing.

When we have hidden pain we may also:

- use illness to keep from having to be too productive. When you are ill, someone else cares for you, and you are "off the hook."
- experience unrelenting anxiety even though our lives appear to be moving along smoothly.
- be unable to enjoy successes or be unwilling to risk new endeavors out of fear of success or fear of failure.
- withdraw from those who love us, appearing cold, aloof, indifferent, self assured—for protection when we feel threatened, insecure and frightened.

The woman who does not pay close attention to her emotions and feelings is most likely to face an emotional winter. Her hidden sorrows and shameful places in her past are like boils that need to be lanced.

However, we would prefer to put the blame on something in the present rather than look for the underlying trigger that fuels the present reaction. When we do not face primary pain (loss of a love, abuse of the past, the loss of parent or sibling to death, the divorce of our parents), we inevitably create situations which cause secondary pain. Remember, secondary pain is any pain incurred from avoidance of feelings or facing our fears.

I met Leslie in an industrial setting and was fascinated by her vibrance. Her story describes how unattended primary pain creates secondary pain.

"I graduated from college with a degree in mining engineering. In my firstmining job, I was hired as their first female manager, overseeing thirty-five men. There were obvious strikes against my success. I was five feet tall, petite, and female. I was raised to believe that if you are fair and kind, people will respond in kind. No one told me how vicious some of the mine cultures could be. The men bored holes in the women's wash room. Another manager did everything he could to get me fired. He spread false rumors about me after pretending to be my friend.

"One night, after I was there a year, I vowed, 'I'm not going to let anyone get to me anymore. I'm going to give back what I get.' From then on I got tough. If someone pushed, I pushed harder. I learned to talk as tough as any of them. But I became someone I didn't want my parents to see. I became someone I didn't even know. As a result, I'm tougher than I need to be, I don't trust many people, and I have little charity for the men in my life.

"Currently I'm a manager in a plant. I have the ability to organize things and see that a product gets through the plant efficiently. I have no tolerance for inefficiency or politics. I've been tough a long time. Now, I'm being considered for advancement, but I've hit a wall. I've been told unless I get my temper under control, I'm not moving anywhere.

"When I feel undermined, not listened to, demeaned by my peers, I blow my stack. I go from calm to volcanic in seconds. All I see is the injustice; I rarely see the impact on others."

One of Leslie's sources for primary pain was the harassment and sorrow from her experiences in the mines. Because she could not face the pain of what she had become, she just kept moving into new, more challenging work places. When her undealt-with anger leeched into her relationships at work, her job advancement was threatened. The fear of a job loss, the shame of being singled out is called secondary pain. By being all business with her peers, she also experienced the loneliness of isolation. By taking care of the primary pain, she will decrease the stress of secondary pain and have more resilience for day-to-day coping and living.

Often the only way an individual is willing to break the denial is when the pain of going forward is greater than the pain of stopping and asking "what is going on?" When a woman consistently denies unpleasant feelings—from annoyance to loneliness to outrage—or neglects her inner self, she drains significant funds from her emotional and physical bank account. It may take a wake-up call either emotionally or physically, to persuade her to slow down and change her direction.

Other Causes of Grief

Accumulated Losses

Accumulated losses and multiple changes in a woman's life intensify her winter seasons. In the mid-sixties two social psychologists, Thomas Holmes and Richard Rahe, developed what they called a "Social Readjustment Scale" which listed the most stress-producing events in our lives. They had a sample of 2,400 men and women list a variety of life's events in order from most stressful to least. They postulated that the greater the number of major changes in an individual's life, the more prone she will be to a major illness, depression, and/or burnout.

On Holmes and Rahe's original list the death of a spouse was ranked as the most stress-producing event in a person's life and was assigned a stress value of 100 points (see Figure 5-1). In 1967 divorce was ranked as the second most stressful event and was assigned 73 stress points. At the end of the listing, individuals were asked to add up the number of changes and losses they had experienced in a calendar year. As you can see the chart includes both tragic and joyful events. The one thing they have in common is that they all involve change.

Too many changes within a limited time period become life-threatening. Holmes and Rahe discovered that people with scores over 300 points had an 80 percent chance of contracting a major illness, being in a major accident, or becoming depressed. Those whose scores were between 150 and 300 points were 50 percent at risk of falling ill within two years.

In 1990, Georgia Witkin, the author of *The Female Stress Syndrome* gave the same stress scale to 2,400 women, asking them to list the same life events in order of most to least stressful (see New Point Value Figure

LIFE EVENT	New Point Value [1]	Old Point Value [2]
Death of Spouse	99	100
Divorce	91	73
Marital Separation	78	65
Jail term	72	63
Death of close family member	84	63
Personal injury or illness	68	53
Marriage	85	50
Fired at work	83	47
Marital reconciliation	57	45
Retirement	68	45
Change in health of family member	56	44
Pregnancy	78	40
Sex difficulties	53	39
Gain of new family member	51	39
Business readjustment	50	39
Change of financial state	61	38
Death of close friend	68	37
Change to a different line of work	51	36
Change in number of arguments with spouse	46	35
Mortgage over $10,000	48	31
Foreclosure of mortgage or loan	55	30
Change in responsibilities at work	46	29
Son or daughter leaving home	41	29
Trouble with in-laws	43	29
Outstanding personal achievement	38	28
Spouse begins or stops work	58	26
Begin or end school	45	26
Change in living conditions	42	25
Revision of personal habits	44	24
Trouble with boss	45	23
Change in work hours or conditions	36	20
Change in residence	47	20
Change in school	36	20
Change in recreation	26	19
Change in church activities	26	19
Change in social activities	26	18
Mortgage or loan less than $10,000	27	17
Change in sleeping habits	27	16
Change in number of family get-togethers	15	15
Change in eating habits	29	15
Vacation	43	13
Christmas	56	12
Minor Violations of law	30	11

Figure 5.1: Social Readjustment Rating Scale

5-1). According to her results, life in the nineties is more stressful for women than thirty years ago. The new stressors have not replaced the old ones.

In addition to the traditional home pressures, a woman is now as worried about financial considerations and work related stress. In an age where many women share the financial burden with their spouses and where single family homes are on the increase, women faced with a job loss or financial change are under more stress than thirty years ago. The scores are up from a value of 47 to 83 on job loss. Wilkins discovered new stress-producing items that women ranked with high points: a disabled child yielded 97 points; single parenting, 96, remarriage, 89, depression, 89, and a child's illness, 87. Because the working mom is still the chief nurturer and manager at home, a child's illness produces stress for her. A study released in the fall of 1993 found that in families where both parents are working 85 percent of the work around the home is still done by women. Other high point stressors are infertility, a spouse's illness, crime victimization, parenting parents, and raising teens.

Burnout

During the drought that had California in its grip for seven years, I watched mighty, ancient California oaks wither and die on the hillsides next to a major freeway. As the water table declined, the trees became vulnerable to disease and decay as car pollution and the stress of cold and heat battered at their ancient frames. Over time, the trees slowly died, first losing leaf and then limb. Likewise, ongoing periods of stress and change leave us vulnerable for burnout and disease.

Stress is inevitable. Although we cannot eliminate environmental stressors, we can learn how to manage our stress and prevent burnout. It is therefore important to distinguish between good stress and bad stress. Good stress spurs us on to achieve, to improve relationships, to risk. Bad stress leaves us exhausted and does not alter with a good night's sleep.

When our bodies become overloaded, we head for burnout. According to Herbert Freudenberger,

> Burnout is a wearing down and wearing out of energy. It is an exhaustion born of excessive demands which may be self-imposed or externally imposed by families, jobs, friends, (spouses), value systems or society, which deplete one's energy, coping mechanisms, and internal resources. It is a feeling state which is accompanied by an overload of stress, and which eventually impacts on one's motivation, attitudes and behavior. [3]

And, as such, burnout can usher in a winter season.

Understanding Grief

The winter woman learns how to navigate the waters of grieving. The swimmer in the ocean must learn how to navigate the waves, or she will be dashed and churned about by the crashing breakers. The swimmer learns she must dive into an oncoming wave or squat down and allow the wave to crash over her head to avoid a thrashing. Likewise, the grieving woman must dive into the pain of her loss in order to avoid the thrashing of secondary pain. She also discovers

- there is a time for grieving.
- her culture and family traditions affect how she grieves.
- ungrieved losses produce secondary pain.
- losses can be hidden, communal and accumulated.
- burnout can usher in a winter season.

In the next section we will learn how to dive through the grief cycle by examining the stages of the grieving process.

Reflection

Examine your attitudes about grief in these journal entries.

1. Compare the change points in your life in the past year to those in Figure 5-1. What do you observe? Record the changes on Figure 5-1 that you have experienced in the past year and add up the points on the printed chart. What did you discover about the stress events in your life?

2. Have you ever experienced a winter season of loss? Record as much as you wish about that season. If you have never gone through a winter, you may wish to record a loss that you have experienced and the feelings attached to the memory.

Chapter Six

A Season of Grief

❧

*Humpty Dumpty sat on a wall. Humpty Dumpty had a great fall.
All the King's horses and all King's men couldn't put Humpty together again.*

Children learn about loss and the nature of death through their play and stories. The nursery rhyme "Humpty Dumpty" teaches a child that there is loss in this life that no earthly power can alter: "all the king's horses and all the king's men couldn't put Humpty together again." The loved animal, person, condition in our life, age, stage, life style, is gone. But although we may recognize our loss, it still has a powerful hold on our very being.

Even though we may have major losses in our past and may not have been allowed or taught how to grieve them, we can still live productive, functional lives. These past hurts, though, increase our vulnerability for stress and decrease our capacity for coping with successive loss. The Institute of Medicine[1] finds that some individuals will experience more acute physical and mental trauma following a major loss than others. A major loss that occurs during one of the following situations increases a person's risk of becoming physically and/or emotionally ill in the future:

- An individual who has a poor prior history of mental or physical health.
- The younger one is when one experiences major loss.
- If a relationship of a husband or wife at the time of death was particularly ambivalent or dependent.
- Those who experience loss without a social support network.

Researchers have attempted to understand physiologically what occurs in our bodies as a result of trauma. Some use the illustration that emotional trauma does to the nervous system and emotions what a sledge hammer would do to the head. Pretty shattering! As close as we can understand the brain cells are literally traumatized and excited when abuse, loss, or violation occurs to us. The pain input, sent along the nerve endings, is so powerful that it excites the brain in a way that the memory stays fixed and frozen with all of the details of color, shape, sound, feeling just as it entered. If a compassionate person is able to assist the adult or child talk about the events and help her express her feelings, the brain wound can be lanced, opened, and drained of its poison. If not, the brain surrounds the trauma much as an oyster surrounds the invasive grain of sand.

The emotional content of a loss is as powerful as the physiological. We do not just feel our pain, but we interpret it as well. Anne's dad took a new job which required him to travel extensively. When he left, she felt abandoned. No one explained where he went and why he was gone so long. On weekends he would appear for a day and a half, grumpy, angry, exhausted. In her five-year-old mind she figured that it must have been something she had done wrong. "If only I were a perfect little girl, Daddy would come home again and be nice."

Anne believed a lie. She was not to blame for her daddy's leaving or for his grumpiness. She had a false picture of her worth because no one told her the truth. The truth was her daddy left the family to earn a living and could not be emotionally present for his children when he was home. In order to feel free of this loss of value and childhood, Anne must grieve the losses. As she does this, her brain wound will begin to heal. She will then need to replace the lie with the truth by telling herself something like this: "I was not to blame for my dad's inability to handle stress. I was not a 'bad' little girl. In fact, I am a very sensitive person, and it hurt to be yelled at when I did nothing wrong."

Loss-Recovery Wheel

We must remember to actively mourn in order to break open the electrically charged material lodged in our brains, to dissipate its impact, and restore us to health. Our journey through the grief wheel gives us a model for understanding grief's cyclical nature. The intensity of the passage through each stage depends, of course, on the importance of the loss. As we noted in the last chapter, death and divorce are life-change events that produce an enormous amount of stress. However, each of us experiences other losses that cause a deep sense of grief. Some of these are loss of innocence by childhood sexual abuse, loss of friendship, loss of job, and loss of value because of emotional and physical abuse.

When we face a loss by death, certain factors affect our ability to face and deal with loss—the age of the deceased, how close the person was to us, whether the death is sudden or a prolonged one. Violent, unexpected death poses particular difficulty since deep anger often accompanies such a loss. The death of a child leaves us with the sorrow of an unfinished story. Death after a protracted illness is often accompanied by relief that the sufferer has been released from pain. When we let go of the loved one in stages, our grief is well advanced by the time death occurs.

How long is appropriate to grieve? Grieving takes as long as it takes. We are all unique and with our uniqueness comes as many ways of grieving. Generally, however, the grieving process takes at least a year. During that time we remember birthdays, anniversaries, favorite holidays, and shared events. If we are grieving the loss of a home by fire or our own chronic illness, we may remember other events that occurred in happier times on those anniversary dates. By the second year, the griever has begun to put into place new days of celebration and new patterns, new activities, new people that begin to replace the old.

Does everyone grieve the same way? No. There is a wide range of normal grieving. Dr. Camille Worman, a psychologist at the University of Michigan, discovered that severe distress or depression does not always follow major loss. She states, "People who are grieving often find themselves under a subtle social pressure to show more distress than they may feel close to the loss, on the one hand, and to cheer up and get on with life long before they feel able to do so, on the other. The truth is that there is no universal prescription for how to grieve."[2] In fact, Worman discovered that one common trait of people who did not go into total despair at the time of the loss was that they had a belief system that gave them a broader perspective. A "spiritual outlook lets them see the loss in a way they could accept as part of life's plan, for example, or for some greater purpose." No matter how one grieves or the length of time of one's bereavement, we all must grieve.

C.S. Lewis speaks eloquently of the pain he experienced at the death of his wife when he said in *A Grief Observed*: "How often—will it be for

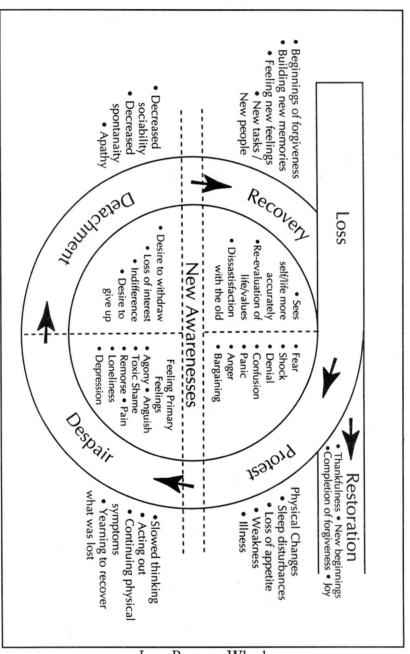

Loss–Recovery Wheel

Figure 6-1

always?—How often will the vast emptiness astonish me like a complete novelty and make me say, 'I never realized my loss till this moment? The same leg is cut off time after time. The first plunge of the knife into the flesh is felt again and again.'"

In another place he described the grief process in these words: "One keeps on emerging from a phase, but it always recurs. Round and round. Everything repeats. Am I going in circles?"

Yes, we could tell him, you are going in circles; that is the nature of grieving. A look at the loss-recovery wheel explains why. Figure 6-1 shows one version of the grief cycle with its four stages between the experience of Loss and Restoration. We may go around the loss-recovery wheel several times. If you look at the illustration, you will see a dotted line cutting the circle in half. When we grieve we often discover new information, or other losses surface. Then round the wheel we spin again.

Each person grieves on her own time-table. Some follow the tasks sequentially and others go from one to another and back again. Some go around the circle many times before they are ready for restoration. Each stage of the grief process (protest, despair, detachment, recovery) has its own emotional and physical characteristics. In addition there are tasks for each stage that, when completed, draw the winter woman closer to renewed life.

In order for us to successfully navigate the winter storms we must

- accept the reality of the loss.
- experience the pain of grief.
- adjust to an environment in which what's been lost (lost love, child, friend, vision of self) no longer exists.
- withdraw emotional energy from the old and reinvest it in the new (new job, new relationship, new vision of self).

The grief wheel diagram and its tasks are designed to help us understand more fully the nature of grieving. When we are in the middle of a loss, we most likely will not say, "Well, here I am in stage one. Let me get out my handbook and see what I'm to do." Let the following be a guide for your own future journey and for understanding the journey of others.

Protest

The first stage on the grief wheel is *protest*. The task is to accept the reality of the loss. The most common expression in this time period is, "Nothing is wrong; nothing has really happened." And yet our whole body is telling us something different. Around 6:30 one morning I received the phone call telling me the husband of one of my dear friends had committed suicide. I think I said something inane to the caller like, "You've got to be kidding. Are you sure?" For days I found myself standing, staring, unattached to the events around me.

Scripture gives many examples of those who mourn, protesting their losses and expressing their confusion. Jeremiah in the book of Lamentations gave a guide to the expression of grief when he wrote:

> Let your tears run down like a river day and night;
> Give yourself no relief
> Let your eyes have no rest.
> Arise, cry aloud in the night
> At the beginning of the night watches;
> Pour out your heart like water
> Before the presence of the Lord;
> Lift up your hands to Him. (Lam. 2:18–19a)

King David also mourned for the way his life had been:

> My tears have been my food day and night,
> While they say to me all day long,
> "Where is your God?"
> These things I remember,
> and I pour out my soul within me.
> For I used to go along with the throng
> and lead them in procession to the house of God,
> With the voice of joy and thanksgiving,
> a multitude keeping festival.
> Why are you in despair, O my soul?
> And why have you become disturbed within me?
> O my God, my soul is in despair within me. (Ps. 42:3–5, 6a)

Both writers validated the importance of shedding tears. David affirmed the appropriateness of asking the tough questions during this time. Even Jesus on the cross faced the crushing emotion of abandonment and aloneness when He cried out, "My God, my God, why have you forsaken me?" If we do not ask the questions, we don't give ourselves the opportunity to have them answered. Some hesitate to be open about their anger, questions, and doubts during this season. But, if it were not okay to question God during this time, why did Jesus, who willingly entered into grief and death, do so?

Naomi, the great-grandmother of King David in the Book of Ruth, epitomizes the winter woman. Her expectation of what life was to be like had been shattered. Her dream had died when her husband and both of her sons died in the land of Moab. They had left Israel during a drought and sought success in a foreign country. When the Book of Ruth opens, Naomi had decided to return to Israel. But she left Moab bitter. She had no hope that life would ever go well for her again. In fact her despair was so deep that she renamed herself: "Do not call me Naomi [meaning "pleasant"]; call me Mara [meaning "bitter"] for the Almighty has made my life very bitter" (v. 20, NIV).

Naomi successfully passed through stage one. She named her loss and did not hide from her feelings. She knew that her life as a married woman, as a mother was over. She had lost all that she held dear.

Women who try to short circuit their grief and do not successfully go through this stage of protest remain in denial. They may close themselves off to the facts of the loss, the meaning of the loss, or the irreversibility of the loss. One mother I met refuses to discuss her father's illness and death nor admit her daughter's former drug abuse. This woman has not successfully navigated the stage one task of accepting reality.

Despair

The second stage of the grief wheel is *despair* and the task is to experience the pain of the loss. An appropriate statement for this stage is, "I know I can't make it; I'm not sure I'm going to survive." The goal of this stage is to experience the pain until it fades. A statement typical of one not facing despair is, "I'm doing just fine." A woman who pretends the problem does not affect her is likely to have an extended winter by creating situations that draw secondary pain to her.

In this task the griever yearns to recover what was lost. The emotions are deep. We use words like "anguish" or "agony." At this juncture we may lash out verbally and act out the anger. Or we may withdraw, turning our thoughts and pain inward. The electricity has no place to flow when turned inward. We call this inward despondency depression. We also may want to escape as King David did:

> . . . Oh, that I had wings like a dove!
> I would fly away and be at rest.
> Behold, I would wander far away,
> I would lodge in the wilderness.
> I would hasten to my place of refuge
> From the stormy wind and tempest. (Ps. 55:6–8)

One way we short-circuit grief in this stage is to deny our pain and the seriousness of the loss. Helen's husband of forty-five years divorced her. Shortly thereafter, he died. Instead of facing her feelings of loss, she visited all of her five children. She went to Europe and to China. Between trips she would be at home for a few months and then off she would go again. Everyone commented on how well she was adjusting. After one particularly long trip, she returned very weary and depressed. Normal amounts of sleep did not help her regain her vigor. She began to have disturbing dreams about being left on desert islands and abandoned in front of on-coming vehicles. Finally, her daughter urged her to go for help. As she slowly faced the reality of her loss and her pain, the depression lifted. She had tried to short-circuit the process of grief, and she experienced what we call a delayed grief reaction.

Another way task two can be short circuited is to enter into a period of exaggerated grief. The griever refuses to care for herself. She becomes increasingly helpless, demanding assistance in the tiniest tasks. She may refuse to try new things or care for her physical appearance. Even two or three years after the initial loss, she will spend her days crying.

During this stage of grieving, despair leads many people to cry out to God for comfort and answers. Naomi was deeply aware that she did not feel God's presence. Her despair led her to return to her spiritual and family roots, to the place of blessing "when she heard . . . that the Lord had come to the aid of his people by providing food for them" (1:6, NIV). Many of us yearn to find meaning in the losses of our lives, and like Naomi we may seek to find a place of blessing.

Detachment

Stage three is *detachment* and the task is to adjust to an environment in which the loss exists. When a partner is gone, we must undertake new tasks. Someone has to mow the lawn, balance the checkbook, take out the garbage. If we have lost a long-term friendship, we get used to not calling her or avoiding haunts where we had lunch or shopped or played tennis.

During this time we experience an emptiness, a deadness, a numbness. There is a desire to withdraw, a loss of interest in normal activities, a desire to give up. The support system that rallied to assist us when the loss was most intense has dissolved, and everyone goes back to life as usual—everyone but us, that is. During this time, when the one who grieves withdraws, helpers are very important. I encourage clients going through divorce to either visit or join a divorce recovery support group. It may be a time to see movies, read mindless novels, and accept this as a period when the brain cells and the body are in the repair shop.

We sense others around us want us back to "normal." We want to be back to "normal" also. But no matter how hard we try to do "it" differently, we can't. We would never tell a friend who is on the operating table for cancer or for open heart surgery, "You've been there too long. Get up and get on with life." We recognize in the physical realm that our bodies take time to heal. Our emotions and minds need time to heal as well.

We can compare this stage of detachment to a winter field lying fallow, waiting for spring's sun and warmth. The snows have melted, but the land is still cold. Although the field has been plowed, it is not a season for planting or new growth. It is a season of waiting.

In this stage of detachment Naomi was able to assist Ruth, her daughter-in-law, in creating a life for herself in Israel. Ruth was devoted to Naomi and had returned to Bethlehem with her, desiring her companionship and her God more than she desired the familiarity of her own land. Naomi taught Ruth how to find food for them. She may not have had hope for herself, but in this fallow time in her life, Naomi was able to assist Ruth in bringing joy and hope to her life. She taught her how to approach her kinsman, Boaz, who eventually recognized Ruth's value and chose her to be his wife. By her actions, Naomi showed that she moved from the bitterness of "I'll never make it. All of life is sorrow" to "Even if my life's hope is over, maybe there's hope for someone else."

In order to grow through each stage of the recovery cycle we must be aware of how the grieving process can be delayed. At the transition between detachment and recovery, the numb feelings begin to thaw. Grief may be delayed as we grieve for different aspects of what we have lost. As we thaw, we remember different things we will miss. We can go through the wheel many times on different levels and for different aspects of the loss.

Grief can be delayed in another way at this stage. The simple grief of a specific loss begins to merge with past, ungrieved, below-the-surface losses. Hillary's story is an example.

On the surface Hillary's sorrow is an ongoing struggle with infertility and the sorrow for not having children. In fact the journey of infertility testing and surgeries is not a joyful, exciting series of events. But rather, is a painful, often frustrating and exhausting one—and it is particularly sorrowful when the events do not lead to conception.

Hillary appeared on the outside as a person who was unable to accept the fact she could not conceive and was unable to put the grief to rest.

After my husband and I had been married for two years, we tried to have children. All I ever wanted was to be a wife and a mom. It was what I was raised to believe women did when they grew up. After a couple of years of unsuccessful trying, we went to a fertility specialist in a town near us. Every aspect of our lives was focused on getting pregnant. Even our most intimate times became controlled and dictated by the day of the month and the clock.

Through it all I was in incredible emotional pain. I cried constantly . I felt so trapped, so shamed that we couldn't have a child. I hated going to church and I dreaded people's comments: "Where's your faith, Hillary?" or "Maybe it's not God's will for you to have a child." Or they would offer advice. All they wanted to do was fix me. Only a very few could be empathic and say, "I don't know how you are coping. It must be so hard. How can I help?"

The medical things were harsh and severe—I would even say, cruel. Finally, after one particularly painful procedure, I lost faith in my doctor and decided "no more!" In time we decided to adopt. We now have an adorable little boy.

But my journey isn't over. When I'm in a vulnerable time of month or when stress increases, I grieve again for not being able to have my own children. For a time I am at peace. And then unexpectedly I notice every pregnant woman around and plunge into remorse and depression, crying and grieving all over again. No matter what I do, I can't get through this grief."

Much to my amazement, as I got to know her better, she revealed a similar story to Gsil's. When Hillary was thirteen years old, her younger sister became suddenly ill and died within ten days. She collapsed and cried hysterically at the time. But her parents were unable to give her the comfort she needed as they had spiritualized their own sorrow by saying "It's all in God's plan." "God is a good God and has only our best in mind for us." How can one fight God? From the funeral on, no one cried in front of anyone else, no one mentioned her name and all of the pictures of her mysteriously disappeared. Is it possible that as Hillary rounds this grief wheel over and over for the babies she has never borne, that she is grieving at a very deep level for the sister she was not allowed to grieve?

When a person does not follow a relatively normal grieving pattern and the grief lingers or is more intense than would be expected for the circumstances, it is always appropriate to ask, "What else have I lost that might be adding to my sorrow?" Once the resting and withdrawal of the detachment phase fades, the mourner is beginning to move into the fourth stage, recovery.

Recovery

Stage four on the grief wheel is *recovery* and the task is to withdraw emotional energy from the old and reinvest it in the new. Instead of thinking about what could have been, our thoughts turn to new friendships, new homes, new relationships, new jobs, new endeavors. Our increased ability to withdraw emotional energy from the old and reinvest in other relationships is a growing sign of healthy adjustment. We learn to trust again. We see ourselves and life more accurately. We reevaluate our choices and our values. We become dissatisfied with the old, and we celebrate new feelings. We actually begin to believe we can make it. We begin to build new memories and to enter into forgiveness where needed.

While nights are still chilled and snow mounds resist the sun's rays, acacia and forsythia bloom, heralds of the coming spring. Naomi, the prototype of the winter woman, moved toward recovery as she assisted Ruth in the customs of her people and aided her in seeking her kinsman Boaz's favor. The season of restoration took many months. But ultimately, Naomi's losses were redeemed in the birth of Ruth and Boaz's child, Obed, who was the grandfather of King David. The women of her community recognized the blessing of this baby when they said: "May he be to you a restorer of life and a sustainer of your old age" (Ruth 4:14).

As Obed's nurse, she gained a sense of purpose and meaning that restored her hope.

In addition to feeling a new sense of joy and life, the recovery stage is a time to practice changing thought patterns and habits that leave us attached to the old. After Tammy's divorce, she had a difficult time not thinking about her ex-husband even though he had remarried. She would concoct elaborate measures to engage him in conversation about their children, attempt to get him alone, and in general found ways to stay connected to him. Many of their conversations were arguments over the children and over money. "Although the encounters were anything but pleasant," she admits, "I forced him to stay connected to me. I'm not sure what I would think about if I didn't focus on him and our past history together." This obsession with her ex-husband prevented her from risking and moving into a new life.

Disengagement from the old and reinvestment in the new is hard work. At a deeper level Tammy is determined not to let go of her ex-husband and has great difficulty coming to terms with her new life. Until she chooses to reinvest her energy into new relationships, her job, friendships, or other endeavors, her thoughts about him will rule her.

However, when she decides to let go, Tammy would benefit from a technique called *thought stopping*. The first step is to set a timer for five minutes. During that time, she will practice not thinking about him at all. Every time a thought about him would enter, she would practice doing something different: call a friend and not talk about him, plan an outing for herself, think about something pleasant just for herself, or think about what she will fix for dinner. The next step is to set the alarm for ten minutes. She may need to be accountable to someone else in her resolve not to call him or be involved in his life.

As the energy to embrace the new bubbles up, we have the energy to face our own complicity in our losses. When the alcoholic enters an AA meeting, she must name her condition: "My name is Karen. I'm an alcoholic." She must admit she needs divine assistance to go on. One of the crucial steps in recovery in a twelve step program is step number four which is "a fearless moral inventory." Whether we have experienced a death, divorce, or loss by natural disaster, our personal spirit has been touched in such a way that we will never be the same. Part of our new personal awareness is how we have wounded others. The AA program insists that its members take personal responsibility for their behavior rather than blaming others for their plight.

"How can I be blamed for the death of my child or for my husband's affair?" you might ask. No, those are not your responsibility.

When we have been touched by grief, we become more sensitive to the moving of the Holy Spirit in our lives and of His desire to move more deeply into the fabric of our being. As He does so, we become aware of our need for His tender touch of healing and forgiving.

In fact, our awareness of how we have wounded others is a painful part of recovery from loss. As we enter into the stage of recovery and move on into restoration, we will be more able to begin the process of forgiveness of ourselves and others.

A winter season, according to our model, comes ultimately to an end.

Chronic Loss

When a woman struggles with a debilitating illness or is the caretaker of someone who is chronically ill, she is challenged by many trips around the loss-recovery wheel.

Lynne is a poet. When she was forty-four, she and her husband divorced. Shortly thereafter, she was diagnosed with Parkinson's disease. She strives relatively successfully to have a positive attitude toward the disease and the limits it puts on her. However, she faces a lifetime of adjusting to a disease that is unrelentingly progressive. Each time she loses mobility or thinks more slowly than the day before, she comes face to face with her fear of being alone, encased in a body that does not move, with a mind that still thinks and a spirit that still feels. But with each turn of the wheel, Lynne has learned to appreciate her strengths and acknowledge her limitations. She has learned to graciously ask for and receive help. Above all, she has learned that in the midst of pain, in the midst of her fear, she is not alone. She has learned to recognize the calming touch of the Spirit so that each new roadblock does not send her into quite the depth of despair as the one previously.

When a woman cares for a loved one who has a chronic illness or disability, she also faces recurring seasons of evaluation and transition. Susan is a talented graphic designer whose son has been physically disabled from birth. Although she handles his disability with a positive and loving attitude, her heart sorrows at each stage of his development. "The loss keeps coming. As he enters his teen years, we are faced with different challenges from when he was younger. How do we handle his emerging sexuality? We grieve because he won't be able to enjoy high school sports, go to dances, have a girl friend. Just when I think I've accepted his disability, he enters a new stage and I feel overwhelmed, sorrowful and angry."

When Winter Comes to a Friend

It is often hard for someone in need to ask for assistance. Most women are used to giving and supporting. It may be difficult to ask for what they need. It may be difficult even to know what they need. Below I've listed suggestions and strategies that others have found helpful for walking beside a person in a grieving season. The items below may also spur your creativity since this is by no means a complete list of ideas.

The most valuable thing we have to offer our grieving friend is our presence. What the individual needs most is an acknowledgement of the grief and the pain he or she is going through. Beyond that, there are some practical ways you can help. First, ask yourself, "What are my gifts and what am I comfortable doing?" Giving with resentment benefits no one. Next, ask the person, "What do you need?" Be prepared with several suggestions of things you could do. Even better, ask specific questions like, "Do you need me to pick up anything from the grocery store for you?" Finally, be sensitive to the specific needs and stage of mourning your friend is going through.

Physical Support

As you read through the list below, think of friends, neighbors, and family members who may have losses not related to death. A friend who is divorcing, who is going to counseling and is grieving family losses, who faces chronic illness will need your gestures of care as well. The needs of these latter losses may not appear as obvious, but they are as real.

- Bring a main dish or a meal.
- Organize a group of friends to bring in meals on a regular basis. Do not forget needs will last after the initial phases of a crisis.
- Send cards, notes, and scripture verses that are non-condemning.
- Take young children overnight; on day trips, or for a few hours.

- Send flowers. Balloons are wonderful when our friend acknowledges a new milestone achieved. Otherwise they may be too frivolous.
- Make calls to the bank, insurance carriers, funeral home when a loved one has died.
- Be a spokesperson or intermediary by answering the phone and screening calls.
- Shop for groceries; run errands.
- Clean up dishes or the house.
- Search out support groups and services
- After the initial crisis phase has passed, continue to be available. Take the person to lunch, a movie. Do not neglect them when the crisis has passed.
- Continue to ask what is helpful and what is not.

Emotional Support

Be with her while she cries and pass the tissues. It is important to remember that we do not have to fix our friends. Letting her be angry, upset, sad, mad, irrational is an important part of lending support.

- Give her hug or hold her as she cries (when appropriate to do so).
- Share a poem, scripture, or other writing as an expression of sympathy. Later on, share information on the grieving process. Books and support groups can be helpful.
- Collect any remembrance, photo, letter, or other "treasure" you have saved of the person who has died and give it to the one who is grieving.
- Encourage her to talk about her feelings.
- Share briefly, when appropriate, your own experience of loss.

A Grieving Woman

The winter woman is a grieving woman. She has been plunged into a season that she did not ask for, nor is she well prepared for. As she embraces her pain and does not run from it, she moves around the grief wheel from protest, to despair, to detachment and eventually emerges into recovery. If she denies her pain and the importance of her loss, she merely delays the inevitable. Denial delays the grieving process and contributes to an increase of secondary pain. In time the winter woman understands with the psalmist that crying comes in the night, but joy in the morning. A spring of new beginnings does indeed follow winter.

Reflection

1. How old were you when you faced your first major loss? Do you remember? Was it a pet animal or a major move? Was it a death of a close family member? Was it a change in family living standard that took Daddy away from the home more often? Can you remember how you felt? Were you able to tell anyone? Do you remember if anyone tried to explain the changes or the losses to you?

2. In the winter of your despair, what were some of the tough questions you asked or wish you could have asked? Have you ever wondered why something has happened to you, or asked, "Where are You, God?" or "How could a loving God allow tragedy to happen?" Write down some of your own questions.

Chapter Seven

The Winter of Life

❦

One summer we were inundated with flies—big horse flies. Every time the door opened, several would swoosh in. We couldn't eat on the patio without a flyswatter nearby. I had no idea where the swarms were coming from. Then, one of our friends jokingly asked, "What are you growing in your garden this year, maggots?" *Maggots . . . garden . . . compost . . . oh no,* my thoughts raced. *Is that what those crazy, white, wormy things are in my compost pile?* Sure enough, my wonderful attempts at recycling had gone sour. I had created a fly-breeding habitat!

I had successfully built a compost pile in the past. All of our non-fat, non-meat garbage was mixed with shredded paper and garden clippings. My compost pile needed heavy doses of air (oxygen) and light. Deep in the center of the mass heat built up as part of the transformation process from garbage and garden refuse to nutrients to replenish the soil. But, that year, instead of fertilizer I got rotten garbage and maggots! I had not tended the compost diligently that season—too much to do, too many commitments, too little time. I took short cuts and hoped it would all work out. But it didn't!

Likewise, we must tend our compost pile of losses and disappointments, failures, and sins so we can produce nutrients for more lush blooms in our next season. Often women, as they face the change in their bodies, in their hair color, body shape, stamina, and age, feel more like garbage and refuse than useful fertilizer to grow things beautiful. If they have not tended their compost piles, the payoff is maggots of disappointment, bitterness, discouragement, and isolation.

The ultimate passage of our lives is entering into our final winter season. And like the grieving woman, an older woman also has tasks to perform and challenges to meet. Some of the questions the woman in her final winter asks are these: "What has been my purpose for being? Do I have meaning when I can no longer perform and when I'm no longer attractive? Now how do I measure my value and worth? How do I want to be remembered? What do I want to leave behind after I am gone?" Not all of our journey of aging needs to be as a grieving winter woman. Just as a woman in the spring of her life can experience a season of winter, so a winter woman can enjoy a spring of new beginnings. The aging woman will thrive in her winter years when she

- chooses integrity over despair.
- accepts her losses.
- faces the reality of her condition.
- prepares her heart for death.

Choosing Integrity Over Despair

Unlike other transitions in a woman's life, we do not get to choose growing older. We may not be able to slow the aging process; however, we can choose our attitude toward aging and the meaning we give to it. Erik Erikson calls this the crisis of choosing integrity over despair.

I have been growing older since the day I was born. I am older than I was ten years ago, but I still do not consider myself old. At what age do we consider an individual old? Is age a condition and/or a state of mind? If it is a state of mind, isn't it possible that we can become old before our time? I am reminded of a profound saying, "Age is a case of mind over matter; if you don't mind, it doesn't matter." But old we do become. We also must distinguish between growing older, which is inevitable, and acting old. An individual who acts old is rigid in outlook and thinking, bitter about her unfulfilled life, limited in vision, chooses safety over exploring new possibilities, and often lives in despair and hopelessness. She is more interested in her own affairs than the affairs of others and chooses isolation rather than involvement. Her soul withers before her body is ready to die.

The woman of vision ages well. She inhabits her own rooms and builds her own sense of purpose. She continually gives back to life with one more project to plan, one more letter to write, one more book to read or write, one more person to meet, one more baby to rock, one more goal to meet. And, with an attitude of joy and an anticipation for the new, she inhabits her days. The well known author, Pearl Buck, said on her eightieth birthday, "Would I wish to be young again? No, for I have learned too much to wish to lose it. I am a far more valuable person today than I was 50 years ago, or 30 years ago, or even 10. I have learned so much more since I was 70! I believe I can honestly say that I have learned more in the last 10 years than in any previous decade."[1] Erikson would say this woman has chosen integrity over despair.

A woman in her elder years becomes more of what she has always been but without the masks of propriety and convention. My Grandmother Berger became irascible following a series of nibbly strokes in her mid-seventies. She was used to being in control and exerting her will. As she aged, these traits intensified: she would refuse medical treatment except from her doctor son, and would insist on "helping" by trying to be the mistress in her daughter-in-laws' homes. However, other traits also persisted as she aged. As a young woman she had moved to Boston to be one of the first Salvation Army lasses. Her love for God and her dedication to telling others of His love persisted even after she lost her memory of who we were and what was current. When it was no longer safe to have Grandmother in an unsupervised environment, my parents moved her to a nursing home. When we visited, we would find her visiting her neighbors and telling them about Jesus's love. Her servant's heart won over despair as she pitched in to "help" the nurses with someone in need. They adored her upbeat, loving spirit. Age often brings with it a loss of meaning, loneliness, and unfulfilled yearnings. These can be exaggerated for the woman who has not found peace within, accep-tance apart from another's value of her, or assurance of God's perspective of her worth. The woman who has learned, like the apostle Paul, to say, "I have *learned* to be content in every circumstance," (Phil. 4:11) can experience her losses of age, grieve them, and continue to find meaning in her life. If we have learned in the middle of earlier storms who God is and to listen to what He is saying, we will again be comforted in knowing He walks with us "through the shadow of [this] death" as well (Ps. 23:4).

A woman of years is an incredible gift to others when she provides experience, wisdom, and maturity. If she is a grandmother, she has the opportunity of giving an emotional and spiritual foundation to her grandchildren.

As we age we may also learn how to love our children and those closest to us without strings attached. We all make mistakes—some big, some not so big, some unknown to us—as mothers. The wise woman becomes receptive to hearing how she may have wounded friend or child. She learns to graciously say, "I'm sorry" and to respect child or friend in the way requested. In fact it is never too late to make amends and for a child to hear that her mother loves and values her. At sixty Peggy was reconciled to her mother just before her mother's death. After years of criticism, demands, lack of appreciation, and competition, Peggy's mother turned to her one day while in the nursing home and said, "Honey, I want you to know how much I love you. I know I haven't shown you or told you how much you mean to me." Something had turned deep within this mother's heart so that her last weeks on earth became a blessing to her daughter. The sorrow at her death was for the wasted years, but Peggy was freed from her feelings of abandonment, rejection, and bitterness.

Paul Tournier claims that the power in old age is to see the hand of God in all of the significant events of our lives. And, no matter how successful we are, we will feel empty and not quite fulfilled if we have abandoned our first call, the inner leading of the Holy Spirit. Tournier says,

> It is the idea that life is a gift which implies responsibility, that God-be he known or unknown-expects something very definite of us, and not just anything. God loves diversity. Each person has a call on her life, has her own story to tell that has unique meaning and universal meaning.[2]

In the hand of the master weaver all the threads of our lives create a unique tapestry of beauty. Each pattern, each color contains a story that, when told, can bless the hearer. What is it God has taught you? Did the lessons come in joy or in sorrow? How did he refine you? How has he spoken to you? What is your story?

Accepting Loss

The last chapter examined the cycle and tasks for grief. These same tasks face us as we grieve our losses to age. Even the woman with a wonderful attitude and spirit toward life becomes overwhelmed at times, exasperated with the aches, pains, and slowed steps. No one relishes more wrinkles, jiggly underarm muscles, age spots, or thinning, whitened hair.

As we age we face the loss of friendships, the loss of mobility, the loss of our youthful appearance. At some point we say goodbye to our partners, our health, our homes, our ability to drive, and our independence.

Although that is not all that aging brings, these losses must be faced. The winter woman's journey through the grief cycle may be similar to the woman who has a chronic illness, except age is not a disease, as Aristotle said, "because it is not contrary to nature." After each loss, she has the option to enter into a new spring of trusting, of faith, of meaning, or of living in despair and hopelessness.

Facing Reality

Cultural myths affect how we view the aging process. Recent studies have shown that fewer than 10 percent of the 30 million Americans over the age of 65 show any significant loss of memory or mental impairment. Also, only 10 percent of people over 65 are confined in any serious way. Only 5 percent of this age group live in institutions.[3]

No matter how positively one may enter these years, the quality of a woman's life is impacted by certain pressures. In each phase of our lives these affect our well being, but the older adult has less resilience and resources at her disposal to regroup and less time in which to do so. These pressures are the following:

- her finances
- her health and mobility
- her family fractures
- the quality of her relationships, her network of support
- her ability to engage in meaningful "work"

Pressure One: Finances

According to labor statistics, women earn significantly less than men during their work lives. While many earn enough to survive during their productive years, they do not have enough to prepare well beyond social security for their retirement years. Hence, many must work longer to earn enough to maintain financially. In fact, many older Americans live at or below the poverty line. When a woman is able to prepare adequately for retirement, the angst of growing older is eased.

Pressure Two: Health and Mobility

A woman who has her health can age more gracefully. She is able to be more independent, exercise, and feel "up to" involvement with others. Many chronic health conditions become exaggerated with age. When we are younger, we expect a quick recovery from illnesses. As we age the recovery time lengthens and illnesses become chronic. As the older adult's health decreases and invalidism occurs, she becomes more dependent and life becomes increasingly difficult.

Pressure Three: Emotional Account

In winter we not only draw on our financial retirement accounts, but on our emotional accounts as well. A significant factor in how we grow older is how well we have completed our grieving seasons of the past.

At eighty-three Mrs. T. sought counseling for depression. She was a particularly winsome, charming lady who had had a steady boyfriend for a number of years. Because she had always been able to control everything and everyone in her environment, she had never really faced what it meant to be out of control. As she declined in health, she wanted to move in with her daughter. She had a lovely apartment, was active in church activities, and appeared to have a rich life. But internally she was miserable and unfulfilled. She spoke critically about the choices her children and grandchildren had made. Every positive was met with "yes, I know, dear, but . . ." Then she would insist, "If only I could live with my daughter, then I would be happy. She could take care of me and keep me company and I wouldn't be so miserable." But the daughter, who had tried her entire life to make her mother happy and had "failed," knew this would not heal her mother's historical wounds. The daughter told me one day her mother had never gotten over the death of her own mother when she was very young: "Although she was favored by her dad and brothers and has been given marvelous opportunities in her life, I've yet to see anything that has made her happy."

Mrs. T's life account was full, but because her emotional account was not healed, she became even more bitter and discouraged as she aged.

Our emotional accounts can be filled not only with resolution from the past hurts and losses, but by filling the well with humor and good will. The following is called "The Joys of Aging" and shows Imelda Madden's ability to enter into joy:

I have become quite a frivolous old gal. I'm seeing five gentlemen every day. As soon as I awake, Will Power helps me out of bed. When he leaves, I go see John. Then Charley Horse comes along and when he is here, he takes a lot of my attention. When he leaves, Arthur Ritis shows up and stays the rest of the day. He doesn't like to stay in one place very long so he takes me from joint to joint. After such a busy day, I'm really tired and ready to go to bed with Ben Gay. What a day![4]

Pressure Four: Relational Account or Network Support

A fourth factor impacting how we age is the quality of our relationships. Studies have shown that women who involve themselves in a multi-generational environment with friends of all ages are less lonely and less self-absorbed even when the conditions of health and wealth are not optimal. Not only is she given support by others, she in turn can lend moral support, love, and kindnesses. She can find meaning and value in these relationships. She is also not as bereft of companionship when age peers become ill and die. Several aging mothers I know live close to their grown daughters and assist them with house chores, babysitting, and house sitting when the family is gone. One of these women, who is in her late seventies has volunteered for years at her grandaughter's schools, contributing her skills and benefiting from the vibrant school environment. Other women choose to live in neighborhoods rather than in retirement communities. Church and civic groups provide women of all ages an environment in which to contribute, and cross the age lines.

By investing deeply in relationships with women of all ages, she finds meaning in her own life apart from her roles as mother and wife. A woman who sees herself only by these roles has one of the most difficult times adjusting to aging when her husband dies, when she is divorced and/or her children invest in their own lives and may move away. Research on women in general indicates that women with multiple roles are less depressed and less discouraged than women who have only one or two roles defining their value.

However, loneliness is ranked the highest of the ills that plague the older woman. The following poem states it eloquently:

Minnie Remembers

God,
My hands are old.
I've never said that out loud before
but they are.
I was so proud of them once,
they were soft
like the velvet smoothness of a firm,
ripe peach.
Now the softness is more like a worn out
body that has served me too well!
How long has it been since someone
touched me
Twenty years?
Twenty years I've been a widow.
Respected.
Smiled at.
But never touched.
Never held so close that loneliness
was blotted out.
I remember how my mother used to hold me,
God.
When I was hurt in spirit or flesh,
she would gather me close,
stroke my silky hair
and caress my back with her warm hands.
O God, I'm so lonely!
I remember the first boy who ever kissed me.
We were both so new at that!
The taste of young lips and popcorn,
the feeling inside of mysteries to come.
I remember Hank and the babies,
How else can I remember them but together? Out of the fumbling,
awkward attempts of new
lovers came the babies.

And as they grew, so did our love.
And, God, Hank didn't seem to mind.
If my body thickened and faded a little.
He still loved it, And touched it,
And we didn't mind if we were no longer beautiful.
And the children hugged me a lot.
O God, I'm lonely!
God why didn't we raise the kids to be silly and affectionate as well as
dignified and proper?
You see, they do their duty.
They drive up in their fine cars,
they come to my room to pay their respects.
They chatter brightly, and reminisce,
But they don't touch me.
they call me "Mom" or "Mother"
or "Grandma."
Never Minnie,
My mother called me Minnie,
So did my friends.
Hank called me Minnie, too.
But they're gone.
And so is Minnie.
And God! She's so lonely.[5]

How can we who live in other seasons reach out to the Minnies in our lives? Linda lives next door to a "Minnie" who is in her nineties and still lives alone. Once a day Linda peeks in to see how "Minnie" is doing, may run an errand for her while she is out, and on occasion takes her for a drive.

"At first I wasn't sure I wanted to be bothered with the responsibility for another person," Linda honestly confessed. "But over time she has become a very vital and important part of my life. She is very respectful of my time and appreciative of what I do for her. I in turn have a relationship that has replaced in part one I didn't have with my own mother." As in everything, it takes time and effort to reach out and support another. But in giving we will be blessed.

Pressure Five: Meaningful Work

Today many married women work full or part-time outside or inside the home even after having children. But the majority of women in their seventies and eighties are women who have never worked outside the home or who may have entered the work force out of necessity after raising a family. According to research, older working women have a better morale than those who have not worked. They also report a higher sense of personal worth and sense of "dignity." They have learned a resilience and are more able to adapt to change than women who have had a restricted view of life.

Meaningful work for another woman might be focused on being an active volunteer in her community (schools, politics, hospital, and other charitable auxiliaries), or in her church. On most days of the week I can walk through our church fellowship hall and see many women of retirement age folding brochures, stuffing envelopes, sorting clothes for the clothes closet, or working to keep the church library in order.

Divisions of Older Adult Years

Like the unfolding stages of childhood, the aging process also has its stages. We can view these divisions by age as well as by ability. Each group has different problems and needs and capabilities. The key is our attitude toward our losses as much as the nature of our losses which will determine the quality of our old age.

Stage one can be called the "productive elder years." These years are characterized by vibrancy and activity. With her own as well as her spouse's retirement, the younger older woman has time and energy to embrace the activities and dreams she could not in more committed years. She is independent, competent, and probably living in her own home, or where she has chosen to retire.

The productive elder years usually begin to end with crises in health, finances, or major losses. This period we will call the "narrowing the focus stage." A season of loss may follow the death of one's spouse—a move into smaller quarters, a selling or giving away of the accumulations of one's life. Others may begin to make decisions for her. Loss of health and stamina begin to impact the mobility and capability of the winter woman. Much of her day is spent caring for her own basic needs or limited by caring for an ailing spouse.

The next developmental stage we will call the "letting go stage." Severe health disabilities begin to impact her involvement outside her home, which affects her mental well being. She becomes dependent on others for transportation and obtaining basic necessities. During this stage a woman's loss of memory, hearing, and sight separates her more and more from the world around her. If she is not in a nurturing setting, her loneliness increases and she may not care well for herself, forgetting to eat or bathe. As a result she will probably move into a more managed care living arrangement, most likely against her will.

The last stage we will call the "good bye stage." It can last days, weeks, or sometimes several years. In this period of time illness and physical disability are so limiting that she is in bed care at home or in a nursing home. As she withdraws physically from life, she withdraws within herself, using all of her energy to survive. Those who love her prepare themselves to say goodbye.

The ability stages are not linked to time frame or ages. Our productive, younger older woman may become ill and die without going through the stages of decline. Or we may find an old older woman who at ninety-five is still keen of mind and health, living independently and productively, and who may die in her sleep.

My own mother became chronically ill after the death of my minister-father when she was seventy. Walking pneumonia turned quickly into pulmonary fibrosis (a chronic lung condition in which the lung becomes rigid and ceases to function). My mother had been called to be a minister's wife and she wore her calling well. But with my father's death, not only did she lose her spouse and partner, but also much of the meaning to her life and her identity.

She fought disability and refused to give up. Convinced that she would be healed, she took her drivers' license exam with a portable oxygen tank four months before her death, attended her grandnephew's swim meets, and kept several speaking engagements on her calendar.

Not knowing how ill she was, she continued to prepare for life. Although she could not live alone and needed abundant rest, she chose to move near us. For the short term we were able to hire someone to live with her. Even though she was on full oxygen and on a portable tank, she dressed everyday, lay on the couch instead of staying in bed, and took care of her personal needs.

Not knowing she had only two weeks to live, she tried to establish a new doctor relationship near her new home. I went into the consultation room with her after he had examined her and we both heard reality for the first time. "Mrs. Berger," the doctor began," I don't know how you are doing what you do. I have never seen anyone as sick as you who is not hospitalized. If you had come to me sooner, maybe we could have done something for you. I'm sorry." The words "you are dying" hung unspoken in the air.

Quietly we walked to the car. I asked, "Mom, how are you doing?" Tears welled up in her eyes, she caught her breath, apologized, and said, "It's a little hard to take. I really didn't know I was so bad off. I guess I'm not going to make it." We didn't speak again about it. I wanted her to cry, pour it out. I wanted to cry and hold her, but I had to drive. Powerless, stunned, helpless, I drove silently to her home.

Over the next weeks, she got up daily, dressed herself, and cared for her essential needs. She also asked lots of questions of God: "Isn't there anything I can still do or a treatment I can take to live? Why now, Lord? I still have messages of Your love to give and grandbabies to rock and know."

The day before she died, my cousin June and I had been to the flea market. We bounced in to show her our treasures. I wanted to stay, but Mom had another visitor who just stayed on. I reassured her I'd be over the next day. She had that look in her eyes that pleaded for me to stay, but I was young and foolish. How I wish I had.

About eight o'clock the next morning, her nurse, Charlotte, called to tell me she had died.

Several months later Charlotte added to the story of that morning: "When I heard your mother stir, I called to see if she needed assistance. She responded, 'No.'" I lay there waiting. I felt restless. I called. She didn't answer. So I got up and walked to her door. As I stood there in the doorway, I saw a light in the dark January morning fill the corner of the room by the closet and move slowly to the bed, hover over your mother and then it returned to the closet and was gone. I couldn't move for several moments. When I could enter, the room was still and your mother was gone. I didn't tell you earlier because I thought you might think I was strange."

No, I hadn't thought she was strange. Her story comforted me. Dying from a lung disease can be very frightening though not painful. I knew Jesus had come and taken her home—without stress, without pain, in peace. I remembered wondering if I would ever remember her face without the oxygen tube, without the mark of death.

My persistent question throughout those last weeks wasn't, "Why is she dying," but rather, "Why does she have to struggle and suffer after all she's been through, Lord? Why can't she be given a few more years of joy and fulfillment?" The answer was surprising to me. Deep in my spirit I heard the Father's voice, "My child, I'm preparing her for glory."

Scripture affirms the ultimate hope of a new spring following death. The apostle Paul says we do not "grieve as do the rest who have no hope" (1 Thess. 4:13). My mother did not want to let go of life. If she had had a choice, she would have chosen more years of active living, loving, and giving. But she also had the hope of joy in reuniting with my father, her parents and siblings, and her son. In answer to my "why," I was reminded of what Paul said to the Corinthians:

> Therefore we do not lose heart. Though outwardly we are wasting away, yet inwardly we are being renewed day by day. For our light and momentary troubles are achieving for us an eternal glory that far outweights them all. So we fix our eyes not on what is seen, but on what is unseen. For what is seen is temporary, but what is unseen is eternal. (2 Cor. 4:16–18, NIV)

I value the legacy my mother left to me: She died as she had lived, with gentleness, outward focus, and a hope that tomorrow would come, bringing renewed life and new energy.

The Final Winter

The aging woman who has successfully weathered many seasons has prepared well for winter. She has developed a solid support system to share life's joys and losses. She has actively forgiven and healed from historical pain. Even the darkest threads, those shameful errors, have contributed to the beauty of the tapestry of her life. She knows God walks in the dark of new tunnels even when she cannot see His ways or His purposes. And in that knowing, she feels safe asking her questions and knowing she will find meaning and joy in this season as she prepares for her final journey home.

Reflection

1. If you are a woman of age, what do you struggle with and what have you enjoyed most as you've aged? If you are in another age season, what do you welcome, fear, or dread about growing older?

2. What do you admire in older women you have known?

Part III

The Spring Woman

When the grass disappears, the new growth is seen.

(Prov. 27:25)

Chapter Eight

The Nature of
New Beginnings

❦

hile the skies are still dark and gray, the air still crisp, spring comes. Forsythia and acacia herald spring's arrival. As I turn toward the farm, I am confronted by a blazing field of mustard. Trees have burst into bloom. In my garden, daffodils and crocuses, hyacinth and tulips appear in early spring. In later spring, roses flourish. Warmth and cold play leap frog through the days. Color replaces the dark grays of winter. There is hope.

The spring woman finds joy and excitement in the thrill of new beginnings. She rejoices in the abundance of all things and finds herself worshipping easily for the beauty and blessings around her. No matter what her personality type, whether she radiates for all to see and hear her joy or quietly shares it with one or two close friends, a woman in the season of spring rejoices that winter has passed and she has been given a new beginning.

We are at once child and woman, vulnerable and tough, innocent and experienced. We have a child's passion and curiosity and an adult's tempering and rules. In the season of spring we are the essence of joy, excitement, yearning and impatience, full of feeling and life.

The spring woman chooses to let go of winter and inhabit spring. She chooses hope, good will, joy, and forgiveness. She chooses to let go of the past in order to live in the present. But like seeds planted by a farmer, she is subject to the laws of the universe that are controlled by God. She plants and God works deeply within her to accomplish more than she could possibly imagine.

Thus we can describe the tasks of the spring woman as follows:

- The spring woman moves out of winter into spring by embracing the child of the past, by letting go of fear, and by actively forgiving
- The spring woman formulates a dream.

Spring Stories

Some of us enter a spring of new beginnings after a winter season. Others have an abundance of spring experiences without the devastation of a winter season. For several of her young adult years, Heather battled with depression and fear. After nine years of marriage, she and her husband were eager to have a child, but were afraid of risking conception while she was on medication. After careful fetal monitoring, she delivered a gorgeous, healthy little girl. Carrying and giving birth to a child is a spring event. In Heather's case the joy was doubled as the fear melted into praise.

Fulfilling a long cherished dream is a spring experience. One morning Carolyn began a session with, "Am I crazy for wanting to finish my degree at forty-five years of age? Will it be a waste of time to go to school? Is there time left to do something with it?" For weeks she had been choosing classes, budgeting her resources, and strategizing with her husband. Her eyes sparkled and danced as she spoke of her choices and her fears.

Finding ways to fulfill our own dreams is a spring task. Maryanne had planned to marry right after college, raise a family, and work part-time. But her dream had changed. For twenty-five years she had been at the top of her profession. But she kept waiting for Mr. Right before she "settled down." Each time she explored the possibility of buying her own place to live, her mother would warn her, "No man wants an independent woman who owns her own home." So she settled for a small apartment and saved her salary for travel and the future. "On my forty-eighth birthday I finally got IT," she confided. "Mr. Right may never come along. I am tired of apartment living and not owning my own place." During the following months, Maryanne not only bought and furnished a lovely condo, but also discovered "Mr. Right" who had been working in the office next to her for twenty years. When she trusted in her own wisdom, something shifted. She was finally ready to receive her "Mr. Right."

Transition into Spring

For some women it is hard to move out of winter into spring. It is difficult for them to become childlike, to play, and to try new endeavors. I am one of those women. I say to myself, "I should be doing something productive," or "Let the children do such and so. I'll watch."

As we look at the grief recovery wheel we can see that the stage called Recovery is a time of beginning new activities, meeting new people, and the beginning of forgiveness. If this task is not met, around the grief wheel we go once again. But once these tasks are completed, we can still choose not to enter into joy. We can block joy by clinging to negative self talk, complaining, finding fault in ourselves and others, stagnating instead of risking. Melancholy becomes familiar. We choose safety over life.

The Spring Woman Embraces the Child of the Past

To move out of winter and embrace spring we must understand how a competent side of us can co-exist with an immature and struggling side. On the one hand we may encounter the new with excitement and a sense of competence. On the other, we may hear voices in our head saying, "Do you really think you can be happy and do things well? Think again!" We are in many ways capable and successful adults and, at the same time, a part of us acts very young, immature and scared. This younger part we can label our "inner child."

Monica's story helps illustrate this struggle between a self-image of competence in one area and feeling totally inadequate in another. Monica is a competent educator who developed a clinical program for child development in a Southern state. Her work was used as a model for other programs. She knew she was professionally competent. But when she had children her self-confidence dropped. Professional knowledge and private application were alien bedfellows.

Part of any new endeavor is acknowledging the learning curve. Competence in one area does not guarantee quick learning and competence in other areas of our lives. Second, our private lives harken back to childhood memories and habits. Monica had been raised by two adults who had never grown up themselves. Their needs, desires, and pleasures dominated the home to the exclusion of Monica's needs. Mom watched T.V. all day, beer in hand, while little Monica wandered from room to room, creating play for herself. When Monica became a mother, she had to contend with an uncared for, unnurtured little Monica within her who had no competent mother model.

Monica is experiencing the dichotomy between her competent adult self and the wounded, yearning child. We also experience that part when we pout, selfishly guard our resources, gossip or lie to protect our reputation, or when we experience the positive qualities of childhood (i.e. unabashed play, wide-eyed innocence, and fantasy.) Sometimes we feel embarrassed, weird, out of control, or foolish. Unfortunately when we feel inadequate our thought process goes something like this: "If I act this foolish, or am this incompetent, all those other parts of me must be false." Or, we might say, "I may show well on the outside, but if you knew what I was really like on the inside, you wouldn't like me." What we are experiencing is an inadequacy of what we call the "inner child." Entering into spring is discovering and accepting those parts of our personality we call the "inner child" while embracing the stability and competence of adulthood. In fact, adult identity integrates the qualities of child—the ability to play, the openness to change, the ability to trust, and the enjoyment in exploration.

Importance of the Inner Child

Jesus supports the importance of accepting the qualities of child as adults when He says "truly I say to you, unless you repent [change, turn around] and become like little children [trusting, lowly, loving, vulnerable, forgiving] you can never enter the kingdom of heaven. Whoever then humbles himself as this child, he is the greatest in the kingdom of heaven" (Matt. 18:2-10, ANT). You might say, "Those words do not fit my view of child. When I was a child, I had no voice, I was not blessed, nor could I trust." However, in spring, in this place called recovery and in this time of restoring what was lost, we must learn to trust, love and be safely vulnerable if we are to become victors rather than victims. One way to do that is to become stronger adults who can care for the child within us who is not capable of protecting herself.

When we speak of the inner child, some people think we are talking about a separate entity living in our body or a separate personality who acts apart from our will. We are merely labeling the less competent, often petulant or exuberant, sometimes immature and out of control side of us "the child."

Embracing the Child of the Past

Brain researchers tell us we can free the gnarled neurons in our brain when we face the details of the painful events.[1] It is important to break the belief system that accompanied the wounding: "Because this happened to me, I am an unloved child. Nothing will go well for me. I am unworthy to be loved or chosen. I am dirty." What does the child need to hear instead?

Bonnie tells her story this way. "I played the piano for years, but never progressed as I would have liked. As a college student I would return home and yearn to play. But I wouldn't if my father was around. If he overheard and complimented me, I would immediately stop. Was I a rebellious, obstinant, unloving daughter? I certainly acted that way. Only later did I connect this event with a historical wound.

"When my father was pastor of a little church, he wanted to make prayer meetings enjoyable and relevant to the children. Each week a different child performed a musical piece or gave a reading. All of my friends performed. Sometimes twice. But I was never asked.

"When I was older, I asked him, 'Dad, why did you overlook me on those Wednesday prayer meeting nights?'" He honestly replied, 'Because you hated to practice. I was afraid you would perform poorly and I would be embarrassed.'

"Recently I wrote out what I wish he could have said to me: 'Honey, you know all the children are participating at church. I would love for you to have a turn. Would you like to pick a date and then you and Bob (my teacher) can work on a piece? I know practicing is hard and isn't fun. But I also know you can do a good job. It is also okay with me if you choose not to do it.' He would have looked me confidently in the eyes and given me a big hug."

Bonnie's daddy couldn't do that. But she could say that to the child of the past, and she could forgive her father for not being able to do so. The act of changing the message is crucial in order to break the child's hold on the adult.

When we acknowledge we have an immature side and name it as our inner child, we allow ourselves permission to enjoy the competent part of our nature. Craig and Susan continued to wound each other in their fights until they grasped the image of the inner child. "Now," Sue reports, "we can laugh mid-way through and say 'who let those kids loose?' Knowing I have a kid inside that still has to grow up is a big relief. I really couldn't see myself as competent at work or at home as long as I felt so young inside. Now I can separate out what's child and give credit to what's adult."

Disciplining the Inner Child

Many individuals were not parented in a healthy way. Some were overindulged. Some were ignored. Some were abused. Our task as adults is to learn healthy parenting techniques and reparent the child of the past. The wounded child needs both loving affirmation and discipline as any child does. *Self talk* is a wonderful tool in this process.

Some of the techniques may seem strange when we approach this journey from a strictly right brain, intellectual viewpoint. One such technique is talking to the child. When Claire gets off the phone with her mother, she is often angry and wants to throw things. In those moments she takes a minute to breathe deeply to slow herself down and then asks herself, "What do you need?" "I need to be heard. I'm never heard by her," is often the response she gets. But more importantly, she gives her inner child permission to be angry and to be listened to by a caring adult. Self talk is an important component in this work. The competent adult Claire tells the child, "I know you are hurting, but you may not yell at your mother or do damage to anything when you are angry. You may hit the bed or throw eggs at the back fence. But you may not use bad language or say hurtful things to her or anyone else." Claire is teaching herself other strategies for dealing with her anger with her mother. As she builds up a repertoire of appropriate behaviors, she feels more adult, less out of control, and more competent. The goal of understanding the inner child is not self absorption or more self introspection, but the integration of all of the parts. We need to be reminded that the present is not the past. As we learn to trust the power of God and know we have the ability to make healthy choices, we can more readily leave the past behind.

The Spring Woman Lets Go of Fear

If a woman chooses to leave winter and enter into spring, she must remove the "toxic waste" of her life. Holding on to fears, grudges, hurts, bitterness, and slights are toxic to our spirits. We may seal the toxic material in acceptable storage drums, but when the seals loosen, the waste leaks out and pollutes not only our own well being, but the well being of others.

Fear keeps us from entering into joy. Whether it is a fear of rejection, a fear of failure, a fear of success, a fear of death, a fear of being overwhelmed, or a fear of losing, fear destroys. Fear attaches itself to our soul like velcro. Outside my office door is a lovely hedge of bamboo and juniper bushes. Threaded throughout are masses of ivy. When I look indiscriminately, I see a hedge of green. But on closer exam, the ivy is taking over. Likewise, fear wraps itself around our souls, indistinguishable on the surface from self. But fear is not our character. It is not our Self.

Maxine became so accustomed to her fears that they became part of her soul. One of her many fears is the fear of driving in the city. "I hate crowded places, narrow, busy streets and crowds. When someone suggests a fun activity, I'll get all excited. But when they say it's in the city, my automatic response is, 'Oh that's a shame. I won't be able to make it.' My responses are so automatic, that I don't even notice how much my life is limited by my fears."

If we are to enter into spring and rid ourselves of fear, we must

- identify and name our fears.
- recognize where and how fear entered.
- fall out of agreement with fear.
- implement strategies for freedom.

Identify and Name Our Fears

Maxine had to say, "I'm afraid of the big city and it limits my life," before she could begin the task of ridding herself of the limitation. If she chose to, she could hide behind the logic that big cities are not pleasant and she does not want to go there. But that would be camouflage. When fear does not legitimately rescue us from an imminently dangerous situation, it becomes destructive and debilitating.

When we love another person deeply, the threat is always there that the person will die or leave. Even though in our heads we might agree with the old adage, "It's better to have loved and lost than never to have loved at all," our hearts often say, "I've been hurt; why risk? Why trust?" But if we say, "I'm afraid I will be abandoned, left alone, be rejected," we can better understand what we fear. Whenever my son would try a new adventure, I would think, "What's the worst thing that could happen? Can I cope?" He jumps off cliffs, deep sea dives, and wants to jump out of an airplane. I, on the other hand, have been afraid of riding roller coasters. I had to name my fear—"fear of losing a child to death"—before I could grapple with a reasoned response to his activities.

Recognize Where and How Fear Entered

Maxine grew up the middle child of five. Often left to her own devices, she made very rigid rules for her life since no one gave her the guidelines she needed for safety, dress, or behavior. She recalls always being afraid of saying or doing the wrong thing. An often-cited research study on preschool children and boundaries took place in a nursery school setting. One group of children was placed in a schoolyard around which was a strong fence. The second group of children played in a yard with no fence. The first group of children played in all parts of the yard freely and enthusiastically. The second group of children huddled together close to the buildings and to their teacher. Well defined limits in behavior and in our physical environment give us freedom to explore and live with less anxiety. Likewise, children with few boundaries or expectations must create their own boundaries. When doing so, they often create rigid, rule-driven self restrictions that lead to anxiety in more free environments.

Once I was able to name my fear when my son would do fun, risky behaviors, I was easily able to trace it to the death of my baby brother. I was afraid of someone I loved dying. Other women are limited by phobias until they acknowledge serious abuse or other traumatic incidences that occurred to them as children. Once acknowledged and dealt with, the fear recedes. For some of us, a strong fearful response is a wake-up call that a deeper issue needs to be examined.

Fall out of Agreement with the Fear

When we are able to say, "This fear is not me. It came unbidden and I don't want it any more," then we are more able to fall out of agreement with it. If we say, "Oh, I'm just an old scaredy cat," we stand in agreement that it is okay for fear to live in us. In the direct measure of our fear, we limit our faith in God and that life will go well for us. It was a milestone for Maxine to say, "I want to be free to go to the city." It takes courage for the divorced or widowed woman to say, "I'm willing to risk a new relationship," or for the woman in debt to say, "I'm willing to do what it takes to be financially responsible." We may even have to say out loud, "No, fear, you will not control my life. I choose God's gifts of love, power, and a sound mind."

We are not to fall out of agreement with the fear that forces us to change our ways. If we have overdrawn our checkbook, we should be appropriately afraid of the consequences. If we speed, we may feel legitimately afraid of getting a ticket. We need the flight response that propels us out of imminent danger. However, the fear that stalks us and paralyzes us from attending to life and its tasks, robs us of joy and inhibits the budding of spring in our souls.

Implement Strategies for Freedom

When we see that we have choices, we can develop a deeper sense of well-being. We can have a healthy sense of our own personal power instead of feeling helpless and out of control. When I fell out of agreement with the fear of losing a child, a very powerful shift came in my spirit that surprised me. We were hiking at Big Sur on the California coast and came upon a sheer rock that jutted out into the surf from a sandy beach. My daughter scampered up to the ledges above, calling back to us to join her. Knowing my hesitation with "risky" endeavors, my husband graciously asked if I minded if he followed her. I replied no. Disgruntled, I sat at the base and looked up. I was no longer comfortable waiting and watching.

The climb to the first ledge was easy. Slowly and methodically I picked and chose footholds in the rocky face. The wind blew steadily and the salty air stung my skin. But I wasn't turning around. Nor did I look down. Finally, I reached the top and gloried in the incredible vista of the coast line, the fading sun, and the magnificent spray of wave meeting rock. I was challenged, but the feeling of fear for my children's well being was not there. In fact, I was experiencing a freedom from the fear that had limited *my own* ability to explore.

Maxine decided if she broke the task of driving to the city into small enough parts, she could overcome her fear. "I think I can do it by going up there when the traffic is light and when I don't have a destination or a time limit. I'll also make sure I take along a good map." Maxine is gaining a sense of mastery over her own world. As she does so, she is choosing spring.

Conclusion

In order to enter fully into the joy of new beginnings we need to understand the power the child within us has over our well being. We need to speak truth about our value to ourselves and change the messages we believed from the past. As we develop an appreciation for our value, we are more able to embrace the joy of spring. In addition, we are more able to enter into spring when we acknowledge the areas in which fear controls our lives. As we identify and label honestly the areas where we limit ourselves out of fear, we allow room to embrace joy.

One more task will move us out of winter and into a spring of new beginnings. In the next chapter we will see how letting go of bitterness and choosing to forgive brings joy and prepares us to leave winter and embrace spring.

Reflection

1. What words shout "spring" to you? Can you recall a spring season or a spring event in your life? Record it as vividly as you can. What feelings do you experience as you remember?

2. What fears limit you from entering into spring and enjoying the abundance of life? Where does darkness still tie you in knots? When you have time, take one of the fear limits and practice the steps to freedom.

Chapter Nine

The Freedom of Forgiveness

✿

Spring is a time of planting. Prior to sowing seed, the soil is nourished with fertilizer and conditioners. One of the nourishments for the seeds of hope, joy, and love God sows in our own lives is forgiveness. In the latter stage of the recovery process questions about forgiveness begin to emerge. If I forgive, does it mean I was not hurt as badly as I feel? Does it make the person who hurt me right and me wrong? Does it mean I have to be in relationship with someone who is not safe? How can I forgive when the other person never asks forgiveness from me? After the hurt has been acknowledged, the pain has been felt, and after the grieving occurs, we must begin the process of forgiveness.

We must not only forgive the major hurts and losses in our lives, but all the little annoyances as well. Any occurrence that blights our soul or causes a painful reaction needs forgiveness. Often our own inability to accept life as it is causes us pain. Part of life and healing is accepting life as it is; accepting a situation the way it is (was) and not the way we may want it to be, and accepting a person as he or she is, not as we may want him to be.

As a teenager, I remember disciplining myself to ask my parents for forgiveness every time we had a fight. I also remember being very disappointed when they never asked forgiveness from me. The act of forgiveness didn't always bring peace or renewed fellowship. Then as a young mom I would rigidly insist that my children ask each other for forgiveness when they fought. I failed to understand the process of forgiveness and to acknowledge the right of my children to choose whether they wanted to forgive or not. I could not allow my children or my parents the freedom to choose because I was uncomfortable with the tension in the household when there was a lack of resolution. My children tried to teach me that they had to feel their anger and resentment and work out in their own way the hurt before they could go to forgiveness.

A Definition of Forgiveness

The dictionary says forgiveness means to give up resentment against or the desire to punish. Scripture states clearly that there is a direct relationship between our ability to forgive another person and our receiving and accepting forgiveness: "And when you stand praying, forgive, if you have anything against anyone; so that your Father also who is in heaven may forgive you your transgressions" (Mark 11:25). The Lord's prayer reads: "forgive us our debts as we also have forgiven our debtors. . . . For if you forgive men for their transgressions, your heavenly Father will also forgive you. But if you do not forgive men, then your Father will not forgive your transgressions." (Matt.18:21–25) Apparently the only way to heal the pain that will not heal itself is to forgive the person who hurts us. Forgiving has the power to stop the reruns of the pain and frees us from the bondage to the offender.[1]

When we fail to forgive from our heart (from the center of our will), the need to get even or be justified overwhelms our choices and behaviors. In physics one immutable law says, "For every action there is an equal and opposite reaction." When I am wounded I react with words or punish with withdrawal and coldness. My child, friend, or spouse responds in kind or with hurt and the cycle begins to roll. On the other hand, I may respond kindly, hold my temper when hurt, and not let my offender know I have been wounded. But where does the tension go? When I hold it in, I may direct my frustration on someone innocent.

Forgiveness is a process rather than an event, however. The process of forgiveness is a decision of the will that has many layers. We can forgive the grocery clerk for overcharging us and we can have trouble forgiving a brother for being abusive. We can forgive and take it back, forgive and become angry again, until eventually the feeling matches the decision and freedom and peace prevail.

Feelings of revenge, bitterness, and unforgiveness ultimately hurt us more than they hurt the other person. Often we feel, "I'm never going to let go of my anger. I'll get even by not forgiving. I'll show him or her." Meanwhile, the other person is pursuing his or her own life and is not affected by our unforgiveness. But we are. What Jesus mandates is always in our best interest. "Be angry, and yet do not sin: do not let the sun go down on your anger" (Eph. 4:26) is not a line to make us feel guilty, but rather a way of being that brings us sleep and peace.

When we refuse to forgive a person, we actually become more bonded to him or her. The one we want distance from becomes the focal point of our thought life and sometimes of our behavior. We allow ourselves to become victims to our anger and hurt. This in turn keeps the anger and bitterness alive and growing. We may even be blocked from receiving blessing in the area where we cannot or will not forgive. For example, you may be legitimately angry with your father for abusing you. But the anger is still too strong to forgive him. At the same time you want acceptance from your male boss at work, but you show clearly in your attitude that you think his decisions are stupid and you do not respect him. Your anger at your father is transferred to your boss. Until the issue with your dad is resolved, it will be difficult to receive what you yearn for from your boss or other authority figures.

And, as a result, forgiveness breaks the power of the enemy in our lives. Forgiveness and right action begin the process of restoration and conformity to God's image. As this occurs, blessings begin to flow. We have more energy to think, to plan, to love and enjoy life rather than focusing obsessively on the misdeeds of the other. The enemy no longer has permission to rob us of joy and divide us from others.

During a seminar for adult children of alcoholics, I was asked, "How can we forgive when the deeds against us were so wrong? Wouldn't I be saying that it was okay for my dad to be abusive and hit me when he was drunk if I forgave him? Do I then pretend that nothing ever happened and go back into keeping the secret? I would rather never forgive than do that"

Forgiveness does not mean that the deed was right and good. Forgiveness means that we acknowledge that the deed was indeed horrible, sinful, evil, dastardly, hurtful. There would be no need for forgiveness or repentance if there had been no violation. We acknowledge that the deed was wrong and we choose with divine assistance to act in obedience to forgive.

Forgiveness and right action can coexist. A woman may choose to forgive her father, grandfather, brother, or neighbor of the sexual molestation and still report him to the authorities and bring charges against him so that he will not be able to hurt other children. Setting boundaries and limits on another's behavior to avoid being reabused or to protect one's own children from endangerment can coexist with forgiveness. One can forgive and limit the amount of time one spends with the toxic individual. When we know we are in healthy control, we can better forgive the other. We are no longer victims.

Janet and her sisters were continually hurt by their father's selfish and hurtful behavior when he had been drinking. They told him over and over again not to drink before they came to visit. But he persisted. Finally, instead of telling Dad what he needed to do to change, they told him: "Dad, we love you and want to be with you. And if you want to drink that is your choice. But if you have been drinking before we get together, and you act rude to us, we are going to get up and leave." In making such a statement, these women were able to reclaim control over their own choices rather than continually feeling helpless and angry over their father's lack of consideration.

Forgiveness does not mean re-entry or relationship with an abusive person. One should not seek the presence of the other if it is not safe to be with them. By remaining safe, one is freer to forgive since unforgiveness often serves as a protection when an individual feels helpless. Unforgiveness keeps the abused person from being reabused or helps the mother protect her child from danger until she and the child are safe. Several women I have met over the years could not enter into forgiveness until the fear of reabuse had passed with the death of a father, brother or uncle who had molested them.

Forgiveness is not forgiveness if it eventually does not bring peace. If relief and peace have not occurred we may be entering into the process prematurely before the grieving has been undertaken and feelings felt, or one may be asking for forgiveness or forgiving the wrong. We may ask forgiveness for being angry rather than giving ourselves permission to be angry, sad, hurt, grieving and going through the pain.

A corollary may be that the unforgiving spirit is a symptom of a deep hurt not yet dealt with. The current sorrow has torn the scab off a wound from childhood that needs surgery and healing. Finally, we might not receive relief because we are assuming all of the responsibility for the conflict or blaming the entire conflict on another. I spoke to a divorce recovery group recently, and afterward a young woman approached me. She stated honestly that she really didn't want to face the issue of forgiveness because it felt so good to be totally in the right and blame everything on her ex-spouse. Forgiveness that does not ultimately bring peace is incomplete.

Forgiveness is not a substitute for bad behavior or for an unexamined life. When an adult has lived in an unsafe environment as a child, she learns protective behaviors. She may have learned to over control, to think in "black and white" or all-or-nothing terms, to demand her own way, or to use illness to avoid responsibility. She may have become passive instead of expressing her wants and needs, or she may have withdrawn out of fear instead of confronting the problems. In adult life these behaviors create dis-ease. So while we learn to actively forgive the wounding of the past, we must also learn responsible, effective adult skills at coping with life. We are responsible for changing our thought life and behavior in order to stop the rampage of pain.

Forgiving Others: The Process

I love to garden. When we moved into our present home, the rose bushes were overgrown and entangled with suckers. Suckers and huge branches drain energy from the plants. In February the major task of rose care is to prune each bush so that the strength of the bush does not go toward maintaining a structure but can be spent on new growth and blooming when May comes. Likewise, unforgiveness drains the strength from our personal spirit as the overgrowth and suckers do to the bloom of roses.

Catherine Marshall in her book *Something More* helped me understand the power in forgiveness. She quoted a conversation she had had with the South African pastor, David DuPleisse:

In my life I've found this forgiveness business a key to getting prayers answered. A couple of years ago I was going through one of those prayers-not-getting-beyond-the-ceiling periods and I prayed, "Lord, I don't have enough faith. Give me the gift of faith."

"It isn't your faith," the reply came. "I can see faith even if it's as small as a mustard seed. No, it's something else. . . .When you stand praying— forgive if ye have aught against any. That's your trouble. That's why your prayers aren't answered. You go about with a lot of aughts against alot of anys. (Mark 11:25)"[2]

The words pierced deeply. My toxic storage containers were badly leaking. To admit that the responsibility for being free lay in my power was very humbling. I had given that responsibility to all those known and unknown forces beyond my control. I was an expert at remembering conversations and analyzing who was wrong and who was right. Of course, I always came up on having done the "right thing." My husband and I are both very good at arguing our positions. But resolution comes only when we both are willing to take ownership, without excuse, for our own complicity. Alcoholics Anonymous addresses this human tendency to blame others and exonerate our own actions in the fourth step. The fourth step calls for a "fearless moral inventory" of all the misdeeds I have done that have impacted others. The steps further encourage confessing these wrongs to another person and, where possible, reconcile and making reparations.

I have found the following process to work well in confronting the task of forgiveness.

Change Is an Act of the Will

The process of forgiveness means actively taking time to list the hurts, name the resentments, and let them go as the Mark passage on forgiveness admonishes. Catherine Marshall suggested setting aside a half hour a day to the task of listing everything I had against anyone. I could do that. In fact, I felt relief in being given permission to name and acknowledge the wrongs and slights I had stored. One day I focused primarily on the annoyances and bothersome memories of the past. My father did not earn much as a minister, but he had a heart for the poor and downtrodden. He gave out of a meager storehouse, but always joyfully. However, I resented his giving to others because it took away from what I felt was my due. So on the list went my daddy for giving the family of twelve my new little red wagon with the detachable sides. Also included on the list was my grandmother for loving and preferring to live with my six cousins rather than with us, and my parents for having had only one child and no siblings for me. When I was six my friend Joan would trick me into eating my peanuts faster than she ate hers. Minor? Incidental?

To the adult, yes, but to a six year old it was a betrayal. From that betrayal part of me learned to distrust. If I remembered it, it went on the list.

The list grew as the days passed. I wrote that every time I would approach the New Testament I could not read the epistles of Paul. I heard condemnation, chauvinism, and arrogance in his "voice." Thomas Hardy, the Victorian novelist and poet, went on the list for writing such depressing novels. I was angry with him for the way children were treated and where love never turned out "correctly." My college roommates went on the list for misjudging my intentions and for all the misunderstandings that come in the course of normal living. I included the broken relationships with boyfriends and arguments with my parents. Anything that still caused anger, resentment or pain went on the list.

As I looked over my list, I realized that reality and my feelings and perceptions were often not the same. But my perceptions had become my reality and had need of being forgiven. I also discovered that I had developed habit patterns of being critical and easily wounded, patterns I needed to break.

Confession Precedes Healing

I find it easier to find fault in another than to bear the responsibility for my own wrong doing. First John 1:19 says, "If we confess our sins, He is faithful and just to forgive us our sins and to cleanse us from all unrighteousness." I needed to ask the Lord for forgiveness for holding on to the bitterness and judgment toward the specific person or event. In addition, where appropriate I had to ask myself "in which of these cases and in what way do I need to be forgiven?" These offenses toward others went on a separate list.

The Act of Forgiveness Is a Choice.

Sometimes we are able to forgive positionally, but not specifically. We might pray, "Lord, make me willing to forgive. I want to forgive, but I can't yet." Some of the items on my list were easy. I took a colored marking pen and lined out all of the items that I could easily let go of. Then I openly acknowledged that I was not ready to let this or that one go yet.

Finally I was ready to pray, "Lord, I choose to let go of being angry and hurt by this situation (or person). I choose to hand over to You any consequences that need to occur in the other person's life. In addition, I pray that You will cut the cord of connection between me and this person (or event) and set us both free."

As the weeks passed, I recopied the list several times until most of the items had been forgiven.

Blessing Lifts the Spirit

When the forgiving process for the items the Lord brought to mind was complete, I began praising the Father for the individual who had wounded me and asked blessing on the person in the precise area of the hurt (where it was appropriate.) As a child I was very jealous of my cousin. Her father was wealthy; mine was poor. Our grandmother was overt in her love for her; I felt slighted by her. As adults my cousin and I have become quite close friends. Therefore, it was very important to me that I not allow anything to interfere with our relationship, especially circumstances that neither she nor I had had any control over as children.

A few years after my initial act of forgiveness, the old attack of covetousness returned with a vengeance while we were visiting in her home. I was only able to break the power of it by once again confessing my covetousness and choosing, albeit through gritted teeth, to pray, "Lord, bless her more abundantly with this world's goods, with friendships and blessings in her family." Instantly the hurt lifted. I felt warmth toward her and a restoration of good will.

Rituals Work

The final stage in the process for me was a formal, ritualistic wiping out of the old. I tore the lists into shreds and burned them in the fireplace. Although I remember, (as if looking at a black and white photograph some of the items on those lists) the sting, the conversations, the obsessional thoughts are gone. Since that initial list burning, I have had to go through the process on several other occasions. It is much easier to keep my daily accounts straight when the ledger is not filled with debt.

Reparations and Reconciliation Bring Closure

Much of what I had to forgive was based on my own perception of reality. Those I needed to forgive were, for the most part, unaware of my resentments and bitterness. Therefore, it would have been foolish and hurtful to the other person to say, "Would you please forgive me for being angry with you when you hurt me?" The ninth step in the Twelve Step program reads, "We made direct amends to such people wherever possible; except when to do so would injure them or others." However, when the walls of friendship have been broken down and there is a cloud over relationships, it is important to go to the other for reconciliation.

After a women's seminar, several of us met monthly to do the "homework" assigned. One of the challenges was to actively seek reconciliation with those we had wronged before the seminar repeated the following year. I had a number of individuals on my list. By this time my parents had died, but nonetheless, I needed to acknowledge my wrongdoing in several key areas. Privately and quietly, I spoke out loud as if I were talking to them and asked them for their forgiveness. I named my wrongdoing. I needed to make things right with a cousin. When I was ten I had collected stamps. An older cousin had a fabulous collection of old stamps and one in particular had caught my eye—and had "stuck" to my finger. Every time I looked at it, I felt ashamed. During this time period, I retrieved it from my stamp box and returned it to her with a note of explanation and apology.

A week before the year was up, I had one more person on my list to seek out. My old roommate was living in our area for only a few months. I called and invited myself over. Over tea, we chatted breezily about everything except what I had come for. For the life of me I could not figure out what I was going to say to her. Up until the very last moment I could not think of a single thing where I had been wrong. Looking back on us as young college women, I could see how poor our communication and conflict resolution skills had been.

Finally, as I prepared to leave, I gave her a hug, wished her well and the Lord dropped the words into my mouth, " Would you please forgive me for not being the kind of friend you needed over these years?"

Although I hear about her from time to time, we have not met since our tea in her living room The nattering conversations, the bitterness, the judgments, died on that day. Reconciliation and restitution bring closure. Reconciliation also implies that we begin to see the person we have offended or who has offended us from God's viewpoint. What is his or her history? Can I separate the deed done from the person? What can I do to bless the person rather than curse him or her? What ways can I build a bridge to this person? What positive qualities does this person have?

Though many of these illustrations may seem trite by comparison to the wounding of your spirit, we still must rid ourselves of the toxic material we carry around with us in order to give us more resilience to withstand "bad weather" and enter into spring.

Forgiveness is a process. In summary we must

- experience the feelings of loss guilt, shame, sorrow, pain.
- state honestly our "aughts against anys."
- forgive what is possible but leave what can't be done immediately and return to finish the job at a later time.
- do a "fearless moral inventory" of our own misdeeds.
- do acts of restitution and reconciliation where appropriate and safe to do so.

Forgiving Ourselves

We must also put ourselves on the list of the "aughts against anys." A noted psychiatrist stated that two thirds of mental hospital wards would be empty if patients could only experience forgiveness of self.

When in healthy working order, guilt is God's built-in mechanism for correction. Healthy shame and self-directed anger are crucial for us to confront our own sinful nature and seek restoration and forgiveness. If I do not see the pain I cause another or feel the pain of my misdeeds, then I will not change and will continue to cause pain to others.

Part of the letting-go process is to sit quietly, relive the painful memory, and accept forgiveness. I suggest the following steps.

First, select a time when you will not be interrupted and a safe place to relive the memory that creates the guilt and shame. For some of you, it will be important to do this in the presence of a trusted counselor who can assist you if the memory is too painful. You may want to ask yourself, "What do I need to do to let go of this skeleton once and for all?"

Second, slowly walk your adult self into the picture that is painful. Go slowly. For some people, walking into the scene with a trusted person is vital. For the Christian, seeing Jesus in the scene brings peace. Remember we are trying to relieve the ball of electric energy in our memory bank so that our brains can be relieved of the blockage.

Third, ask yourself these questions: What do you see? What do you feel? What are you hearing? You may hear a voice saying, "Are you ready to give and receive love and not hide behind your resentments?" "Are you ready to forgive yourself instead of blaming others?" It is very hard to face the reality that we have contributed to a good portion of the struggle of life because we would not, could not, did not forgive ourselves.

Finally, you must plant a new seed, a new message, in your personal spirit. What do you need someone to say to give you relief? Whom do you need to say it? Write it out or say it out loud. Then you need to plant the seed that says, "I am loved and forgiven."

Bitter Root Removal

One day I noticed a pattern. My thirteen-year-old son and I would repeat painful exchanges. I would react instead of act in disciplining him. He would retreat in anger and hurt. Inside, I was furious with him most of the time. It wasn't the typical junior high mentality that upset me, but rather I was disturbed by my attitude that no matter what he did, I could see nothing right. I had always had a very special relationship with this child. We had had conflicts, but we had always been able to work them through. This was new. My concern deepened when Todd innocently told me a description he had given of me for an assignment. He saw me as an angel flying over him, but instead of blessings, I was throwing rocks at him.

When a branch on a tree fails to bloom in spring and leaves don't appear, we can trace the trouble to a dying root. Spring was coming and I had a dead limb in my life. Persistent annoyances in one area of our lives and repeated patterns of resentments indicate root damage in our souls.

Beneath the patterns are decisions we have made in our hearts about the way life will go for us. Some are self-fulfilling prophecies. If I believe something will be so, I will ignore all contrary evidence and what I expected emerges. Then I can say, "See, I told you so."

But judgments sown in childhood have a greater power than just a selective viewing of reality. A vow made deep in a child's soul takes on a life of its own. "The seed we sow may be tiny—an anger, a resentment held against some family member as a child—and forgotten. The longer it remains undetected or neglected, the larger it grows. We may sow a ping-pong ball and reap a nine-story bowling ball."[3] Or we sow the wind and reap the whirlwind.

We cannot ignore the laws of the universe: "What we sow we will reap." Scripture gives us another cause-and-effect verse that is vital for us to consider. The only commandment with promise says this: "Honor your father and your mother . . . that your days may be prolonged and that it may go well with you in the land which the Lord your God gives you" (Deut. 5:16). If we read it another way, can we say, "in the areas where I cannot and do not honor my mother or my father, my life will not be prolonged and things will not go well for me in the place where God leads?"

What does honoring mean? Does it mean believing everything a parent tells us? Does it mean doing everything as adults a parent may ask of us? Can I be angry with them and still honor them?

We may honor our parents by being kind, sending seasonal cards, writing letters, making phone calls, performing appropriate tasks. But if in our spirit, we have judged them, in the area we have judged, we will reap a negative.

I was seeing a pattern, but in those days I was incredulous that a resentment toward one or both of my parents was at the root of my struggles with my son. The summer I learned about these laws, I asked the Holy Spirit to reveal clearly to me what judgment there might be that was operating in my life. I was certainly not being successful at changing my mental attitude or my behavior. No matter how hard I tried, I kept yelling at Todd and resenting him.

Two nights before my husband returned from a lengthy business trip, I woke crying from deep sleep. I heard the Lord's voice say, "Child, as a little two year old, you blamed your father for 'killing' your baby brother. You said in your spirit, 'If my daddy can't take care of a little baby, then I'm not going to let him take care of me.'" The reaping began in junior high when I remember believing that he was incompetent and "could never do anything right." I could never understand why I couldn't be proud of my daddy. He was a good man, successful in his work, and very kind. Other girls adored their fathers. What was wrong with me?

My father had his faults, but he did not kill my brother. But I blamed him. I needed to be forgiven and to forgive my father for what the inner child believed to be true. Then, I needed to stop sowing criticism and judgment toward my son and the other men in my life. I had to choose to accept their way of doing things without saying in my mind, "Oh, how stupid." I do not have to like or accept their choices, but I also do not have the right to judge them.

Once we have identified behaviors and attitudes that don't serve us or others well, or when we see life not going well, we must ask, "What is the inner vow that is holding these behaviors and structures in place?" Some of these vows might be similar to the following:

- "If I trust anyone, I will be abandoned and hurt. So I won't trust."
- "I'll give and give and give but no one will see it nor will I get any credit for what I do. I will always be hurt by those closest to me."
- "I'm unworthy and don't deserve success, happiness, joy. If any good should come my way, I'll reject it."
- "I have to do it all because no one else will do it right."
- "No one will take advantage of me again, ever!"
- "If I get close to and trust someone, he will abandon me."

Diana's parents spoke little and minimally explained their decisions, thoughts, and beliefs to her as she was growing up. Before her senior year in high school, they told her that she would have to drop out of sports and focus on her studies because her grades were so poor. Diana silently protested the withdrawal of what gave her the most joy and what connected her with friends. She vowed, "I'll show them. They may keep me from sports, but they can't make me study." Although the decision was never that clearly made, the evidence for such a vow was clear. She never studied and her grades fell. She got into college but did poorly in several classes and was uninterested in completing a four-year college program. Finally she finished a two-year medical program. She told me when I met her, "I don't read and I'm not a good student."

In time I had her bring in her high school report cards as we had identified her senior year as a turning point year for her. What was the truth about her ability? All through a very academic high school she had all B's, one C, and a smattering of A's. This was a non-reader? I sent her home to make a list of the vows she made surrounding her parent's decision and to make a statement of what was truth. In fact, she even went to them and for the first time confronted them on this decision, asking questions she had been too afraid to ask before. She also was able to tell them the impact their decision had had on her. She also confessed the vows she had made. The result? Each time I meet with her she is reading another book; she's decided to return to school to explore options for a career change. Her final grade in her most recent class was an A!

A Season to Forgive

"For everything there is a season and a time for every purpose under heaven." The season of forgiveness and of letting go of fear may come around again and again as we gain wisdom and deeper understanding of ourselves and others. We must continue to grasp the image of a cycle of changing seasons. If we do not accomplish everything we wish for today, there will be tomorrow and another season.

The waves of the sea hurtle their power against cliff and shore, recede, regroup, and cycle once more, hitting the rock in release of power and energy, as hands lifted skyward in praise. Likewise we may feel a release of power and joy as we let go of some of our fears and resentments in forgiveness. We can enter into the excitement and anticipation of new beginnings as we explore the other tasks of the Spring woman.

Reflection

1. What patterns are you unable to break? Is it possible the child of your past has judged one or both of your parents in the exact area of your pattern of frustration?

2. Identify the pattern in a relationship or a thought process that does not serve you well.

3. Ask yourself, "Is it possible these same patterns existed between me and my parents as I grew up?"

4. What judgment might I have made toward a parent? The judgment takes the form of a belief or a vow.

5. Once the source of the vow is discovered, apply the process of forgiveness to this bitter root.

Chapter Ten

A Season of Awakenings

*O*ne of the major tasks of the spring woman is to formulate a dream and to see how that dream reflects the purpose, vision, and meaning of her life. As she does so she enters into a season of spiritual awakening and seeks support from others who support and encourage her in both the season of dreaming and the season of implementation.

Dreaming the Dream

What was one of your childhood wishes? As a child I wished for a fluffy white Persian kitten, a pony of my very own, and I wished to marry the boy of my sixteen-year-old dreams. None were fulfilled. My father brought home a scrawny, flea bitten stray; there was no room in a San Francisco flat for a pony; and the love of my life married someone else. There were many others that did come true: My daddy always came home safely from his travels, the first boy I really cared for in junior high liked me back, and I went to the college of my choice.

Childhood dreams come and go. Depending on the nature of our dreams and the decisions we make about them, we either retain the hope that dreams can come true, or we lose hope that we will receive what we yearn for. Children who come out of woundedness often fail to realize that they even have the ability to dream. Many of us give up, however, when we have prayed or hoped or dreamed and we don't receive what we want. Some honest questions we might ask ourselves are these: "Do I believe dreams really come true?" "How could I rekindle the fire to dream again when other dreams have been deferred, delayed, altered, or have actually died?"

The spring woman chooses to leave winter by facing her fears and choosing to forgive herself and others. Her third major task is to learn how to dream. The woman who dreams

- enters into joy.
- dreams her own dream.
- seeks the support, friendship, and encouragement of others.
- enters a season of spiritual beginnings

The Spring Woman Enters into Joy

No matter whether we are embarking on our adult journey in our early twenties or facing our last spring, we can be spring women as we enter into the joy of new beginnings. The teenage Mary, the mother of Jesus, and her post mid-life cousin, Elizabeth, are examples of women in springtime. Both were women dreaming their own dreams in the midst of everyday events. Certainly neither of them had any idea that their normal yearnings and desires could be transformed into such profound calls on their individual lives.

Mary, we can imagine, was dreaming of her upcoming engagement and marriage to Joseph. But then the power of God offered her a new vision, a new dream and she responded, "Be it done to me according to your word." And Elizabeth yearned to have the shame of infertility lifted from her spirit, even though she was too old to have a child. Not only was her shame lifted, but she was given the profound responsibility, along with her priestly husband, Zacharias, of preparing John the Baptist for his unique mission of stirring up the spiritual climate in Israel in preparation for the coming of Messiah. What a powerful illustration of God working through our natural yearnings to give our lives a deeper, more profound meaning and purpose than we can conceive.

The Spring Woman Dreams Her Own Dream

In addition to entering into joy and seeking the support, friendship and encouragement of others, the spring woman dreams her own dream as she

- makes choices.
- searches for meaning in her tasks.
- discovers the process of dreaming her own dream.

Over the years women have not been given cultural models or encouragement to dream their own dreams. We read as children the fairy tales of young girls on the verge of entering into the fullness and challenges of womanhood who are stricken by evil and fall asleep only to be awakened by a handsome prince. How can we awaken and show up to life with or without a prince in our lives? How do we form our own dreams? One mid-life woman said at a conference, "I've spent so many years supporting my husband's dreams and launching my children's dreams, I don't know which are theirs and which are mine."

Making Choices

Research on women, as we discussed in chapter 2, indicates that a young woman may put off the decision of a career until after she has made the decision to marry. But for the woman between eighteen and thirty, choices today are more complicated than for young women in earlier decades. She recognizes that she has a variety of choices and a more flexible time frame in which to accomplish career and family goals. But having more choices doesn't necessarily mean life is easier. A spring woman in her twenties told me once, "If I choose a career and love it, I may not have time or energy for a marriage. My fear is I will be old and alone if I don't make marriage a priority." To form a marriage and have children may be her primary choice. However, we see more and more young women delaying the choice for family until they have selected a career. In a society where job security and the economy are so volatile, many counselors are encouraging women to be well trained even though they may choose marriage and family.

Several single women I know chose to work at a "job" right out of high school rather than choosing a career because their goal was to be married. After ten years being single, one says, "I wish someone could have convinced me at eighteen that I needed skills because there's no guarantee any of us will be married. Now, it's taking more time and effort to complete my college degree *and* work."

An individual who gets stuck in a choice that limits her options is said to be in *foreclosure*. The way we foreclose on our options is by getting married right out of high school, getting pregnant and raising a child with or without a partner while still in our teens, or by getting a job and running up bills so that we have to keep working at an unsatisfying job just to keep even. If a woman actively chooses her marriage, children, and the type of job, she will be more fulfilled and better able to explore a dream and discover herself within the choices she has made.

Often I hear stories of women who didn't have the luxury to dream and plan for a future. They were in difficult home situations and marriage was the only acceptable way to escape. Others, due to financial need were forced to support themselves. For many others, there were no mentors or guides to encourage them to explore the options available for young women. Even those of us who were privileged enough to go to college, often chose "acceptable" female job options—teaching, nursing, social work, physical, speech, or occupational therapies. In my college experience the rare woman went for a career in business, politics, or medicine—careers that may have taken a longer training period.

Most women believed they would work for a few years and then raise a family. Most did not believe they would raise a family and work. Joan worked part-time as a speech pathologist once her children entered school. She comments at fifty: "Now I have the energy and verve to choose a career because I know my abilities and what I love to do. I wonder what else I would have chosen if I had been exposed to more choices? Now I'm not sure it's worth the effort to start over." It isn't so much what the choices are that we make as women, but rather that we have explored the options and know that we have choices?

The exciting part about the cycles of our lives is that it is never too late to be a spring woman. In fact, statistics reveal that most individuals will change the course of their career life at least three, if not more, times. So our training needs to be not only in skill development, but also in learning how to go through change. No matter what the choices have been or what the limitations we perceive we have in our lives, in God's economy, nothing is ever wasted.

Finding Meaning

Finding our dream in the broadest sense of the word is finding out why we were created, what unique contribution our unique selves have for the world we inhabit. It is believing that I am not an accident. I am as unique as my fingerprints. In the incredible intricacies of human interaction, I play my part and hold a place that has meaning. In addition we are challenged to believe that God moves personally and uniquely in the nit and grit of our lives to accomplish a very special plan for our time here on earth.

A call or a mission is the core motivation in our lives. We may be "called" to a line of work in a certain location to accomplish a certain purpose. For the Christian, the call is not only to fulfill our own destiny, joy, and well being, but also to yield to what we perceive is God's plan. His call blesses us and blesses others through us. In all that we do we are each called to demonstrate God's love, compassion, and power to a hurting world. *How* we do that and *where* we do it is the challenge of dreaming and discovering the desires of our own heart.

The call on our lives may be general rather than connected to a specific career location. Jesus read the following as His mission statement in the Galilean synagogue:

The Spirit of the Lord God is upon me,
Because the Lord has anointed me
To bring good news to the afflicted.
He has sent me to bind up the broken-hearted. . . .
To proclaim the favorable year of the Lord
And the day of vengeance of our God.
To comfort all who mourn,
To grant those who mourn in Zion
Giving them a garland instead of ashes,
The oil of gladness instead of mourning,
The mantle of praise instead of a spirit of fainting.
So they will be called oaks of righteousness,
The planting of the Lord, that He may be glorified. (Isaiah 61:1–3)

As we begin formulating a dream and discovering our call, we must first think specifically and then generally. The journey is to unfold meaning and a dream. Once we come to believe that we have purpose, we may not see clearly what all the parts are. We must avoid the narrow view that says, "If I can't see it, it must not be real." We must remember spring is a seed planting time, not a harvesting season. The apostle Paul gave expression to this when he said, "Now I see through a glass darkly, but then face to face. Now I know in part, but then I will know even as I am also known" (2 Cor. 13:12). There will be full revelation ultimately, but we can expect an unfolding revelation throughout our lives of what our purpose is. The more we know, the more we understand. The more we understand, the more our faith grows and the more we are willing to risk and dream some more.

The Process of Dreaming

Step One: Seek God First. Our dream unfolds from a twofold relationship of acknowledging God's presence in our lives (our understanding of who God is) and understanding and accepting our abilities, talents, and gifts. If we choose to be God's child, He promises that all the details of our lives will be dealt with if we seek him first (Prov. 3). Probably the clearest picture of this bonding of God's will and our own is expressed by the apostle Paul when he says, "Be anxious for nothing, but in everything by prayer and supplication with thanksgiving let your requests be made known to God" (Phil. 4:6).[1] We are encouraged to dream, describe specifically what we desire, and explain it clearly to the Father. In the process of understanding our heart's desires, we work with God at a core level to bring to pass His will for our lives. But until we stop, listen, and look inward, we will miss our call. The result of this honesty, is the promise for peace and supplied needs: "And the peace of God, which surpasses all comprehension, will guard your hearts and your minds in Christ Jesus" (Phil.4:7).

Step Two: Dream Specifically. A number of years ago I read Corrie ten Boom's book *The Hiding Place,* about her family's experience hiding Jews during World War II. The story records their capture and removal to concentration camps in Germany. When she and her sister Betsy were sent off together to the concentration camp, Ravensbruck, they conducted Bible studies and prayer groups amid the flea-infested barracks.

During those days Betsy became ill and died, but not before imparting to Corrie a dream for post-war victims. She saw a grand building with gardens and lawns which created a peaceful place for the restoration of broken souls. Every night they would add details to the picture. Betsy never doubted that Corrie would fulfill the dream if she could see it in her own mind's eye.

After the war, Corrie sought to complete the dream. Within a year of her release from the camp, Corrie found an old manor house that exactly matched the one they had envisioned. For several years individuals damaged and war weary were renewed and restored in the gardens of Betsy's dream. Corrie's call in life was not to run a respite home forever. Her call was to "bind up the broken hearted" and to preach the power of forgiveness and healing to broken souls. But she first had to learn that God inhabits the dreams of His people and that He is trustworthy.

Do visions and dreams only come true for saints in prison, or can we appropriate that same power that makes dreams come true? I have discovered that the clearer the picture in my mind, the more likely it is that what I seek I will find.

I have always been fascinated by "house" stories. When my children were little we were looking for a bigger home. I was in a small support group and asked for prayer to find the right house. I was almost apologetic as so many others in the group had deeper concerns. My request seemed so trivial. But one friend reassured me by saying, "Normajean, it is vitally important to God where we raise our children and where He chooses to plant us so He can bless us."

I had never prayed as specifically as I did for this house. Duane and I listed and pictured all the details we wanted: four bedrooms, two baths, family room, near tennis courts (that was his contribution). I needed rose bushes in the back yard, within a certain price range. "Also, I prayed, "if it isn't too much to ask, I really would prefer not looking into my neighbor's kitchen window from mine." Once the list was complete, we continued looking. Within two weeks, we saw an ad in the paper. I couldn't believe my eyes. Not only did it meet our basic needs, but the property backed up to a park that had four tennis courts and my kitchen window looked out on a row of redwood trees.

Step Three: Relinquish the Results. A year later I faced another opportunity to pray and dream. But this time the Lord taught me about the principle of relinquishment. My husband got a job teaching at a private school in Honolulu, Hawaii. Again I began praying for where we would live. We put out requests for information. Then we began dreaming about what we really wanted: we wanted all the comforts of our new home on the mainland, plus we wanted to be away from the city and up in the foothills. We also needed a car and we listed the amount of money we could afford per month.

What we normally could have afforded for the amount we had allocated was a two bedroom apartment near town. While we waited, we heard of a home in the hills that matched our dream list, but the price was too high. We also had the option of living on the school campus in a two bedroom apartment. When we got no reply to our inquiries, I made plans to go to Hawaii to househunt. I prayed that God's choice would be our choice. While there I visited the house. I loved it, but they were firm in their price. As I returned to the apartment on the school campus, I prayed, "Lord, You know I would prefer that house on the hill with all its space. But if Your will is for us to live in this two-bedroom apartment, I will be content with whatever You choose." No sooner than I had said, "Amen," than there was a knock on the door. The homeowner stood there offering us the house at the lower price and included a car for our use!

The hardest part of being in partnership with God is believing that His ways ultimately do work. Whether the dream is a place to live, a yearing for a spouse, a job, education, or healing, our peace comes when we can honestly let go of the final outcome to God. By relinquishing, we can't loose. We let go of how life ought to be, and we are then able to accept and enjoy life as it is.

The key is relinquishment, not capitulation. We are still saying, "This is important and I'll keep working toward it until You make it clear I'm moving too fast and in the wrong direction." As Catherine Marshall said:

> It is certainly the Creator's will that the desires and talents that He Himself has planted in us be realized. God is supremely concerned about the fulfillment of the great person he envisions each of us to be. he wants us to catch from Him some of His vision for us. After all, isn't that what prayer is, men cooperating with God in bringing from heaven to earth His wondrously good plans for us?[2]

Step Four: Accept Reality. Because we want something very much, we think we should have what we desire if we just work hard enough. So we pine away, missing out on what we do have by yearning for what we don't have. Midway through our stay in Hawaii, we toyed with the idea of establishing our home there instead of returning to the mainland after our year commitment. We prayed, sought employment opportunities, and then had a tough decision to make. Because our children were still little, I did not want to have to work full time to make ends meet, which island living mandated.

Even though it was a wise choice to return home, I was angry, lonely, and frustrated once we returned. I had no energy to reconnect with old friends or find new ones. Because the anger had no place to go, I swallowed it and mucked about in depression through winter and into early spring. One evening I gave vent to my anger and frustration to God as I stood looking out over the row of redwood trees behind our home. "Lord, I liked us in Hawaii. You gave us precious friends; we felt part of a wonderful community of people; and now You've taken it all away. And I don't want to be here!" Quietly and clearly I heard, "My child, I can bless you here as abundantly as I did in Hawaii. I have not abandoned you." With that gentle statement, I knew I had a choice to get on with life, accept it as it was, or continue to be stuck in discouragement and depression. The doors were closed on Hawaii. Was I willing to turn and walk through the door open for me?

I had to face the reality of our living situation. As I chose to let go of the old, I embraced a new reality: I could be blessed wherever I lived. I began to see that either He will change my limited view, or He will refine the vision in order to fulfill the dream.

Learning to Dream

A first task of learning to dream is identifying the desires of our hearts. This level of dreaming is a journey of becoming more clearly defined as women. It takes courage to say, "I want," "I need," "I yearn for," "I love." If I define my desires in clear, precise, unambiguous language, I am really making a declaration about who I am and my uniqueness. It's not by accident that we dream in spring after the winter of grief. Old structures and belief systems may have to die before we are ready to dream and to be prepared to act to fulfill our dreams.

Some of the desires of our heart may be very concrete and personal: "I need to find a job that pays twelve dollars an hour," or "My family needs to find a place to live in a month." Others may be more abstract. We may yearn for inner peace when we are under stress or desire to know God more personally, or contribute in some way to alleviate society's ills. I have found as I struggle with the concrete and see how clearly God unfolds His answers, my faith is built and I can begin to see a pattern in my life. The task is to "dreamstorm."

Every good manager will lead her group through a process of brain-storming when a new direction is needed. When we brainstorm no suggestion or idea is right or wrong, good or bad. Likewise when we practice dreaming, we must feel free to write without censure anything our heart desires. Whether in a special section of your journal or in a separate dreaming journal, practice recording the desires of your heart and your dreams. After a period of time, review your lists and see if you can discover any broad themes.

Dream Stoppers. If you have a hard time being specific and clear about your desires and your contributions, you are not alone. Many of us have voices in our heads that often counter the positive moves we choose to make. Consider for a moment some detractors to believing in God's ability to move on our spirits.

- A woman's family history may have taught her *a list of don'ts*—don't trust, don't feel, don't talk. As a result the child tends to dream another's dream. She may try to fulfill Mom or Dad's dream in order to make the parent happy. The child, however, ends up not knowing what she feels or thinks or likes or desires and ends up not knowing how to dream her own dream.

- We may move too fast. We may not stand still long enough to ask ourselves, or God, the tough questions. "Am I in the right job?" "Do I like or am I fulfilled in what I'm doing?" "Am I ignoring God's urging and leading?"

- We may be afraid of success or of failure; of never receiving anything of real value; of being thought egocentric or selfish; of making a wrong decision. We may say, "I've had so many past failed dreams; it's safer not to dream."

- We may not be able to believe that God is who He says He is and that what He says he will do. Often we transfer to God our fear and distrust and disappointment learned from a faithless, human parent.

- We may have learned all-or-nothing thinking. We may say, "Unless I can have it exactly the way I want it, I don't want any part of it." I knew a woman who had a list of expectations for her husband only God could match. When her husband failed at any one of them, and, of course it was inevitable he would, she was punitive and rejecting. If she couldn't have it all, she would reject the whole.

- We may be impatient and balk at the discipline required to dream and to wait for it to come true. "What do you mean prune me, refine me, prepare me to receive my dream? I want what I want yesterday!"
- We limit God's power in us to grow the dream seed when we confess the opposite in our spirits. "Oh, others may get what they want, but I'll never get." or "I'm not worthy to receive . . ." Jesus says clearly, "Therefore, I say to you, all things for which you pray and ask, believe that you have received them and they shall be granted you." It's as if we were to plant the seed and then dig it up saying, "no, I shouldn't plant that seed here." If it does not get left in the ground, it can't grow.
- We hear a voice in our head saying a variety of negative things. "Who do you think you are thinking you can dream?" or "What right do you have to get good things?" or "You're too stupid to figure this out."

What Makes Your Heart Sing? Once we've identified some of the fears and blocks to dreaming, I ask my clients, "What makes your heart sing?" Several steps are involved in the process of answering that question. First, I ask them to identify things that they love and that give them joy. Visual images, experiences, people, objects, places to visit are all possibilities for their list. One client brought in a beautiful notebook she had compiled of elegant English gardens and colored pictures of Victorian scenes and handcrafts. When she looks at her notebook, she gives a big sigh and can rest. Another woman put together a tape of her favorite classical music pieces. Another walks miles a day in the woods near her home, and a fourth takes photographs of the natural beauty in her world.

Second, define things you *do* that bring you joy. Ask, "What are my gifts and talents? What do I do well? What am I not particularly good at, but I love to do? What do other people say I'm good at? What have I done that I am particularly pleased with? What do I enjoy doing?" By writing the answers to these and then talking about them with a trusted friend or mentor, you will discover a clearer picture of your value.

Giving Wings to Your Dreams

In the back of my planner I carry around several 3x5 cards on which I have boldly written my heart's desire in several areas. One card is a finances card, another is a card for career dreams, and a third is for family needs. The financial card included having the opportunity for us to travel without having to pay. Since my counseling practice was in its fledgling stages and we were looking at college educations for our two teenagers, travel was not in our budget. I figured the only way we could go anywhere was if someone else paid.

After writing out my desires and praying, "Lord, these are my yearnings; I yield them to You," I set the card aside and didn't look at it until I was preparing for a recent Bible Study. As I calculated the time between my writing and God's provision, I was startled to discover that it had taken only months. Shortly after writing out my request, my husband began traveling in the summers, teaching statistics in various parts of the country. Soon he added other professional obligations that added to the travel miles. He has accumulated so many frequent flier miles that I now join him when I can. Our daughter had earned her way to Japan for a summer stay and spent a study year in Italy. While she was there, my husband sent me over to visit her with his earned miles. And our son criss-crosses the United States for various water polo competitions annually, financially covered by various institutions. If I do not formulate a clear vision, I wander around without hope and without definition.

Keep Your Feet on the Ground

If you pick up any health product these days, you'll read a list of cautions: May Cause Drowsiness. Do Not Operate Heavy Machinery While Taking This Medication. The following may not be exactly cautions, but I want us to be clear about what dreaming is and what it isn't.

Giving ourselves permission to dream is not the same as making up stories and fantasies about what we wish our lives could be like. In a fantasy we build unreal scenarios; we write a script in which we and others live. We are the writer and the director of what we wish could happen in real life—but doesn't. We use fantasy to escape the reality of our own existence. When we return to the real world from a fantasy, we can be discouraged and disappointed that real people—our spouses, children, friends, co-workers—don't match those in our made-up world. No real person can live up to the perfection we create in our minds. Dreaming is not fantasy.

Telling our inmost wants and desires to God does not imply that God is a genie who will appear when we rub the magic lamp and instantly grant us every passing fancy. Rather it is learning the incredible inter-weaving of His will, desires, and yearnings for us and our understanding of our own. The goal is to learn to hear His voice in us *and* to be courageous enough to discover our own. It's risking saying, "Here's what I yearn for," and at the same time recognizing the answer could very well be no. I may want a gorgeous, million dollar mansion. But in reality I may not want to do what it takes to earn enough to buy one. Does that mean God doesn't answer prayer? No, it means once I am courageous enough to say, "This is what I want," I am willing to accept reality. Now God can do whatever He chooses. But unless that desire does not fade, I can scratch it off my wish list.

In her book *Adventures in Prayer*,[4] Catherine Marshall encourages us to run our dreaming prayers through a series of tests to determine if our dreams spring from our selfish human will rather than God's will.

- Will my dream fulfill the talents, the temperament, and the emotional needs which God has planted in my being? This is not easy to answer. It involves knowing as few of us do.
- Does my dream involve taking anything or any person belonging to someone else? Would its fulfillment hurt any other human being? If so, you can be fairly sure that this particular dream is not God's will for you.
- Am I willing to make all my relationships with other people right? If I hold resentments, grudges, bitterness—no matter how justified—these wrong emotions will cut me off from God, the source of creativity. Furthermore, no dream can be achieved in a vacuum of human relationships. Even one such wrong relationship can cut the channel of power.
- Do I want this dream with my whole heart? Dreams are not usually brought to fruition in divided personalities; only the whole heart will be willing to do its part toward implementing the dream.
- Am I willing to wait patiently for God's timing?
- Am I dreaming big? The bigger the dream and the more persons it will benefit, the more apt it is to stem from the infinite designs of God.

Behind our dreams and wishes may be a deeper yearning of our personal spirit. As we examine honestly our desires and see the patterns, we must also ask, "What yearning will this satisfy?" The dreaming may also emerge from a vow that needs breaking. For example, if all of my dreams center around money and acquiring things, maybe I have vowed, "I'll never be poor again no matter what."

By knowing the deeper roots, we may discover God healing or filling that need in ways other than by giving us the "thing" for which we've asked. So when we don't "get" what we are specifically asking for, a closer look reveals He may be answering in a way we didn't expect. The real desire of our heart may be to be accepted, to be loved, to be valued rather than to get things.

The Spring Woman Seeks the Support, Friendship, and Encouragement of Others

One of the tasks of the spring woman is to seek mentors and support networks. Whether we find them in our work environment or as models for parenting and homemaking, women benefit greatly when they learn from other women. Debbie, at fifty-five, has actively sought older women as confidants—her mother, her father's sister, and her eighty-year-old housekeeper. Each woman was professionally competent and blended the professional with the feminine pursuits of home and creativity. She said, "Although my relationship with each woman was mutually benefi- cial, I always knew they were there for me and would take time to discuss my concerns. I could trust them to give me honest feedback."

In our own culture we see the results of women struggling alone with the transitions in their lives. Most of us have wonderful dreams and excellent perceptions and ideas, but we need someone to listen, encour- age, and affirm our journey. In order to alleviate some of the sources of female depression, experts encourage women to find ways of being connected with each other. As we have noted earlier, women of past generations often grew up and raised children in the context of commu- nity and long-term relationships. The support network of family and community was strong. Today those support alliances have weakened and we are only loosely connected with those with whom we work and live. Whether we are spring women developing our adult identity or spring women entering a new area of growth, we need mentors—other women who have walked the road ahead of us, who can give us encouragement and guidance, who can be cheerleaders for our new beginnings.

The Spring Woman Enters into a Season of Spiritual Beginnings

Those who are sensitive to the patterns of life often yearn to understand the meanings behind the patterns. Whether we have had a strong religious upbringing or come to an awareness of the power of God as adults, we begin to see a divine hand plowing our fields with us.

Heidi had always approached the subject of religion intellectually. Over the years she had studied most of the major religions and prided herself on not being biased in favor of any of them. However, after thirty years of marriage she was divorced. Although she was a successful business woman and had good relationships with her children, she was restless and dissatisfied inside. As she went through a time of transition, she called out to God and said, "If you really do exist, I want to know You." One whole weekend she decided she would come to terms with this issue of faith, determined to figure out if Jesus Christ was God or not. For two days she sat in her bed and read the Bible. As she read, her spirit stirred inside her and she began to cry. She struggled and asked all of the hard questions: "God, do You exist? If You exist, why is there pain in this world? If You exist, how do I get to know You?" By the end of the weekend, she knew she had to make a choice. She finally gave up and said, "What do I have to lose? I choose you and choose to believe Jesus is who scripture claims him to be." With those words, a deep calm settled over her spirit. Although she has many questions, the core one is settled. The words, "I've come home," best fit how she feels now.

A Gallop Poll claims 95 percent of Americans believe in God, but only 35 percent report having a relationship with a personal God whose principles guide their lives. Whether we are adults or children, the personal encounter begins with our willingness to acknowledge that we have access to God through His Son Jesus and can have a partnership in life with Him. A spiritual awakening is a spring event.

Spiritual Renewal

Once we encounter God in a personal way, we discover many levels of intimacy with God. As we read Mary and Elizabeth's story in the Gospel of Luke account, there is no doubt that the two women have different, but equally powerful, personal spiritual experiences. Both are part of their respective religious communities. In fact, Elizabeth is the wife of a respected religious leader. Although each has an established belief, they are led into a deeper encounter with the power of the Spirit of God. The angel appears to Mary, announces God's intention, and explains, "The power of the Most High will overshadow you." When Mary goes to visit Elizabeth, the Spirt of God comes on her, and she begins a spontaneous outpouring of praise to God for the miracle of Mary's baby. Mary, in turn, responds to the joyful moving of the Spirit in her own spirit.

Giving Praise

We may be bored with form and ritual, be complacent with old ways of viewing things, and yearn for a fresh breeze to blow through our personal spirit. However, we too can be overshadowed by the power of the Most High when we seek spiritual renewal. Scripture comes alive. We hear God's voice speaking more clearly. We see life through a new lens. When I sought to understand what had kept Christianity vibrant for two thousand years, I was first introduced to the praise principle of the Spirit. Whether we feel like giving praise or not, we will be set free to think and act more clearly and will release the power of the Spirit in our lives when we give praise for all things (Eph. 5:20).

As with most things important, I learned how this principle works in the mundane events of life not in my lofty spiritual moments. I tried praising instead of swearing when I stubbed my toe or bumped my crazy bone. I gave praise for red signals and altered plans, arguments with my spouse and disappointments with friends. I remember one particularly hectic Thursday afternoon. I had rushed home from work to take Todd on his paper route, pick Gretchen up from a school activity, and race Todd across town for a swim meet. We were running late and I was getting more and more frantic. The angrier and more frustrated I became, the more the traffic slowed and every signal turned red.

"If you kids didn't have so many activities, I would have a calmer life!" I bellowed. *Give praise for the red lights,* a quiet inner voice said. "What?" my spirit almost shouted. *Give praise for the red lights,* the voice repeated. I took a big deep breath, swallowed hard, and prayed, "Lord, thank You for the red lights. I let go of the time. I let go of when we get there." "Todd, I'm sorry I lost it. This isn't your problem. It's mine." I repented. By giving praise I was willing to let whatever happens happen. But as soon as I relinquished control and accepted life as it was, the traffic smoothed out and lights turned green. But with either outcome, we won when I let go.

Every day I confront the question, "Lord, do I give praise for these horrible stories of child abuse, depression, death, and loss that have so terribly wounded your children?" *No, child,* comes His patient answer. *You are not giving praise for the evil of these events. Evil is not good. But I want you to give praise for all things. In so doing you release My power to bring good out of evil, joy out of sorrow, and release you from bitterness.* God never wants us to confuse evil with good. Nor does He say we are to be glad evil exists. What He does want us to do is to release the hold our bitterness and lack of forgiveness has on our spirit. We need to give praise for the power of God to overcome evil with good, to change the circumstances, and to give us strength in the midst of crisis. Praise frees our spirit to accept God's vision—His ability to make something new and good out of the old. And praise ushers us into a deeper understanding of the power of God to fight evil in practical ways.

Season of Revival

We have all experienced boredom in our lives, our relationships, and our faith. We may take others for granted and the patterns of religiosity and churchiosity may replace the eager expectations of former joy and excitement of our faith. Sometimes the transitions of our lives and the winter seasons churn up the old patterns and we turn again to seek a season of spiritual revival, which is a spring event. Webster's Dictionary says revival means "to come back to life or consciousness, or to flourish again after a decline." Even in this season, the spring woman may need mentors and support to encourage and bless her along this road.

Mary and Elizabeth, prototypes of spring women, model for us the joy of new beginnings as they see their dreams fulfilled, as they choose to enter into joy, as they celebrate together, and as they experience the power of the Spirit in their lives

The Time of Seed Planting

The spring woman celebrates letting go of the old ways and welcomes the season of new beginnings. She knows that if she has planted well during these months of preparation and dreaming, she has the hope of an abundant harvest in her personal spirit in the seasons to follow.

Have you ever watched cotton candy made? The vendor takes a white tube and passes it around the vat of swirly, sticky, angel-hair, fine candy threads. The threads build up and up around the central core. Seasons are like that. Each season builds on the previous ones, and each time we go around another cycle, we become wiser.

Reflection

1. Try listing some of the elements of a dream that you've had hidden behind the boxes in the attic of your mind?

2. Can you describe one desire of your heart? Pay close attention to how you feel as you write it down.

3. What dream stoppers are familiar ones to you? You may wish to write out your own.

4. What makes your heart sing?

Part IV

The Summer Woman

When we die and go to heaven,
Our Maker is not going to say,
"Why didn't you discover the cure for
such and such." The only thing we're going
to be asked at that precious moment is, "Why
didn't you become you?"

Wiesel

Chapter Eleven

A Season of Balance

❧

*I*n late spring I watch the corn stalks grow tall in military precision at the corner farm. The farm workers stake the tomato vines and cultivate the fields. As spring fades into summer, the owner props open the wood slat shutter which protects the counter of the yellow produce shed. By July 4 the local corn crop is ready for eating. Over the weeks to follow the bins are laden with beans, squash, lettuce, tomatoes, and apricots. Flies drone and bees hum around the doorways. Summer arrives!

Summer is a time of fresh fruit and early harvest. The vibrancy of spring changes to summer's long, warm, easy-going days. Summer storms hit, but quickly are replaced by the sun's warmth. Summer is a season of flowering, of richness, of personhood. It is a time when a woman faces who she is and what she wants with confidence in pursuing her goals. It is a time for reevaluating former goals and dreams. It is also a time of deepening friendships and understanding the importance of the mother-daughter relationship. It is an active time. The summer woman is at once independent and interdependent, individuated and connected. She has an accurate perception of her strengths and weaknesses. She values herself and is nurtured by the value others have of her. Balance is a key word.

When I learned to dream, I discovered I was in partnership with God. He worked with me to shape my dreams according to His will. Likewise, the summer woman develops a sense of self-worth and value in partnership with her Creator.

As in each other season, the woman in summer has tasks to perform. The summer woman demonstrates her ego strength when she

- weathers transitions, reevaluates her dreams, and celebrates her choices.
- finds emotional balance.
- finds her own unique voice.
- discovers the mirrors that define her.

Before we elaborate on the tasks of the summer woman, consider a summer model. If you are familiar with the woman in Proverbs 31, you have probably noticed how unbelievable and unattainable her accomplishments are. However, I see her as a powerful picture of the woman in the summer season of her life. She is a woman of balance.

Take a minute to read the description of this woman. What do you notice first about her? You may be drawn, as I was, to all that she does. There are times when I become frustrated when I read about her because I fall so short of her to-do list. However, when I really look closely at this section of Proverbs, I notice that it is not her *doing* the author wants us to notice, but rather her *being*, the quality of the woman she is. Her doing is not the only measure of this woman's worth. But her doing reflects her strength of character, which allows her the freedom, the joy, the energy to accomplish what she sets her heart to do within the confines of her culture. Even though this woman is a married woman, the character strength she displays is a model for us whether we are single or married.

A woman in summer acknowledges her worth and takes pleasure in what she does. This woman of worth "works with her hands in delight" (v. 13) and "smiles at the future" (v. 25) because she wisely prepares domestically and financially. We see her confidence in her business dealings as she buys a field and plants a vineyard. She is not so self-absorbed that she fails to attend to the needs of her household, including those who serve her. She also gives to those within her community who are in need of her assistance. To accomplish her tasks with a heart of joy, we assume she has let go of the pain of her past.

Her doing flows out of a heart whose values are clear. The last part of the chapter tells us her secret. "Charm is deceitful and beauty is vain, but a woman who fears the Lord, she shall be praised" (v. 30). Her *doing* comes out of a center that understands the power of God in the everyday. The fear of the Lord is not the fear of which we have spoken earlier; this expression might be better translated "awe" or "respect" as opposed to "terror" or "panic." She is a woman who understands the importance of putting God first, of inviting Him into the details of her life, and of following His directives.

She has her own life, but she intertwines it into the life of her family. As she chooses what makes her heart sing, her family is blessed. In research on the roles of women it was discovered that women who choose their jobs and tasks and who had a number of different roles (mother, wife, business woman, volunteer, friend, daughter, to name a few) reported being happier than those women who had limited roles and did not feel they had chosen those. Non-working women who did not have children at home reported a significantly higher number of physical symptoms and more depression than any other group examined. Men who are employed in high status jobs are the most symptom-free. Women in high status jobs are equally symptom-free when compared to women and men in work positions which lack satisfaction and are perceived as valueless. Women who have focused their entire lives on raising children feel as if there is no self left when they are gone. These women are then challenged to find new tasks and new dreams to define themselves.

Although we wish our sense of value came from within, we learn our worth by the value others put on what we do. For the working woman, a pay check, promotions, pay raises are all powerful measures of progress and worth. Lynne is a new mother. She had been a very well paid and highly regarded clinician in a world-renowned medical center. She wisely is reevaluating what will give her a sense of well-being now that she isn't working. "No one praises you for a clean toilet! I'll keep the toilet clean, but I'm also going to upgrade my professional career by going to school." More and more young women who were professional summer women have delayed having children. As they start on the "mommy track," they have to reevaluate what gives them self-worth as the measure of their value shifts. Several who continue to work part-time have negotiated with their bosses to work several days out of their homes or have begun home-based businesses. They are creatively applying to a home focus the skills they learned in the work force. And some, having worked for a number of years, are eager to set the work world aside to focus entirely on home endeavors. Again, it isn't what a woman chooses that is crucial to her self worth, but that she knows she has choices. Crucial, too, is the awareness that we can always make new choices.

The importance of financial well-being is not to be minimized when we speak of a summer self. Another woman I know felt she had nothing to offer in the adult world. "After raising four children, I only knew the language of children and of other moms. When my children were all in school, I took a part time job. Just having a pay check, knowing I was contributing to alleviate our financial need, and seeing I was a capable adult, improved my feeling of value." No matter how we look at it, if a woman has the ability to earn money, it gives her a sense of independence and freedom. It is not unusual to encounter a woman who stays in an abusive marriage relationship in large part because she has no financial skills to live independently. For other women, having a sense of mastery at whatever they choose to do is the deciding issue for having a sense of self.

The Proverbs 31 woman is fortunate to have a husband who encourages his wife's endeavors and who feels blessed rather than threatened by her. They have a unity of purpose even though their tasks are different. She has an identity separate from his which is rooted in her own talents; she has an identity with him and without him. They are interdependent. Sometimes husbands, due to their own wounding and struggles, feel threatened by their wives' fulfillment. It is difficult to maintain a sense of personhood in the face of opposition and sometimes outright anger. However, a woman must seek God's will for her life and resist putting her husband in God's position. Often a woman will believe the negative words of husband or parent rather than seek God's view of her worth. At the same time, a wise woman does not go out of her way to antagonize and create a crisis in her home.

A friend, who has balanced well home and a business, commented recently on the importance of encouragement. "I love my work and feel very connected to my children. But my husband refuses to accept the fact that I'm working and successful. I struggled with guilt for a time. Was I being ungodly for doing what I was doing, especially when he so clearly disapproved? Slowly I've come to realize it's about him, not me. But it is very sad and stressful not to have his support. I know I need someone in my corner encouraging me. So, it's been important for me to find friends who can go "that-a-girl. Keep up the good work!" The Proverbs 31 woman senses her value not only by knowing the power of God and the delight she takes in her tasks, but she is also renewed and encouraged by her husband and children's love and support. And, when the primary relationships aren't there, women can give the gift of encouragement to each other.

Developing Ego Strength

Each of the seasons we can experience many times in our lives. A woman's adult cycle of development is based on the premise that we grow through transitions and upheavals. Life is not static nor does it fit neatly into stages and patterns each following logically on the previous. Because women are by nature empathic and relational, our lives are impacted not only by the events in our own lives, but also by the events in the lives of those with whom we relate.

The development of a woman's self-worth and value emerges out of the vicissitudes of life, as well as from those events and belief patterns she has learned in childhood. The spring woman learned to listen closely to the messages she received throughout childhood and began to understand she could learn to give herself new messages for the old. The summer woman's journey is to allow those new affirming messages to nurture her and to develop not only a head knowledge, but a heart knowledge that she is a special creation with all her warts, wrinkles, cellulite, and hidden shames. She demonstrates ego strength.

Weathering Transitions

The summer woman is not exempted from transitions, but she sees them as part of the fabric of life. She may be shaken for a time, but she knows she will grow through these as well. Hanauma Bay on the Island of Oahu is one of my favorite snorkeling beaches and is a marvelous picture of this process. The old volcanic crater is a magnificent sculpted bowl of volcanic rock. From the park above, a trail slopes steeply to the beach below. From the shore's edge you can see the shaded outline of dark coral reefs below the surface and an occasional flutter and shadow of fish. However, once I've donned snorkel and mask, the underwater world comes into sharp focus. In the water close to shore I can see schools of tiny flitting fish, an occasional brightly painted purple or yellow fish and massive outcroppings of coral. But none of the fish or the coral compares to the vast array of species and the magnificent colors of creatures in the deep waters on the other side of the reef.

Crossing the reef is risky. A surge of the water or the crash of a wave can send the snorkeler scraping on rough coral. On the other side, the water is clear and deep. Multi-colored fish swim around the outcroppings of coral. I can see the sharp pointed mouth and teeth of a moray eel hiding its long body in a dark crevice. A group of large purple fish circle me and swim on. Bright yellow angel fish flit and dart, sucking on the coral's sharp edges.

Like any transition, the reef can be a barrier or a gateway to the riches that lie beyond. The summer woman is a woman who is willing to risk the barrier, knowing short-term pain will bring long-term gain. She is a woman who is "fully human and fully alive," to quote John Powell. His description of fully alive individuals describes women in summer:

> They obviously experience failure as well as success. They are open to both pain and pleasure. They have many questions and some answers. They cry and they laugh. They dream and they hope. The only things that remain alien to their experience of life are passivity and apathy. They say a strong "yes" to life and a resounding "amen" to love. They feel the strong stings of growing—of going from the old into the new . . . They are always moving, growing, beings-in-process.[1]

I think it is accurate to say that a summer woman has faced several transitions and at least one winter of self-evaluation as she looks at her past decisions, dreams, resentments, and disappointments.

My daughter Gretchen and I spoke recently about the transition she is in and how she views herself. Several years ago she recognized she was depressed and was overreacting to the normal challenges of life. She chose to go to counseling. Although she is only twenty-one, I consider her a young summer woman. Last year she spent studying art history in Italy. Upon returning she hoped to apply and enter the university system at the winter quarter. Due to financial cutbacks, however, winter admissions were closed. As a result, she could not return to school for a year. She spoke of this summer season in this way: "I feel very comfortable and confident with the choices I've made this year. At the same time I'm definitely out of sync with my peers. I'm working, but not toward a career. I'm not connected with academics which have defined my purpose for years and I'm not easily part of a group. I guess I'm experiencing sadness and joy both at the same time.

"Not being in school makes me very sad and sometimes depressed. On the other hand, I really know I can be and do anything I set my mind to. I could be an excellent pianist or graphic designer if I wanted to. I also know I've accomplished things that make me feel very good about myself. I'm self-assured in my abilities and I like the way I'm leading the year of waiting. At least I'm not stagnating. I know I'm in a good place when I enjoy what I'm doing *as I'm doing it,* that I feel what I do is worthwhile and that I am making a difference. You know what it feels like? It feels like I'm floating in warm ocean waters. . . settled, contented."

I love the emphasis she gave to how she did what she did. She enjoys her tasks and commitments *as she is doing them.* She allows herself to be nurtured by what she chooses. As we all will, Gretchen will continue to encounter challenges in life. And she will continue to learn how to face disappointment and loss. She will learn to face her weaknesses and embrace her strengths. As she develops her adult identity, she may plunge into many other seasons. The successive seasons will be richer if she is able to remember the characteristics that define her in this season.

Evaluating the Dreams

If the spring woman begins the dream, the summer woman implements strategies to fulfill it. She reevaluates old dreams to see if they still have meaning. A woman I know who is in her fifties has been sowing seeds in many creative areas for a number of years. Her harvest is plentiful; in fact, she is overwhelmed. She teaches at the local junior college, has her own business, and teaches others to create their own businesses. Like any competent tiller of the soil who weeds out the overcrowded rows so that stronger plants may thrive, she has had to weed out and focus on what parts of her business are most important. As a summer woman, she reevaluates her goals and values, and refines her dream.

Making Choices

The summer woman understands her value as she makes choices in her life.

The following list of questions is designed for you to gain a better understanding of how you value yourself, your attitudes toward self-acceptance and what you have learned that has created the self you are today.

- Have I learned to be self-confident knowing that no matter what struggles life poses, life will go well for me? Or have I learned that life is dangerous and will always be painful and difficult?
- Have I learned skills that serve me well to cope with the many roles I have as a woman in my culture? Or have I learned to be dependent, expecting others to make me happy?
- Have I learned the value of being female? Or do I hide my femininity out of fear of being taken advantage of?
- Do I feel confident and self-assured or have I learned to feel confidence is being arrogant?
- Do I allow myself to get excited over the good things in my life, and my accomplishments? Or do I feel guilty when I'm happy and successful?
- Do I allow myself to admit when I'm wrong as well as to acknowledge when I am right? Or have I learned to listen to an internal critic that says I have no worth?
- Have I learned that I have control over the circumstances of my life where possible? Or have I learned to adapt to the circumstances that come my way so I won't be rejected?
- Have I been taught, and have I incorporated into my belief system, that I am loved by a heavenly Father who cares about my daily life? Or do I believe He is an angry father waiting to punish me when I make a mistake?
- Have I learned I have value apart from my doing, that my feelings are valid and that my thoughts are worthy to express? Or do I hide my thoughts and discount my perceptions and feelings for fear no one will hear or agree with me?
- Have I learned to say an appropriate yes and a clear no without feeling guilty?

If you chose the first of the pairs as most like you, you are demonstrating qualities of ego strength. The list is, in no way, all the questions we can ask ourselves.

The Summer Woman Is a Woman of Balance

When the positives of the above list reflect how we see ourselves, we are becoming more the balanced woman of summer. We are finely tuned creatures, a marvelous blend of mind, body, and soul. What occurs in any one part of our being impacts the other parts. If we are negligent in caring for any part, the whole is impacted.

The newest "disease" of the American woman is fatigue. Fatigue singles out women two to one over men. According to New York psychiatrist Leslie Powers, 60 to 80 percent of all doctor visits for fatigue turn out to have an emotional or stress connection.[2] I've indicated earlier that 85 percent of women in two-income families still do 85 percent of the domestic work. We must also take into account the increasing number of women who are the head of the household and sole parent. She has incredible demands placed on her.

We must also look at the physical facts. Women's bodies have less muscle mass in which to store glycogen, and hence have fewer reserves than males. In addition, their bodies are depleted monthly due to hormonal shifts and iron depletions. Women have a significantly higher incidence of anemia and thyroid problems. Because our lungs are smaller, we do not have the oxygen store of our larger male counterpart. Although fatigue isn't really a "disease," it is a primary symptom that we are out of balance and something in our lives needs evaluating.

Archibald Hart in his book *Adrenalin and Stress* has coined the word for our stressed out age, "the hurried sickness." The more we have to do, the higher the levels of epinephrine our adrenal glands pump out and the more our internal organs wear out. The adrenal system goes into action when we need extra energy to run from danger or when we need focus to fight off an attacker. In modern society we may not use the "flight" or "fight" mechanism for physical survival, but we tap into it as we race madly about running errands between work, dinner, and our evening meetings. What we don't anticipate and plan for can cost us dearly. What we can do is learn to understand our own ability to cope with stress and learn strategies to keep the monster tamed.

A summer woman of balance:

- faces her historical wounds.
- evaluates priorities and adjusts her activities to fit.
- values her body, health and appearance.
- learns to set boundaries not barriers.
- nurtures her personal spirit.

Faces Her Historical Wounds

Let us identify those parts that drain a woman's emotional reservoir. If we have been actively working through winter and spring, we will be pleasantly surprised that we are well on our way to managing our stress. What we haven't dealt with can impact our ability to cope with day-to-day stressors. Let's assume we have ten levels in our well of well-being. Imagine the first five are filled with the toxic waste of abuse, unforgiveness, bitterness, anger, and unbroken vows. We now have only five levels to handle the vicissitudes of life. We also know that those first five levels are anything but dormant. We expend incredible energy keeping those memories and feelings from surfacing.

In order to improve her ability to cope with the stressors of life, the summer woman has:

- grieved her losses.
- faced her anger.
- forgiven where she can and is aware of what she can't.
- practices new "message tapes" about her worth.
- has begun to dream her own dreams.

Corrine understands the power of dealing with the past in giving her freedom in the present. "I am just now able to face how rigid and harsh I have been. I always believed there was a right and wrong way to do everything. The right way, of course, was my way. I would become angry and upset when things didn't go my way. In fact before I grieved my losses, I could not hold down a full time job and could barely cope with working sporadically part time. I can tell my ability to cope with stress has increased since I am now working full time and enjoying it."

Evaluates Priorities and Adjusts Activities

When we feel out of control, we have lost our perspective and our priorities are askew. We need an honest evaluation about what we value in life and whether what we are doing matches our priorities. If the stress of work and caring for small children is not mixing well with social life and business travel, a woman has some hard decisions to make. The women of the eighties believed they could have it all and do it all and do it perfectly. Women are becoming more realistic. One woman commented at a recent seminar, "I may be capable of doing it all well, but is it worth the exhaustion and the lack of enjoyment? I have to really examine whether how I do what I do is worth the effort."

A first step is to make a date with yourself. At that time you may want to write down all of your commitments. Second, write out a list of the things in life you value or are priorities to you: husband, friends, children, God, work, accomplishing things, giving to others, making a lovely home, cooking, exercising. Next, put this list in order by priority. Then put the calendar for the month in front of you and ask yourself, "How many events on this calendar match my first three or four stated values or priorities?" You may discover—as many do—that much of the busyness of life is not rewarding or nurturing because it does not match our priorities.

Some questions you might ask yourself are these: Will this activity or commitment really matter ten years or five years from now? If I do this, will it take away from doing well what has real value for me? "A merry heart does good like medicine," the writer of Proverbs proclaims. Wise advice! Often it is not just our to-do list that needs reevaluating and pruning, but our attitude does as well. Once we choose to commit, we will feel less stress if we choose a positive, joyful attitude. Researchers have discovered that when our attitude turns to positive thoughts, the "hurry" drug (adrenalin) decreases, heart rate declines, and breathing deepens.

Besides pruning and prioritizing our activities and changing our attitudes toward what we do, we need to make solving a nagging problem a priority. Often individuals come to counseling saying their whole lives are out of control. But, in reality, there is one nagging problem in the family, in their relationships, or on the job. By having regular heart-to-heart talks with yourself, you may be more tuned in to your own feelings and to the stressful elements in your life. If there is a current crisis, allow it to rise to the top of the priority list and then spend energy solving it.

By focusing appropriate attention, you will feel more in control and less stressful. For several years Yvette's son had not been doing well in school. The lower his grades, the higher the tension. Finally, she took time off from work and sought professional help. The counselor suggested her son be tested for learning disabilities since there had been no observable trauma or crisis that had preceded the decline in performance. "I wasn't excited that he might have learning disabilities, but I was greatly relieved to be finally able to plan a course of action." Stress reduces when we make a nagging problem a priority.

We also must make ourselves a priority. I encourage busy clients to put themselves in their daily schedules. Stay-at-home moms need to put themselves on the calendar as well. Many women say, "Oh, I couldn't do that. It wouldn't be honest." Or they say, "That would be too selfish when I have so much else to do." We do have a choice to slow down, prioritize our lives, and take time out for thought and reflection. Somehow it's okay for us to get sick so we can say no to an activity or yes to rest. Where have we learned that to do what is good for us is wrong? It is crucial for women who are the primary nurturers of family and others to strengthen themselves so they have a full well out of which others can drink.

In a similar vein, we will build a wall against the ravages of burnout if we choose to enjoy what we do while we are doing it. Otherwise, we need to fearlessly ask ourselves, "Why am I doing this?" In order to reduce unhealthy stress, we also need to focus on the present and resist the temptation to live in the future. We may be in a business meeting or church on Sunday, but we're making mental lists of what we have to do the rest of the day, the rest of the week, or next year.

Finally, a woman of balance knows that she will need extra time to regroup after a period of high stress. After the adrenalin rush, our bodies need to repair. Sometimes we may feel depressed and exhausted. If we understand a repair period is needed, we won't be so hard on ourselves. We will build in repair time after intense stress times. Our balanced summer woman evaluates her priorities, prunes where necessary, and learns to inhabit her moments.

She Values Her Body, Health, and Appearance

Three crucial stress reducers are improved sleep, appropriate exercise, and healthy diet. Dr. Archibald Hart claims sleep deprivation alone creates incredible havoc in our ability to cope with stress. He contends healthy maintenance may mean eight, nine, or more hours of sleep per night. When sleep flees, it is because we have not slowed the adrenaline down early enough, and we may have developed poor sleep habits. He encourages us to avoid heavy exercise before retiring but encourages mild exercise. Reducing the light in a room readies us physiologically for sleep. Also, we should avoid greasy and heavy foods and sleep deprivers such as caffeine, nicotine, and alcohol within four to six hours of bedtime. In addition, sleep experts encourage going to bed and getting up at the same time.

A woman in summer does not ignore her outward appearance. Once we have discovered the colors, styles, and textures of the clothes that enhance our appearance and choose to purchase what we know we look good in, we can let go of self-consciousness. I have found I become more self absorbed when I haven't taken the time to purchase clothes wisely and dress appropriately. The Proverbs 31 woman, who fears the Lord and is praised by her husband, is a wise shopper. She purchases quality ("her clothing is fine linen and purple" [v. 22]—the color of royalty). In other words, she chooses what is flattering. A friend of mine specializes in assisting women to discover the look that enhances their natural beauty. "The women with whom I work find a sense of self-worth when they have the tools for dressing well. They find they save money because they avoid poor choices. I give them a picture of the best they can be."

We cannot ignore the role our hormones play in our emotional well-being. We wish we could be as energized every week as we are on a good hormonal week. For some it's their first week after menses; for others it is the week during ovulation. As a woman ages, her cycle may fluctuate and with it the predictability of hormonal flow. But all of us learned early that life is a roller coaster of subtle emotional changes that we learn to compensate for emotionally. Instead of saying, "Why am I feeling so crummy?" or "Boy, did I ever let that guy have it!" we eventually forget why we were a bit off-center on a given day. Often something happens, and we react with tears, anger, frustration; we blame the other guy. We feel like running away from home. Researchers are discovering that as the stressors in a woman's life increase, pre-menstrual syndrome (PMS) symptoms increase. A major step in monitoring and maintaining control of the impact our hormones have on us is to keep a record of our mood fluctuations on a calendar. We can also record how our bodies react during our cycle. Part of taking control of our lives is to be aware and knowledgeable.[3]

Another aspect of valuing self is being physically fit. The Proverbs 31 woman "girds herself with strength and makes her arms strong" (v. 17). As wise, vibrant women, we must find a way to exercise our bodies. As we become more physically fit, our sense of self increases, and our stress decreases. Of even more importance, physical exercise brings blood to the brain and changes the chemical structure that allows us to think more clearly and ward off depression. Some women walk for an hour three or four times per week with a friend. Others work out at a fitness center. Some women run a certain distance each day. Like any new habit, it takes time to develop a pattern that will work. Whenever we start something new we need to encourage ourselves and avoid being critical when we don't meet our initial expectations. Some women need to be cautioned that exercise in excess can cause weakness, fatigue, and irritability, or what is called "sports anemia."

We must guard against the belief that taking care of self is arrogant and selfish. Henri Nouwen claims arrogance and low self-esteem are two sides of the same coin. When we deny our value, we stay stuck. He observed:

> I have come to realize that the greatest trap in our life is not success, popularity, or power, but self-rejection. . . . Instead of taking a critical look at the circumstances or trying to understand my own and others' limitations, I tend to blame myself—not just for what I did, but for who I am. My dark side says: "I'm no good . . . I deserve to be pushed aside, forgotten, rejected and abandoned."[4]

When we appreciate our positive qualities and accept the importance of being our own unique selves without guilt or arrogance, we move into partnership with our Creator. As a result, we learn to relax and move more calmly through our day.

Nurtures Her Personal Spirit

As we read about the summer woman in Proverbs 31, we are aware of joyfulness in her spirit. Her energy, her sense of value, and her wisdom flow from a well filled first by her Creator. When we choose to nurture our personal spirit, we spend time with God on a daily basis, to know His character and be filled with His spirit. We do this in listening prayer, in active Bible study, and in conscious praise through song and worship. The summer woman learns that she is loved. Out of this knowing comes more authentic living and giving. The psalmist compares this person who delights in the Lord to a "tree firmly planted by streams of water, which yields its fruit in its season, and its leaf does not wither; and in what [she] does, [she] prospers" (Ps. 1:3).

This image pictures us drinking continually because we are planted in His presence. Our emotional balance and quiet strength emerges in direct proportion to the quality of our time on the river bank.

We are given many forms of God's love and nurture. When we choose to allow God to love us and when we choose to nurture ourselves, we will surround ourselves with beauty. My mother was never wealthy, but she knew how to make the common lovely. Each Sunday she set the dinner table with her finest china and silver and made a special dinner whether we had guests or not. My officemate fills our rooms with whatever plants are in bloom each month. Another woman keeps one fresh rose in a beautiful vase on her desk as a reminder to "stop and smell the roses." The writer Barbara Johnson, as she moved out of winter and into spring, would do something special to celebrate life on the first day of each month. Finding ways to nurture your personal spirit do not have to be expensive. But they must be chosen carefully. What you do must count. Otherwise, don't start until you are ready to choose what you love.

A Woman Who Fears the Lord

The woman who discovers emotional balance is working toward becoming all that God intended her to be. She acknowledges her worth and takes pleasure in what she does. She has definite roles but they flow out of a heart whose values are clear. The key to her personhood is her fear of the Lord. As we move into the last two tasks of our summer woman we will examine how she discovers her own unique voice and the influences that have shaped her.

Reflections

1. Practice writing a description of yourself. Pay close attention to your feelings as you attempt this task.

2. The following are some random ideas to begin your creative juices flowing. Remember, whatever you choose and whatever you do, choose carefully and enjoy thoroughly. Let the moments of peace bathe over you and restore you as God works in you to bring you peace in your personal spirit.
   - Take a walk in the hills, country, by the shore, in a park, but out of doors, in nature. Be wise. Select a place that is safe.
   - Buy one rose or a bunch of daisies (they last a long time, so do freesias)
   - Select a lovely cup from your collection or purchase one that will give you joy to use. Pay close attention to its weight, size and color.

- Pause during your day to breathe deeply and offer a prayer of praise, "help", or just to say "Hi" to the Lord.
- Have headphones and tapes handy. Listen to music that rests your soul.
- Have nearby a book with lovely pictures or a book of poetry selected for its visual as well as verbal content.
- Create a place in your imagination, a room in your home or apartment, or a corner that beckons you to rest. Put your favorite treasures there to enjoy. Create your own hiding place to retire to rest and recover.

Chapter Twelve

A Season of Expression

✣

In June the snow in the mighty California Sierras begins to thaw. Driving the back way out of the Lake Tahoe basin, we pass lakes of snow and moving ice. Further down the mountain, the lakes turn into churning streams which gather force as they flow toward the mighty dams, crashing over the man-made spillways. Soon, clear snow water meets the mighty Sacramento River. During our drought years, river biologists were concerned as they watched the salt content move upstream from the San Francisco Bay. As the salinity increased, fish, wildlife, and agriculture were endangered. When the snow water pushes into rivers, it provides a cleansing action that maintains a balanced ecosystem. Without the heavy rains and snow, the river couldn't do its job.

When our lives are in balance, we are cleansed, filled, and replenished by streams of living water that flow from a divine fountainhead. Unlike in nature, our Fountainhead is always pouring water into our lives. We may, however, choose to drink from other streams. Those steams, like rivers during our drought years, do not have enough fresh water to push out the pollutants and debris. We end up drinking polluted water that does not satisfy or nurture us.

The next two tasks of the summer woman—"Demonstrating ego strength in finding her voice" and "learning self by reflection"—are interrelated parts. "Finding our voice" is another way of saying we have found our ability to speak clearly the thoughts that are in our heads. "Finding our voice" also refers to the process of learning to think and reason. We learn that ability initially in our family of origin when we

157

learn to value ourselves by what others mirror of us—how they encourage us to think, feel, and reason. These voices are rivers we tap into, for good or ill, to satisfy our thirst for affirmation and value.

Finding Our Voice

The challenge of the summer woman is to discover her own unique voice. Research suggests that women for the most part speak less often in mixed groups of men and women, contribute less, and are interrupted more often. Her voice is more than the words, tone, and inflection of her speech. When a woman finds her voice, she has found expression for the self. She discovers that she has ideas and feelings and that these have value. Many women monitor their expressions because they do not want to hurt another person's feelings or be rejected. Staying in relationship is more important than giving voice to opinions. On the other hand, we have all known women who say whatever comes into their minds whether it has substance or not, whether it hurts another person or not, or whether it contributes to the moment or not. These behaviors may reflect an unexamined self. The number of words expressed and the volume does not indicate a woman has found her voice. Vocalization is not voice.

However, the more a child engages in conversation with parents and other adults, the more her ability to think, reason and express herself develops. If she is spoken to with interest, appreciated for her opinion and encouraged to form one, she develops patterns of thinking that serve her well. She gains ego strength. On the other hand, if a woman is raised in a home where violence is the rule, alcoholism is the norm, abuse is intense, and verbalizing an opinion is perceived as a threat by her parents, she will learn to be what Mary Field Belenky in *Women's Ways of Knowing* calls "silent women." These women have learned it is not safe to express needs, feelings or ideas and as a result their hearts and minds are not developed, "because it is through speaking and listening that we develop our capacities to talk and to think things through."[1]

I love the example of ego strength depicted by Jesus when He was twelve years old. He and his family had gone to Jerusalem from Nazareth to celebrate the High Holy Days. The temple activities came to a close, and Mary and Joseph packed up and left Jerusalem along with others from their home town. They assumed Jesus was somewhere in the group. However, three days out, they discovered Jesus was missing. So back to Jerusalem they hurried.

Can you imagine the frustration, the anger, the fear, and the confusion as they retraced their steps? Finally, they discovered Jesus in the temple in deep conversation with the temple leaders and elders. I imagine Mary was not the sweet madonna we often see in paintings of her. She was probably furious. "Jesus, what in the world are you doing? Your father and I have been looking all over for you. We've spent five days extra not knowing where you were. And you act like nothing's the matter!" Jesus modeled a picture of ego strength and of self in relationship. "Mother, didn't you know I was to be about my Father's business?" He did not acquiesce, but rather stated very clearly who He was and what He was called to do. Then He returned home with them. He had a sense of self that allowed Him to speak clearly.

Women Speak with Many Voices

Women of all socio-economic, educational, and cultural backgrounds struggle to find their voices. Some must raise them in anger and in groups; some allow others to speak for them; and still others never even know that they have the ability and the right to think, feel, and be heard. Several researchers have identified five categories of women using "voice" to indicate their level of ego strength. These are not stagnant categories, but are fluid. Although the summer woman would fall into the last two of the categories, we must examine each level in order to better understand our own journey and the journey of women we meet.[2] These levels are:

- Level one: The Silent Woman
- Level two: The Responding woman
- Level three: The Awakened woman
- Level four: The Reasoning Woman
- Level five: The Integrated Woman

The Silent Woman

The silent woman has a silent mind and a silent voice. She may yell at her children or gossip with her neighbors, but she does not think about her life, does not know she has choices, and, for the most part, doesn't conceive of any other reality than what she lives. We will find her among the less educated, the poorest, and the most abused for she has no ability to shape her own destiny. Because she is steeped in a dependent, victim mentality, she does not have the power to choose. She sees herself at the whim of external authority whether it be her father, her husband, the police, or the "they" who make the rules.

Her family structure has been abusive and threatening, where violence, not words, was used to bring resolution to problems. There is no discussion of goals, choice, opinion, feelings. Usually women raised in dangerous environments are furious when a sibling or a mother protests—but doesn't have the strength or power to bring about change—since more abuse follows the protest. She tends to marry men who are abusive and continues the family pattern. The father figure is either abusive or absent.

Women raised in silent backgrounds have found ways to emerge and find a voice. Others write a daily journal about their thoughts and feelings. Others find outlets in literature, art, music, or dance which give them self-expression.

The Responding Woman

A woman who is a responder has an active mind, but a silent voice. She believes that she is capable of learning. However, when asked her opinion, she will parrot what any given authority will say. She trusts the knowledge from the "all-knowing external authority" regardless of the person's credibility. When confronted with the discrepancy between two authorities, a woman at this level doesn't try to understand why. Her thinking is very black and white. In her personal life she is compliant and giving to others. If she had the choice to express her desire or hurt someone's feelings, she would keep quiet. The responding woman has no authentic voice of her own and is highly influenced by how others define her. Above all, she wants to be included and not rejected. Her roles also define her: She sees herself as someone's mother, secretary, wife, caretaker.

When we encounter the silent woman or the responder woman, we don't need to correct her at every turn. Rather, we can encourage her to ask questions and to speak what she feels and thinks even if it isn't theologically our way. The summer woman wisely knows that it is okay to ask questions and seek for answers. When she sees this beginning in women, she wisely encourages them and provides a safe haven in which these women can explore new ideas.

The Awakened Woman

The awakened woman is more like a bear disturbed in its den. She awakens with a roar. For years she has existed as a responder until one of several things occurs. A major crisis happens. She may be exposed to new ideas in an academic setting or begin to see other ways of doing things while on the job, or by interacting with other women. She may have found a wise woman who becomes her mentor and accepts and cares for her and sees her value.

The awakened woman is an angry woman. She often has great anger toward men for how she has been treated and begins to distrust all authority. Up until now she trusted everybody but herself; now the pendulum swings and she trusts no one but her gut reaction. Because she has been verbally silent, she has few tools with which to express her anger and hurt. She feels out of control and can sound confused in her thinking.

Millie's husband took her out to a lovely dinner at their favorite restaurant just before Christmas—in order to tell her he had been having an affair for over a year. He told her he wanted her and the boys *and* the other woman. She reported her state of mind in this way: "Now that my world has stopped spinning off its axis, I have become furious at everything. I'm furious at Jim for what he's done. I'm furious at my abusive father. But more than anything I'm furious with myself for being so blind, so compliant, so passive for so long! I prided myself into thinking Jim was the crazy one. And lo and behold, my eyes are opened and I really see how in denial I have been. I'm just as crazy as he is."

Millie is wisely seeking professional assistance to gain a clear perspective. She has been in a very supportive Bible study group with a wonderful female mentor for several years where she feels free to speak and hear how she sounds. Wisely, she's staying attached to her support system, women who allow her to be herself. Even though this group of women struggles with many serious problems of their own, they act collectively with the wisdom of the summer woman as they support, love, and give Millie a place to speak and be heard.

The key step for the awakened woman is to move out of silence. Anger is a powerful force for making personal changes. Unless these women heal from the past, they stay stuck in their anger and isolated because they are afraid to trust. When they start to move, however, they speak of the excitement of growing up and of seeing themselves in a new, more positive way.

The Reasoning Woman

The reasoning woman is a balanced, reflective woman. She doesn't run to extremes, to critical judgment of things she doesn't understand, nor to blind acceptance of what others in authority tell her. She recognizes the importance of the voices of authority and of her own voice. The voice of reason seeks to understand what others think, feel, and believe. Then she thinks deeply about what she believes. When she chooses to move into her own world and leave her parents home, she actively asks penetrating questions of herself: "Where am I going? What do I want out of life? Who am I really? What qualities about me are positive; which are negative? What do I believe?"

She has not had the abandonment and wounding by the males in her life. In most cases, the father voice was benevolent, kind and caring. If her parents are divorced, the father stays in close contact with his children. The parent voices are strong and she finds nurture in those first relationships. However, she still has a difficult time speaking up and out. She finds her voice as she discovers Daddy isn't perfect and as employers, professors, and others treat her as a peer. She moves early in life toward equality with her parents, and her relationship with them is one of reciprocity.

A woman who has had a silent voice in the past can learn to value her ability to think and discover her voice when she finds benevolent mentors. Diana had been a responding woman bordering on silent. When I met her, she was just beginning to notice life was not going well for her, but she had no idea why. Her father, a successful professional, was out of the home or preoccupied with his business affairs. When he was there he pointed out what needed to be improved. No ones opinion was as good as his. Her mother's world centered around his schedule and his needs. Most family dialog was spent in preparing for dad to come home and figuring out athletic schedules for the three children. Diana spent hours in fantasy and quiet in her room or playing sports. As a young adult in her early thirties, she had not yet discovered her own voice.

When I encountered her recently, I noticed a vibrancy to her as she met my look with directness and humor. "Diana," I asked, "what gave you the courage to change?" Her response indicated she was beginning to find her voice. "I know it may sound strange, but I had a male mentor. I have a wonderful boss who really has taken an interest in my well-being. He asks me challenging questions about why I'm doing what I'm doing and points out areas he sees need improving. He even was willing to take time off from work to share his perceptions with my counselor. I trust him because he's a godly man and he doesn't tell me what to do. He's given me the courage to speak boldly to my own dad about some of my needs and concerns from the past. Probably because I practiced with my boss, my dad really heard me when I spoke to him. I've got a long way to go yet, but I'm really excited about where I'm headed!"

Whether the reasoning woman discovers her voice by dialog with her first family or practices with a group of peers, she knows it is vital for her to discuss her ideas and thoughts with others. Some seek out structured studies. Others seek out informal groups of friends with whom they feel connected and close. But the reasoning woman thinks clearly and begins to articulate her own ideas and perceptions to those around her.

The Integrated Woman

A woman becomes an integrated woman after years of practice articulating her own ideas and learning to think clearly with her family and friends. When a woman speaks with this voice, she accepts that conflict and stress in this life is inevitable. We might call her a woman of faith. She learns that incredible paradox of being all that she can be while trusting in God's providence and provision.

She is no longer afraid that she "won't win" in an argument or that her idea won't be accepted. She prefers an environment where everyone shares opinions boldly and openly and where, if a decision needs to be reached, a consensus and synthesis can be achieved. She no longer thinks in black-or-white terms. As she becomes comfortable with her own thoughts and ideas, she is much more tolerant and accepting of other points of view. She knows what she believes, but she does not demand others believe as she does. She is able to say, "I don't know," and not feel embarrassed or inferior.

More importantly, she desires to give out of her full well to those who are less fortunate. Whether she is a working woman at home or in the business world, she seeks ways to reach out with care and concern to those around her. She is able to care and not let the other person's problems overwhelm her. When a woman demonstrates ego strength, she knows how much she can give and when enough is enough. This woman demonstrates she can set boundaries, not barriers, in her relationship with others.

Our integrated woman is also a "fully alive" woman. Some women learn to be fully alive through the work of other seasons, other women were raised in families where they were encouraged to think, reason, and ask questions. In these families, heated verbal debate was a sign of respect and growth rather than a signal for fear and abandonment. Both parents were respected for their intellectual abilities, and their fathers demonstrated a significant ability to express and mirror feelings. The mothers for the most part had worked at least part time in careers outside of the home. Their daughters admired their mothers for their ability to show compassion and love and express their opinions in a reasoned way. The parents showed respect for their children and made it clear they valued their adult children's opinions and ideas.

The relationship with the mother was a significant one for these women. The mothers, for the most part, were also integrated women who helped their daughters put thoughts to words.

As we enter the fullness of a summer season, we must remember we can be a mother model to women who are in need of a mentor. Whether we mentor our own daughters or other women, we must remember that we are growing a mind and a heart as we ask in love, "What are you going through?" and "What do you think about this or that?" And we demonstrate our compassion and love when we patiently listen to the answer with acceptance. The summer woman finds her own unique voice and in turn assists others in finding theirs.

Hearing the Father's Voice

The apostle Paul understood the importance of learning our value by reflection when he wrote to the Corinthian church. He encouraged the church to embrace the importance of living out of a motivation of love (chapter 13). At the end of his discourse he acknowledged that we can only see our worth in bits and pieces, in shadow and shade. But when we look fully into the eyes of the One who loves us fully, we will know ourselves and the mysteries of life fully. We will experience the overwhelming warmth and well-being of being accepted and loved. We will have come home. Paul says, "Now we see but a poor reflection; then we shall see face to face. Now I know in part; then I shall know fully, even as I am fully known" (1 Cor. 13:12). Is it also possible then, that if I look more closely into Jesus' face, into His Word, and seek the knowledge of who He is, I will become more aware of my value and worth?

Paul elaborated still another way our vision and our person changes. When we choose to really look at who Jesus is—His glory and power, His being—we don't have to *do* anything. In that looking *we are being changed into His likeness from one degree of glory to another* (2 Cor. 3:17). In essence the Father begins a reparenting process through the power of the Holy Spirit. Just as the child learned her value by watching and interacting with her primary caregivers, now as she watches, listens, and observes the work of her heavenly Parent on her behalf, she begins to experience a new image of herself. He may send trusting friends and spouses, children and therapists to mirror His love and to make up for the years lost when love was not there in the way she needed it.

The summer woman learns as well to hear the voice of her heavenly Parent. One stormy evening I spoke to a group on listening to the Father's voice. I encouraged them to listen in a variety of ways to the way He "speaks."

- When we feel moved to tears of joy or feel an overwhelming sense of awe at the beauty of a scene or are uplifted in worship, we are hearing His voice and sensing His presence.
- When we feel an urgency in our spirit to do something or to call someone, we are hearing "the Spirit's call. We may be awakened in the middle of the night or be interrupted in our daily pursuits with the feeling we must call someone only to discover that our friend or family member is in deep need or had been thinking of us as well.
- God sends a trusted friend or mentor to our door when we are unable to call out for help or verbalize our need. Each time I passed through a different phase of my spiritual awakening, a dear friend and pastor who lived in Jerusalem, would arrive in town to visit his parents. I'd be praying, "Lord, I need confirmation that where I'm going is of You. Please confirm it with someone I trust." No sooner had those prayers been lifted than within a day Wes would call and ask if we could get together. In Wes's voice I heard reflected and confirmed God's word to me. Whether in our specific need, or for maintenance encouragement, we hear God's voice in those who come near with a timely word of affirmation or correction.
- We may feel a restlessness in our spirit regarding one little problem in our lives which we have ignored. God raises it to the top of the

heap, and later we discover that the timing has been crucial to accomplish the task without serious consequences.

- We hear God's voice as a still small voice. We are often apprehensive to say, "I heard God speak to me." Throughout scripture He engaged His servants in discourse. In modern church history, great saints of the faith have actively pursued listening to God.
- The storm reminded me I had forgotten a very important way God speaks. He speaks through earthquake, wind, and fire as well. When natural disasters occur we become aware of how vulnerable we are, how fleeting life is, and how really out of control we are. In the sensitive heart, such events lead the summer woman to ask, "What do You want me to know and learn at this time?"

As I spoke on this issue to this group, I encouraged them by saying, "Expect to hear God's voice!" With that the storm hit above our heads, lightening flashed and thunder boomed. I'm not used to divine dramatics when I speak, but the point hit home for all of us.

Conclusion

In a summer season we embrace the love God has for us and we choose to be nurtured by it. In our mind's eye we can see His face looking approvingly into ours. We see His eyes of love. If we need correcting, we hear His gentle voice saying, "No, no don't go that way. Go this way." Or, we may hear Him say, "This habit has to go!" In addition to developing an inner ear to hear God's voice affirming us, we develop our own voice and have the ability to think and speak our own thoughts clearly. The summer woman is not only eager to speak but listens with interest to others. She knows that in the interchange of ideas, she will learn and grow and become more fully human and alive.

Reflection

1. How would you describe yourself—as a silent woman, a responding woman, an awakened woman, a reasoning woman, or an integrated woman? Use your journal to explain why you see yourself in this way.

2. What are your heart's desires? Pour them out to God and see how He will answer.

Chapter Thirteen

Reflections of Worth

⚜

T he summer woman learns self by reflection. The more she is valued,
listened to and encouraged to speak her own mind, the more she values
herself. Significant people in our lives become the mirrors into which we
look for acceptance, value, and for the definition of our positive and
negative qualities. What we see mirrored of our worth is also impacted
by how we react and what we choose to believe.

Our ability to appreciate our positive qualities and accept ourselves as
"in process" is a learned ability. Babies are, by their very nature and by
necessity, selfish critters who are primarily on the receiving end of love
and nurture. As they grow and develop, they learn to give back, to
respond, to show empathy, compassion, love. But they do it by reflecting
what they are experiencing from those around them.

We act and someone else reacts. We may be reacted to with a warm
and accepting facial expression or verbal response. Or, we may see
reflected judgment and criticism. A third response, and potentially the
most destructive, is the response of indifference. When a child's defiant
or obedient behavior is met with indifference, the child has difficulty
developing a sense of who she is. Early on the baby coos and laughs and
performs with smiles and attempts to sit, crawl, stand, and walk. The
mother responds with joy and enthusiasm, which increases the child's
efforts to please and move forward. At the same time the child incorpo-
rates into herself the positive images and delights in her own accomplishments. The adult self is conditioned by those early responses to be
accepting or rejecting of herself.

When a woman does not gain a solid sense of personal identity, she cannot regain it by merely wishing it upon herself. Subtly we continue to identify cues in the behavior of others that give us feedback on our value and our competence. Johnson and Ferguson, researchers on female development say this about self esteem:

> Contrary to popular belief, self-esteem does not come about by learning to love yourself, nor is it something you can give yourself. Self-esteem comes, at least initially, from other people loving and valuing you. It also comes from how much we are loved, valued and respected as women in the culture at large.[1]

If we have learned to value ourselves, the input from the broader world will have less power. We have already seen the power of our family of origin in creating an atmosphere for thought. In this next section we will expand the importance of mother and father voices that reflect the character of the summer woman.

The summer woman understands she has had a number of mirrors that have shaped her opinion of herself:

- Her mother
- Her father
- The hidden child of the past

Mothers and Their Adult Daughters

Much of the literature on mothers and daughters focuses primarily on the struggle between them as the daughter attempts to say, "Mother, I'm different from you!" Recently studies have focused on the vitality and the importance of the long term mother-daughter bond. Since our earliest sense of self comes from the interaction between mother and the infant child and the interplay between them as the child matures, it only makes sense that our relationship with our mothers as we enter our adult years would also be vital.

As women live longer, the mother-daughter relationship may be the longest intimate relationship a woman has and may span sixty to seventy years. According to Rosalind Barnett, a psychologist at Wellesley College, when this relationship goes well the daughter reports feeling more positively about herself. Most of the women she studied reported good relationships with their mothers and an expectation that the relationship would grow closer.[2]

Most women yearn for a closeness with their mothers and want to be accepted by them for their unique qualities and abilities, especially those that are different from their mothers. Ultimately the desire is for mutual respect. Women often report being positively influenced and respectful of a mother who has found her voice and seeks to improve the quality of her life. When a mother does not respect her daughter's boundaries—tells her what to do and then tells her what she's done wrong—the daughter chooses less contact. For somem daughters the distance creates anxiety and guilt. But the alternative is conflict, anger, and a loss of her own identity. Where possible most daughters do not back away from a relationship with their mothers, but instead they try to discover safe ways to be in the relationship. How then do we grow this adult relationship as mother or as daughter?

The summer woman establishes her own adult identity within a relationship with her mother by

- facing reality.
- letting go of bitterness and anger.
- embracing the positive.

Facing Reality

One of the tasks of growing up is seeing our mothers realistically. Some of us must choose to acknowledge that our mothers are not perfect. We must see her weaknesses and errors. For others, the challenge is acknowledging our mother's positive qualities.

At forty-five Julia still struggles with feeling like a helpless victim in her mother's presence. She yearns to hear from her mother "good job," or "your art work is terrific." Julia is learning to do things competently on her own even though the affirmation does not come. For the first time in her married life she invited her extended family to Thanksgiving dinner which she prepared with her college-aged daughters. Her mother and father refused to join them. They made the excuse that the distance was too far and they preferred eating out. "Although I was proud of myself for being the adult mother to my own children and for creating a delicious dinner, I was depressed for days because my mother refused to acknowledge me as a grown person. I couldn't show her how grown up

I had become. I'm finally accepting the fact, at least in my head: she can't or won't give me what I need. But that doesn't mean I'm incapable of accomplishing whatever I choose to. I can honestly say to myself 'I'm an excellent artist and I did a fabulous job at Thanksgiving!' "

Little people need parents to be stronger, wiser, bigger, more capable than they are. If a parent isn't, then the child creates an illusion of parental competence in order to feel safe. In the maturing process she must discover her mother's humanity, recognizing both her strengths and her weaknesses. My discovery came early.

One afternoon when I was seven or eight my mother was attempting to discipline me for something I had done wrong. She had wrestled me down the dark hallway from the kitchen to my small bedroom. "Nonni, stop fighting. Turn over! If you don't stop, this is going to hurt more!" she implored as she tried to spank me. I pushed, tugged, kicked, and twisted to get free. Abruptly, with a muffled cry, she released her hold. I spun away and looked at her. Her eyes pooled with tears and silently she walked across the hall to her room and closed the door. In my resistance, I had hurt her. I sat on my bed ashamed, lost, empty. I had won, but it was a hollow victory. I yearned for her to come back and say, "Young lady, that will be the last time you do that." She could then have found a punishment that would have worked. I wanted her to win! Groundings and time outs were not common discipline techniques in those days. Even if they had been, I knew she would have had a hard time holding the line with me. I was too young to find out that I could win over my mother.

As a young child grows into her teen years and beyond, she may demonstrate her unique self in her dress, her mannerisms, her opinions. Again, it is vital for her to say, "Here I am and there you are," to the woman whose very nature is written in her bones. Although most women would prefer less arguing with their mothers, it is in jousting and asserting herself that the daughter's sense of value and ability to be a separate person comes about. I was just beginning to undertake the challenge of being an adult daughter when my mother died. Before her death I took her for granted. Naively I never doubted that she would be there for me "forever." I would race into her life, argue and disagree with her, laugh and unload my burdens and struggles on her, and then bounce away until I needed contact with her again.

When she died I was just beginning to let her "have" her opinions and values without having to challenge them. What would it have been like to have had a non-combative and non-blaming relationship where I could be my own self without feeling guilty that I was not more like her? Though I did not have the opportunity with my mother as daughter, the cycle continues as I now have an adult daughter. I must choose to grow or resist and miss out on a dynamic relationship with her.

Part of facing the reality in a mother-daughter relationship is not just a daughter's responsibility. Mothers must learn to listen to their daughters, back away from advice giving, and learn to accept daughters as they are in order to have as good a relationship as possible. For both mother and daughter the key is leaving the doors open for growth, for change, and for maturity in the other. A daughter needs to realize that her mother has also grown up over the years.

As we attempt to have an adult relationship with our parent or child, we must learn to actively wait. How do we actively wait? Some mothers are estranged from their daughters because of family pain. Daughters choose life styles and beliefs that often are offensive to their mothers and make it difficult to avoid conflict and judgment. Other times mothers feel overly responsible for their daughter's beliefs and choices. They come across as interfering, manipulating and controlling. If you are a mother of an adult daughter—especially if you are currently estranged from her—you may need to learn patience while you wait for her to find her way home again. You can prepare your heart for receiving your daughter when she is ready for an adult relationship by

- Acknowledging your own anger, hurt, disappointments, and frustrations with her over the years. Going through the chapter on forgiveness with your daughter in mind will prepare your heart to be receptive to her advances.
- Acknowledging that you may have been less than a perfect parent and recognize areas where you need forgiveness from her. Be particularly sensitive to areas she has acknowledged have been painful to her.
- Deciding what kind of relationship you want from your time with her and what is possible.
- Choosing to examine the patterns of mothers and daughters in your own family of origin to see how you learned to be a woman.

As a young mother Millie was needy, rigid, depressed, and demanding of her daughter. As Beth grew up, she formed views that were different from her mother's. As a Christian Millie felt it was her responsibility to point out how her daughter's views were not God's views. Although Millie told her she had to make her own choices in life, what Beth heard was not "good news" that made her desire a Christian life. But rather Beth heard fear, judgment, rejection, and criticism for her very being. Her heart's desire was to know that she was loved and accepted for who she was—no matter what she believe.

To Millie's credit, she sought assistance for her rigidity and fear. "It has taken me a long, painful journey back in time to be able to go forward. I totally misunderstood God in my fear. I was so afraid my children would miss an eternity in heaven that I pushed them further away. I finally see that my job is to love them and let God handle the differences. I don't have to agree with all Beth says, but I must respect her enough to listen and try to understand who she is and what she believes. With letting go of Beth, I have more energy to get on with my own life."

Letting Go of Anger and Bitterness

Once the winter season has past, and once the act of forgiveness is accomplished, we must choose to let go of our anger and bitterness. I challenged Karina who had already actively grieved her mother's lack of attention, her crude behavior and lack of protection to her as a child: "How long do you need to be angry and bitter toward your mother?" She came back two weeks later saying, "I was really angry with you for asking me that question. But I really thought about it and realized I had used my anger to punish my mother for all she had not done. And then self-righteously I said, 'See, I'm better than you are.' As a result I have pushed away all of her kind advances to make amends. I haven't wanted to see her good side.

"Finally, I decided to let go of the bitterness and move toward my mother and ask her for help. Instead of acting tough and self-sufficient as I've always done, I asked her to run errands with me. Then I asked if she'd go for a walk in the hills with me. We talked the whole way."

What Karina struggles with is not unusual. The wounding of her childhood spirit was so deep that she could not see her mother through any other eyes but the child's. However, after she grieved her losses and let go of her bitterness, she was able to see that her mother had something to say and had changed as she had aged.

On the other hand, some mothers continue to be toxic to their daughter's well-being. They do not change. They may blame their daughters for any and all problems in the family and they may react selfishly and contentiously. After a daughter has done all she can to form an adult alliance, she must decide what's safe for her and her family and what she can and cannot do. *Only after serious counsel and much prayer,* some daughters may find their only recourse is to see their mothers as little as possible, if at all.

As a mother ages, the responsibility factors increase for her children, especially for daughters if they are caring for their aging parent. If the emotional work of letting go of the resentments and hurts of the past has not been undertaken earlier in life, the pressures mount during the mother's latter years. A daughter may be very angry and resentful when she is expected to care for a mother who did not nurture or care for her when she was a child. The tension can even create intense pressure on the daughter who cares for her elderly parent. Paula Duress, co-author of *Ourselves Growing Older,* has discovered that the burden can have a serous impact on the daughter's health physically and emotionally.[3]

Although Irene has admired and valued the sacrifices her mother made for her after her father died, she had never acknowledged the legitimacy of putting a limit on her mother's demands. Irene's mother lived on and off with her for over thirty years. While Irene's husband worked abroad for several years, she raised her three children through their teen years and catered to her mother's needs and desire. She felt the responsibility for making her mother happy. Inside she became increasingly angry, bitter and frustrated that her mother would not stop demanding when Irene showed signs of exhaustion. Although she valued her mother's assistance, she resented her excessive control, critical spirit, and refusal to listen to Irene's needs.

In caring for her mother's needs, she failed to have a necessary lung exam and, a year later, she discovered she had inoperable cancer. "I don't blame my mother for getting cancer, but I am angry and frustrated that I never knew before that it wasn't my responsibility to make my mother happy. Until now I didn't know it was appropriate to say no to her demands in order to have a healthier relationship. I just stuffed and stuffed my feelings of hurt and resentment. Now she lives with my brother. With her at a distance, I can let go of my anger and talk with her about superficial things. Since I've told her she cannot live with us, she has also been less critical."

Irene discovered her right to her own feelings about her mother and was able, finally, to set boundaries of health for herself. We can let go of anger and bitterness when we know we have other alternatives and choices.

Speaking Truth. What helped both of these women let go of bitterness was an exercise I call "dumping." I encouraged each of them to write a letter, which she was *not* to send, to her parent expressing in any terms she wished her frustration, her anger, her pain over past and present events. The letter was written *as if* she felt free to tell her mother anything she wanted her to hear. When we "dump" we are practicing truth telling and acknowledging our sense of self. It gives us permission to speak what has been taboo. Next, I suggested she read the letter aloud to an empty chair or to a trusted friend. Irene reported, "I finally feel free of the anger. Even though my mother, I know, will never hear all of this, it felt so good to give myself permission to be honest with what I've stuffed."

When the dumping was over, each woman chose what she wanted to actually say to her mother. Irene felt comfortable telling her ninety-two year old mother, "Mom, you cannot come back and live with me because of my health. I need all of my energy to fight this cancer and to get well."

Karina, on the other hand, has decided to take her history chunk by chunk with her mother. She told her mother, "Mom, when you talk crudely about sex, I feel shame. I've felt this way ever since I was a little girl. You both had a sexual remark about everything, including how I developed. When I got older, I didn't care about my body either and thought being sexually active was the thing to do. I have paid a high price for my actions." On that walk, her mother acknowledged how painful that must have been for Karina, and replied, "I'm really sorry, Kar, about the past. But I'm not sure I can change how I talk. It's just how I am."

Karina didn't get everything she wanted, but she has started to reconnect with her mother. Her mother gave as much as she was able at the time. But it was enough to encourage Karina to stay in touch. She can accept the reality: "Mom may never become the mother I want her to be. Now, I must choose what kind of relationship I want with her."

Using Anger to Make Choices. Anger indicates something vital is wrong and needs attention just as a pain in a tooth indicates damage that needs fixing. For the most part, we do not know how to use our anger effectively. We bottle it up and suppress it, displace it onto an innocent and often disconnected target, or vent it loudly and ineffectively. First, we must acknowledge we are capable of being angry. Second, we must label the anger and identify why we are angry and at whom. Only then can we do something about the anger. Scripture acknowledges the validity of anger when Paul states, "Be angry, but sin not. Do not let the sun go down on your wrath, and give no opportunity to the devil" (Eph. 4:26). If we do not deal with the anger, we allow the enemy access to create a greater problem.

When we learn to use anger, we choose to take responsibility for our own ideas and actions rather than blaming someone else for our unhappiness or unfortunate circumstances. Harriet Lerner says, "We begin to use our anger as a vehicle for change when we are able to share our reactions without holding the other person responsible for causing our feelings, and without blaming ourselves for the reactions that other people have in response to our choices and actions. We are responsible for our own behavior. But we are not responsible for other people's reactions."[4] Nor, however, can we control whether the other will approve or change their behavior as a result of our preferences. We can only change our own behavior.

Setting Boundaries. I worked with another woman who, like Irene, did not feel she could tell her mother no. Kristin's mother would come over unannounced, walk in the house without knocking, and stay for hours. Kristin would say, "Mom, I really have a lot to do today." But her mother would respond, "Well, dear, I know you always have a lot to do. But I never see you or the children much and it's so lonely at my place." Kristin's angry feelings did not leave when she tried to forgive her mother, or when she felt sorry for her. She had to learn a new approach.

Instead of feeling stuck in her anger, Kristin used her anger to speak to her mother her desires and to set appropriate boundaries around herself and her family. She learned that it was acceptable and appropriate to say, "Mother, you may not come over to my house without being invited. You may not come into my house without first knocking. You startle me and the children." She learned that her mother was capable of finding social groups and activities to fill her time. And, she did not have to, nor could she, meet all of her mother's emotional needs.

As she set boundaries, her mother increased the words of guilt and shame. This reaction on her mother's part was to be expected. Lerner says others want to shout at us, "Change back!" Her mother tried to pull her back into the old, familiar pattern. But Kristin held her ground kindly and firmly. In time, her mother began to lessen her attack. Kristin's anger lessened as she took back healthy control for her own home and time. She actually began to enjoy her mother when she could choose when she saw her. Susan Forward claims, "Emotional and mental peace comes as a result of releasing yourself from your parent's control."[5] Releasing the anger allows more freedom to honor our mothers and create a positive environment for discovering and appreciating her positive qualities. As we learn the tools to let go of bitterness and anger, we develop a firmer base for defining who we are. We discover we count.

Whenever we try something new, we are apprehensive and anxious. "Will I be rejected by my mother? How will she respond? Will I be embarrassed?" I encourage my clients, and remind myself, that the goal isn't how the other person will respond, but rather breaking the taboo that says I cannot be a person in my mother's presence. In letting go of bitterness and anger we learn

- to speak truth first to ourselves and when appropriate to our mothers.
- to use our anger instead of stuffing or dumping it.
- to set boundaries.
- to make choices.

As a result the positive can emerge when we are no longer practicing defensive moves.

Embracing the Positive

Where possible, it is vital to grow up by staying in relationship with our mothers. Many women have difficulty knowing how to talk with their mothers without conflict. Some of the following suggestions can help you do this in a non-threatening atmosphere. In so doing you will discover more about yourself as well.

- Look at family movies or pictures as a medium for talking about the past. You can ask your mother questions about her life and opinions about her choices as you look at the pictures.
- Ask her what it was like raising you, what you were like at various ages and stages.
- Ask about her relationship to her mother. How did she and her mother get along when she was young? How did she handle her own mother growing older? Did she have a good relationship with her? What were the challenges she faced with her mother?"
- Interview aunts, female cousins, female family friends who know your mother to broaden your view of how women function in your

respective family. How women went through childbirth, when they started menopause, and how the older women in a family coped with the changes in their bodies are all important pieces of information you can gather to understand your mothers and yourself.

- Doing things together to provide an arena for conversation or relationship: shopping, the movies, walks.
- Enlist her help where appropriate and as she is able.
- Ask her opinion on issues and dilemmas you face. Because we ask a person for an opinion does not mean we must do what she suggests.
- Practice giving her your opinion on issues without being defensive or angry.
- Actively seek out and identify the qualities in your mother that you value. Embrace the positive without denying the negative.

A woman might also wish to find joyful ways of giving her daughter a blessing of her presence, her assistance, her attention. What can you contribute to enriching and nourishing the relationship with your daughter? If you've been a distant mom you may try moving gently toward your daughter. If you've been a smother mother, you may need to find ways of giving your daughter space to discover her own voice.

The summer woman accepts her mother's weaknesses and forgives her failures, lets go of childhood expectations, and comes to terms with what's possible. She accepts that her mother is of another era and may never change nor have the vocabulary or education or skills to meet her on the same level. She discovers ways to love and honor her that makes the most of their relationship.

Father as Mirror

Of all the sources for approval and gaining a sense of well-being a father's voice is one of the loudest. Young women who perceive their fathers to be supportive and encouraging embrace their emerging womanhood and weather the rough ego-teen years with relatively few bumps and bruises. Whereas, daughters of fathers with critical voices and a critical eye, have little defense to run behind when the messages of their worth is callously attacked. A father's voice calls his daughter to be the best she can be. His voice of love allows her soul to rest. His balanced authority provides safety. Otherwise, she struggles to find from other men and in other places the approval she yearns for from her father.

Maria's comments reflect the power of Dad's words: "My father's words were a powerful influence on my opinion of myself. He would tell me to go on a diet and commented on every good looking girl on T.V. It embarrassed and shamed me. Although he and my mother were having troubles when I was in sixth grade, I thought his absence from the home and the lack of attention to me was because I was heavy."

To make up for the lack of a father's approval and support, some young adults find success in athletics or academics; others withdraw and never quite find a group or a comfort zone until well into adult life. Others seek male approval by becoming sexually promiscuous. In fact, the low self esteem of many women is due in part to an ongoing tape recording of their father's critical voice playing over and over in their minds. When Jesus was baptised by John the Baptist, His Father's voice reverberated clearly from heaven, "My beloved Son in whom I am well pleased." Likewise, a daughter yearns to hear the word of love and affirmation from her father, demonstrated in word and deed, "my beloved daughter, in whom I am well pleased."

We yearn for fathers to listen to us, to say we look pretty when we do, and to trust they are looking at us as daughters and not sexual objects. We need to have the continued affection even after we become women. We need to know that no matter what, our dads are there for us, willing to support, love, and hold the line for us. We trust that as we mature, they will change so we can have a more equal relationship. Many of the strategies I listed to engage our mothers would also apply in our relationship with fathers.

As we mature and fathers change, which most of them do, we must prepare to work on an adult relationship with them. Most of us yearn to hear our fathers say, "I love you," or "I'm proud of you." But as daughters we can also change the script by trying new ways of interacting with our fathers. Have we been able to tell them, "I love you," or "I'm proud of these things in you, Dad." We can engage them in areas of mutual interest and involve them where possible in our lives.

Jeannie's account gives a good illustrations of this: "I've always wanted direct interaction; my father interacted with humor and teasing. As I roared out the door the day of my wedding to get to the church to dress, my dad followed me to the car and leaned on the open window sill and chatted with me. "Dad," I said, "I've got to go! I'm going to be late." He chatted on about trivia regarding the day's events. I was impatient and getting angry. Finally, he let me go. Over time, instead of being frustrated with that memory, I saw more accurately my father's attempts at saying, 'Good-bye, I love you. This is an important day.' But he couldn't and I didn't get it."

The summer woman chooses to see her father through her father's eyes and to stand in his shoes. She chooses, where safe, to find a language they can both speak. You may say, "That's not fair! I've always had to be the mature one and protect him even though what he did to me and my siblings was wrong." If you have been abused by your father, the journey of reconciliation and relationship may not be possible, especially if he does not acknowledge his wrongdoing or change his behavior. After the grieving has past, you must decide what is safe and what you want in a relationship with your father. You may never receive what you legiti' and let go of what you can't. For most of us, once the bitterness passes, we find new ways to be an adult in our father's presence. We can gain incredible blessing in our relationship with him when we let go of expectation and how things "should be."

The Hidden Child of the Past as Mirror

The child we once were can also be a mirror for finding a positive sense of identity. Can you remember qualities about yourself as a young child that you value? One way to discover these qualities is to remember activities you loved to do whether anyone praised you or encouraged you in them or not.

You may forget many portions of your childhood and need a trigger to start the memories rolling. I would encourage you to begin your search by doing the following:

- Look at photographs and home movies.
- Ask questions of mom or dad or other family members who remember you at that age.
- Return to the neighborhood in which you grew up.
- Create a time line of family events and personal events. Perforated computer paper works the best because it unfolds and folds neatly. Across the top of the page write in the dates from birth until the year you left high school. Under each date list the personal events you remember or others have told you about yourself. Also include

the births of siblings, family deaths, who lived with your family, moves, major changes, hospitalizations, parental absences—any piece of family history that may help you remember your own story. Be patient. This task can be fun if you take it slowly.

History making has many benefits. First, you have a mini-personal history to share with your own children. Second, you can begin to see where trauma years may have occurred for you and why you remember that ten, let's say, was a tough year.

As you remember yourself as a young child, write near the memory or at the bottom of the page under the year, what personal qualities or traits you see in yourself. For example, one woman was struck by how resilient she was when she noticed she had moved ten times between first grade and sixth grade. She remembers making friends quickly and doing well in school. As she saw this part of herself, it gave her a sense of well being. She valued being resilient and competent. She also discovered why she has a difficult time sticking with one set of friends and why she gets bored easily in any one place. Because she wants a group of close friends, her challenge is to work on reversing the habit learned in childhood of picking up and moving on.

Finding Ourselves in the Mirrors

The voices of parents, family, friends, and even television become part of our own inner mental structure. How others have responded to us and mirrored us also become part of our perspective. Throughout this book you have been asked to examine the sources of trauma, your reactions to them, and to question what's true and what isn't about the messages you have been given. Although it is difficult to change the tapes, it is not impossible. If you have learned your worth by reflection, you also can unlearn the old and learn the new by choosing the mirror in which you look. You can choose friends that uplift and encourage. You can choose to believe through those who love you that you have value, and you can choose to teach your inner spirit to look honestly at the negative voice and decide whether it is true or not. You can find new mirrors.

As we choose the mirrors we gaze into, we are in essence choosing the image we want to become. We can find mentors who model for us the essence of womanhood we want to add to our character. We can submit ourselves to a small group of women where we can commit to growing and learning from each other . . . how to trust, how to let go of perform-ance, and how to respond authentically.

In order to fully enter into a summer season, we must harvest the produce sown in earlier seasons. We do that when we learn to accept and embrace our worth by discovering the accuracy of the mirrors that have reflected our value. We can discover the positive image of us as young girls and we can begin to listen to trustworthy new voices. Ultimately, we must learn to listen to the Father's voice and watch the way in which He shows us His favor.

Reflection

1. What is or was important to you in your relationship with your mother/father? What would you change in your relationship with her/him? (If you are also a mother, you might wish to put "daughter" in the above questions.)

2. Create a personal time line of family events as outlined in this chapter. Allow time to record your reactions and observations.

Part V

The Autumn Woman

Those who wait for the LORD
will gain new strength;
They will mount up with wings like eagles,
They will run and not get tired,
They will walk and not become weary.

Isaiah 40:31

Chapter Fourteen

As the Years Turn

❧

*I*n California the shift in the seasons from summer to fall is subtle. The farm on the corner continues to produce corn, peppers, and tomatoes, but slowly the rows of vegetables wither and die. Corn stalks are bundled, tied, and propped against the fence posts outlining the newly formed pumpkin patch. Workers scurry to harvest the remaining corn and produce before the rains and chill descend. Once the produce is in, dry corn stalk, bean, and tomato plants are rototilled into the dry, dusty soil.

Autumn! The season marked by children returning to school, football, the end of daylight savings time, Halloween, and Thanksgiving. The Master Artist paints the leaves and Indian corn with rich golds, oranges, rusts, magentas, and deep burgundies. The final harvest is brought in. What has been sown is reaped. The storehouses are filled in preparation for the season to follow. It is a time in nature of activity and preparation, of energy and purpose during the day. As the days shorten and the nights chill, nighttime is a time for regrouping and reflection.

The autumn woman is also vibrant. No matter what her age or her life experiences, she is committed to giving back to the broader community. She has faith that what she accomplishes has meaning. She also sees the purposes for the winters, summers and springs of her life and begins to see the meaning in former sufferings. She sees the beauty in the intricately woven dark and light hues of her life's tapestry. Like the wisdom of Hebrews 12, she has been through the refiner's fire, she has been trained by discipline, and she yields in autumn the "peaceful fruit of righteousness."

She has learned to find meaning in her life. In summer she learned to find her own voice. In autumn she learns to be renewed in silence. The autumn woman has learned to live in the moment and knows yesterday's "good" is to be cherished, but not clung to so she can enthusiastically embrace the good in today. While the summer woman has learned to accept her value and is free to be herself, the autumn woman acts on what she knows to be true with conviction and wisdom. Although there is some trepidation in asking some of the tough questions of life—why is there suffering? What possible contribution can I make that will make a difference?—she does not lose faith in her God emotionally or spiritually when doubts come. She understands she must ask in order to receive and must search in order to find.

As in the other seasons of her life, the woman in autumn has tasks to accomplish. For the vibrant, dynamic, over-committed super woman in our western culture, these tasks may be more difficult than facing sorrow in her winters, exploding in joy and dreaming in her springs, and finding a sense of personhood and balance in her summers. In these other seasons we are the focus of our own personal growth. In autumn, our basic concern is for others and for the world beyond our own personal well-being.

To be an autumn woman we

- understand the process of growth.
- learn power and peace through personal discipline.
- give out of our storehouse of harvested produce for the benefit of others.

The Process of Growth

I met a young woman at a seminar who asked: "Can I have a mid-life crisis when I'm only twenty-five? I've just broken up with my boyfriend of five years, I missed out on all the fun of dating and being independent during college, and all I want to do now is travel and play. The last thing in the world I want to do is settle down in a relationship or a career." This young woman was definitely having a crisis, but she was not a mid-life woman. What does her dilemma reveal about the complexity of adult development? In order to answer her question we need to review the traditional tasks and the natural expectations for the chronological seasons of a woman's life.

In the traditional way of viewing adult development, researchers postulated we went through predictable age related crises and tasks. Erik Erikson claimed adolescence was the age when we developed our identity. In the early adult years of our twenties and early thirties we learned what it meant to be intimate, or we fell into isolation. One showed the ability to be intimate by marrying and becoming part of a committed group structure. By the time we were in our thirties we had a family and were teaching our own children the values and structures of society. This stage was called generativity, the way in which one generation provided stability to the next. If we did not give to our own children or assist our culture train the next generation, we were stuck in a stage called stagnation in which we became "our own best child,"[1] self-absorbed to the exclusion of the needs of others around us. This was the challenge of the adult in his or her thirties to early forties. The last developmental phase for Erikson is a stage we addressed in chapter 7. After mid-life until death, we have the choice to have integrity, a state of being "wise," mature in judgment with accumulated knowledge used to benefit others, or we fall into despair characterized by discouragement, depression and bitterness.

Although these stages were developed based on research primarily done observing adult men, the qualities of being "adult" are worthy to note. In order to have a fullness of experience and have successful elder years, we must develop our sense of identity, learn to be intimate and connected to significant persons in our lives and be able to give back either to our own children or to the world we inhabit out of our storehouse of harvested wisdom and experience. Women, however, according to research, do not accomplish these tasks in a lockstep manner in predictable decades.

As you will see in the traditional tasks of the age many women can identify with the tasks, but they don't fit the age. In our day it is not news that women in their forties are having babies and retiring from careers to enjoy them which throws a curve ball on stage theory. However, there are challenges in our twenties that are unique to being twenty just as there are challenges in our fifties that are unique to being fifty. Because we have already elaborated the winter season of a woman in years, the following section will focus on the decades from the twenties through the fifties.

The Twenties Experience

What is a "normal" twenties experience? The woman in her twenties has more options than in earlier years. But unlike men, she seeks intimacy with others long before and simultaneously with making college, career and life goals. For many women her choices to succeed in an academic and career environment takes into consideration whether her decisions will enhance or isolate her from her relationships. How she dreams her first dream is impacted by these relationships and their expectations of her. On the one hand she is naive and tentative. On the other, she boldly embraces what's before her with energy and the fresh exuberance of new beginnings. She may not have depth of experience, but she makes up for it with enthusiasm. Her tasks are as follows:

- to form close relationships.
- to formulate her first dream and to take steps to implement it.

If we look at the women and their voices described in chapter 12 we see that women in their twenties make decisions regarding love relationships and their dreams based on their cultural training and home expectations. If she is a silent woman or a responding woman she will see her choices as limited by the expectations of her culture and what is safe. She may never challenge or question her position and status in life. More than likely she will "fall into" a job or marriage rather than seeing she has a choice.

The awakened woman in her twenties will defiantly forge ahead with her own plans whether they fit the cultural standards or not. She may suffer in a different way by making oppositional choices in her twenties since her trust level of others is very low. But her anger gives her energy to succeed and to push herself to outgrow the limitations she sees herself having from her background. She may be driven in academic achievement or in her pursuit of career. She may leave home and relocate in another state from her family of origin. Or she may adopt a lifestyle that is totally different from the one in which she was raised. But often this woman, if she hasn't made marriage choices before she awakened, delays marriage until after she develops a more solid sense of self-worth based on mastering skills in the workforce or in academics. She is also skeptical of commitment and intimacy.

The reasoning woman and the integrated woman see their worlds as less hostile in their twenties and more open to them. They have been encouraged to make choices and they have had mentors along the way to encourage them in choosing. One piece of research indicated that regardless of socio-economic and educational background, women who were raised in families where hostile conflict existed struggled with the self-confidence to seek jobs of status. However, women who were raised in families where conflict challenged them to think—to be heard, to put forth their opinions and ideas, but weren't attacked or put down for them—felt confident to choose jobs of high status.[2] But in most cases these women did not see a divergence between choosing a mate and pursuing a dream.

The birth control pill has also radically opened doors for married women to continue their education or work before deciding to have children, something which was not an option thirty years ago. In some respects it is easier for a woman today to gain a sense of ego identity as she relates to mastering skills and finding self worth on her own rather than seeing herself as a reflection of her husband's ability, or in her children's accomplishments. As she adds roles—wife, mother, friend, worker—she gains a broader sense of her personal worth.

The single woman in her twenties—and I would add in any of the successive discussion of the decades—faces her own unique challenges. She is faced with an ever increasing sexualized society. She must make clear decisions regarding how she chooses to be with a man. If she has a strong religious frame of reference and supportive friends of like mind, she will be able to make choices that are strong and enhance her worth. She will be severely tested to couple without the benefits of a committed marriage relationship if she does not seek out a wide variety of supportive, nurturing relationships—couples, her family, other single friends, both male and female. She is uniquely challenged to deal with the expression of her sexuality in a way that doesn't compromise her faith or wound her personal spirit.

She is also challenged by having to make her own choices as to where to live, what career goals she wishes to pursue and whether or not she wants to pursue marriage. Unlike her married friends, she has a broader arena in which she is forced to let go of dependencies and establish her own identity. Even though women who are married may struggle with loneliness, the loneliness and potential isolation of the single woman (and man) often dominates the horizon. "With whom can I share this tidbit of nonsense? Who in the world really cares about me and would care if I weren't here?" are some questions I've heard singles ask.

Some women miss this season of growth by continuing long past financial necessity to live in their parent's home in large part to avoid the issue of loneliness. As well, many young women are terrified of independence and of being responsible for their own well being, finances, and decisions. Others embrace this season of independence and growth, celebrating new adventures and new challenges before choosing to commit to a long term relationship.

Many women in their twenties are faced with economic conditions of a culture that forces them to seek paid employment even though they are raising children. The challenge for these women, unlike the challenges their mothers faced, is "how do I nurture and care for my children and survive financially?" Experts from money managers to theologians and psychologists encourage women to establish whatever home based business they can while their children are in their formative years. I heard recently a secular talk show psychologist on a southern California radio station say, "If you make a choice to have those babies, it's your responsibility to nurture and raise them not someone else's." This psychologist also is fond of saying, "There are really very simple answers to the problems of life. It's the suffering of implementing the decision we don't want to face."[3]

The task of the woman in her twenties is to make decisions regarding her own dream and implementing the first stages of it whether it is forming a career outside of the home before marriage and children, or choosing marriage and children. A third option is being a working mom with all of its challenges and tensions and successes. But for the woman in her twenties her challenge is to form her first dream and to form a close relationship.

The Thirties Transition

Traditional research indicates that in her thirties a woman is challenged to re-evaluate earlier choices.

- The main task of the thirties transition is to question. "What is life all about?" "Am I fulfilled in the dream I have chosen?" "What am I missing out on?" It is a time to resurrect the dream or alter it.

- The second task is to settle down by investing in the choices one has made and to make long-range goals and plans that fit the dream.

Regardless what choices the woman in her twenties made, in her thirties she begins to wonder "What do I want to do now?" The thirties woman begins to see patterns both of her successes and her failures. Whether based on external changes in her environment or the maturity that comes with living life, the woman in her thirties wants to make her life count. This may mean actively grieving her childhood wounds, and/or making wiser choices regarding friends, career, and life beliefs. She may become angry, as our awakened woman, and find ways to make changes in herself, her life style and her culture. In her mid to late thirties she recognizes that time is passing quickly and if she is going to make changes, she had better begin to plan and act.

If a woman has chosen marriage and children in her twenties, she may begin looking at a career option as her children become more independent. She may begin to ask, "What will I do when my children leave home?" The stay at home mom may become restless and impatient with the sameness of her routine and needs to be encouraged to find challenges that develop her ego identity in addition to her roles of mother and wife. The challenge question is, "How do I develop my God given skills and maintain competence in the roles I've chosen?" Mothers who work even part-time outside of the home report it is much easier to set boundaries around how much they do. Women who do not work outside of the home report, "I never know when enough is enough cleaning, helping, chores. I almost feel guilty sitting down. There are no boundaries of time around my work day." Mothers need as much as any other professional to build herself into her schedule and keep her appointment as respectfully as she would with a friend or her child. The more she respects herself and her time, so will her husband and family.

Women who have chosen not to marry or not to have children early in their marriages begin to face the dilemma of their biological time clocks. "Do I want to have children?" is a crucial question for many. "I feel guilty saying it, but I'm not sure I want children," one woman confided. "Am I selfish?" Other women in their thirties, who actively pursue having children, discover that becoming pregnant isn't as easy as planning a business meeting or making a sale. Their hurried lifestyles don't allow for time alone for rest and play with their husbands. So the decision to have children challenges other values.

The single woman sees the crush of time as she faces the question of marriage or remaining single. Many women (and men in this age group) may wish to be married, but do not have any prospects. One young woman expressed the struggle well: "I don't want to give up the dream of being married, but I can't live my whole life waiting for Mr. Wonderful to come along before I travel or decorate my apartment or enjoy life. I find I keep saying, 'I'll do that when I get married.' So I have deep heart to heart talks with myself. 'Self,' I say. 'You may never get married, so get going and make your own plan. Enjoy what you want to do!' " This young woman can't lose. Her heart may yearn for a partner, but she will at least have a full and rich life while she waits. In each situation, the woman in her thirties is challenged to re-evaluate her former choices and decide what she wants to do with her life.

The second task for the woman in her thirties is to settle down and enjoy the decisions she has made. The rest of this decade is spent developing plans and strategies for fulfilling her re-evaluated dream. Activities for her children, career goals and plans, moves to bigger homes, buying her first home or condo, activities we might put under the heading "doing life" occur in these years.

The woman who does not meet the challenge of finding her own voice during these years, may become depressed and resentful of the structures she blames for holding her back . . . her children, her husband, her parents, her boss, society, her own dependencies and inabilities. At each juncture we have choices that we alone can make in changing the structures of our lives. Risking the disapproval of and facing the fear of withdrawal of love and support of husbands, friends or family, keep many women from moving into new realms.

The fear of loss, not necessarily the reality of loss, keeps women from risking. Or, when she does risk, she risks by being angry with the very people she yearns to support her. And then she may say, "See no one cares about me," when they respond not to her choices, but to her anger. We need to continually reassure ourselves that change is inevitable and, as change happens, relationship structures may shudder and shake. If they are solid, they will survive our changing. If they are not solid, it may take more work to hold them together. The choice is to stay stuck and miserable, or risk the discomfort of change with the hope of a new fulfillment on the other side.

Peter Koestenbaum speaks of a woman's ability to exercise her free will in choice making in this way:

The fact of her free will shows that the solution to the problem of feminine roles is exclusively the individual's responsibility. To blame others for the problem is to run counter to the facts of human experience, it is to run away from the problem . . . A woman freely chooses whether to solve her problem or whether to ignore it, and if she chooses to solve it, she also freely chooses the methods. [4]

After the choice is made to change and grow, the rest of a woman's thirties can be a time of fulfillment and settling in.

Facing the Forties—The Mid-life Dilemma

The mid-life passage which traditional research tells us occurs in ones forties is characterized by stress, conflict, depression, a clash of values and emotions and turmoil.

- The main task that occurs in the forties is facing and resolving the mid-life dilemma.
- The mid-life woman comes to terms with her aging body and a re-evaluation of her sexuality.

Facing and Resolving the Mid-life Dilemma

Mid-life men may depart radically from their old habits of work and family. They may change their careers and/or divorce their wives in favor of a younger woman, citing boredom and disenchantment. Or, moving in the opposite direction, they may give up high paying jobs to dedicate their time to family and benevolent causes. Often health concerns such as a heart attack or a poor cholesterol report, propel a man to self-evaluation and to changes in his life structure.

Women too were reported to go through a major upheaval in mid-life—the forties decade. Whether because of cultural shifts, the change in their husband's life or an internal ticking of her biological clock, the mid-life woman begins to recognize her life is passing quickly by.

When the forties woman awakens to all the things she hasn't been or done, she faces a panic, like a massive earthquake that rumbles deep within and shakes and shatters her well-established, well-ordered world. The woman who awakens recognizes she has choices and that she can choose to make changes. Some women do it with wisdom; others act impulsively and move too quickly to find solutions to her confusion in this time of re-evaluation. Mary was what we might call a "runaway wife." Her panic about the short time she had to "live life" and her feelings of being cheated by life propelled her to make a rash move. She moved out of the family home and into an apartment leaving her husband and teenage children stunned. "The boys didn't need me as much any more. I believed if I stayed, I couldn't change. It was either leave or shrivel up." However, a couple years later, Mary wanted to return home, but there was no one to return to. With regret she reports, "I grew up fast when my husband didn't want me back. Somehow I thought I could go off and do my thing and he would welcome me when I returned. I wrongly blamed him for being my jailer. But when I came to my senses, it was too late." The dilemma is a real one and has no easy answers. Can an individual change while living in structures that appear by their very nature to force the status quo?

On the other hand, another woman who passes through a mid-life evaluation may begin to move out of self absorption which includes a focus on her own family, her own success, her own problems, into a broader mission of concern for the needs of others and her community at large. The more a woman has discovered her own voice in other seasons and decades, the more able she is to find her way through the challenges of this decade without excessive destruction to her existing relationships. We would characterize her as an autumn woman.

Growing older refers to aging, but *being* old is an attitude. Similarly, being in our middle years is an age issue. It merely means we are somewhere between thirty-five and forty-five. One woman, facing her fortieth birthday, humorously commented, "Middle age is ten years older than I am no matter how old I become." Whereas, when we face a mid-life evaluation or crisis we are talking about a stage of adult development which may affect us at a number of different ages in our lives.

The concept of "mid-life crisis" presumed a woman married in her early twenties and had children by her late twenties. She and/or her husband would stabilize their careers in their thirties. If she was a stay-at-home mom, she would evaluate in her thirties how to find meaning for her life once her children enter school. The Forties crisis occurred when both men and women saw life passing them by, woke up to the pain that wouldn't go away from past wounding and desired to make changes to allow for a richer last half of their lives. A woman in her fifties would be faced with an empty nest and would be lost because her main task and role in life was over and would grieve the loss of her child bearing ability in menopause. By sixty-five she faced the predictable crisis retirement brings to her husband and to herself when the external structure changes.

The mid-life crisis model of adult development ignores the life cycle of the unmarried woman and her challenges and ignores the reality that women go through times of transition and change throughout every decade of their lives. Today the woman who delays maternity into her thirties or forties won't have time for a forties crisis as she chases toddlers and plunges into the tasks of carpool and school lunches. In her sixties she will face the crisis of the empty nest and must decide then what will fill her life and bring it meaning in her last chronological decades. The woman who chooses not to marry nor has children, will face another set of crises at different points in her life as she makes those decisions. Social psychologist Carol Tavris says this about our adult growth pattern:

> The transitions approach reminds us that adult concerns aren't settled, once and for all at some critical stage or age. It would be nice if we could acquire a sense of competence in grammar school and keep it forever, if we had only one identity crisis per lifetime, if we always belonged. But adult development is more complicated than that, and also more interesting.[5]

Life evaluations come when the unexpected occurs. We face crises when too many accumulated losses or changes happen in our significant relationships, in our financial stability, and in our ability to control our lives in meaningful work, in health and in our mobility. The more involved in loving and giving , the more the surge of transitions crest and crash over us. The losses attached to relationships are closely connected to a loss of self for women in any decade. And it is these losses, especially when unexpected and unplanned that create a crisis for women.

The transition approach removes guilt and unnecessary confusion. If a woman faces many losses and major changes in her twenties, does that mean something's wrong with her? Hardly! One author postulates, "Eventually, research will show that a mid-twenties mid-life crisis is a lot like chicken pox. If you get it when you're young, you could be immune for the rest of your life."[6] Maybe I should, add, if a woman in her twenties learns how to go through transitions and gains a sense of ego strength because of the challenges, she will be better equipped to handle successive unexpected crises and loss as she matures in years.

Looking at Her Body and Her Sexuality

Even if a woman has found her sense of identity in other seasons, she must face some specific realities in her forties and fifties. One of these realities is of her aging body. The woman in her forties confronts her greying hair, the difficulty of shedding those extra five pounds, or the changes that begin to occur in her menstrual cycle. What she used to accomplish swiftly and easily in her twenties and thirties, in her forties she accomplishes more slowly. One birthday card I found read on the outside, "Hating the way your looks are changing?" On the inside, it said, "Stop looking in the mirror." Wouldn't that be a wonderful way of coping with the changes! One writer, quoting Maggie Scarf, states the dilemma this way:

> The loss of youthful looks is seen by the woman as like the loss of an important relationship. The woman is filled with a sense of emptiness and grief, as though abandoned by her beloved. It may be, however, that what she is pining for, during this complex phase of living, is none other than the youthful, sexually appealing person that she used to be.[7]

The woman whose identity has been based on her looks in previous years will struggle more in this decade than those who have sought self definition in other ways such as her skills and personal relationships.

Another area of challenge may be her sexuality. As the married woman becomes less afraid of pregnancy, as she decides to have no more children, as her children mature, and she balances her life, she may discover she has more desire for intimacy and sexuality. But she may be faced with unsatisfactory habits that may need changing. She may have to give up her sexual fantasies of some perfect man whisking her away on his white horse. Another woman may have to overcome what she feels is her lack of sexual attractiveness as she compares herself to the women in the movies. She is vulnerable to her spouse's opinion, reassured if he continues to seek her out, but feel devalued and rejected if he is critical of her. She and her spouse may have formed poor sexual habits such as delaying sexual times to late at night, or avoiding sex altogether because of busy schedules. Or, she may be silent about what she likes and doesn't like about their sexual behavior.

As she evaluates her sexuality, she may need to make some personal discoveries. There are a number of things she can do. She can

- journal her feelings about her own sexuality and her relationship with her spouse. She might ask herself, "What do I enjoy about our sexual times? What feels good? What doesn't? What do I really want? Do I have the courage to change my part of the dance?" One woman was honest when she said, "I think what I really want is to start all over again . . . new body, new man, new location, new life!" Instead of courageously working through this passage, some women, like Mary, rush to change things and to escape. The challenge of the woman of forty (or thirty, fifty, or sixty) is to breathe life into her own body and spirit while rekindling the smoldering embers of her current relationship.

- broaden her knowledge about her own body and the myths and truths about sexuality. I recommend the Penners' book, *The Gift of Sex*. It covers a wide range of topics and gives very concrete practical information.

- talk with trusted friends about what she is experiencing. Often women suffer guilt and shame for thinking or feeling what they do. They assume they are the only ones with such feelings. Seeking information about our own struggles and questions need not betray our spouse if we are respectful and focus on our own needs.

- learn to express her concerns and desires to her husband and work with him to discover a richer sexual experience. Some couples need to learn to date each other again where they spend time talking and sharing experiences before a woman feels safe or the atmosphere is conducive to discuss changes sexually. Many women complain that they feel more like a service station than a cherished person. If the marriage is also a mid-life marriage, it also may need re-evaluation and remodeling.

Decades of research confirm what women know intuitively. If the relationship is floundering and there is tension between the two, the sexual experience is either non-existent or very inadequate. A woman, for the most part desires affection and emotional closeness in order to enjoy her sexuality. And a man, for the most part needs the sexuality to resolve differences and to draw close.[8] In other words, the mid-life couple are also challenged to discover a resolution to what appears to be a "Catch 22" dilemma.

One of the primary killers of intimacy is not enough quality time spent together. Quality time is time not spent discussing problems or arguing.

It is time spent doing enjoyable things and sharing on a variety of topics. To overcome the habit of not enough time together, I encourage couples

- to put each other on their respective calendars and to respect that date as much as they would a meeting with the president of their company or an evening with friends.
- to spend time alone daily for a debrief of their respective activities. Fifteen minutes may do it. Many women do not feel they are a priority to their spouses. If the couple has scheduled mid-week appointment times, the woman is reassured that she is important and she can relax knowing she will have him all to herself. If daily is difficult, they can set aside a lunch or an evening walk. Relationships too need tending, as do all living things.
- to date each other. Instead of relying on either one or the other to make the plans, I ask the husband to take one weekend and the wife the alternate. Each plans a weekend, or a day, or one evening depending on what they mutually decide is possible, as if she/he were the other person. "What would be fun for my spouse?" Loving the other on the other person's love channel improves good will and clears the way for improved sexuality.

The forties transition traditionally has been heralded as a storm and stress decade of re-evaluation and major changes before the winter winds blow, when our options and possibilities for change decrease. We dust off forgotten dreams and hidden talents and re-evaluate the choices we've made and plan for the future. We must face as well during this decade the reality of our aging bodies and confront a re-emergence of our sexuality. However, as women we are not locked into one mid-life time of evaluation and crisis. But rather our times of re-evaluation and dreaming are dependent on unexpected events and turmoils internal and external we face throughout our seasons. Any set of losses and changes can plunge us into a time of crisis, a winter season. Resolving the winter tasks, like a surfer catching a wave, carries us into a spring of new beginnings.

The Nifty Fifties

The primary task of the woman in her fifties is to complete the meaning she gives to the changes in her body. Sometime in our late forties or early fifties we awaken in the middle of the night on fire and drenching wet. Or the sudden deluge occurs in the middle of a business meeting. Menopause is coming and we know that there are myths and truths that we must learn in order to keep this passage in perspective.

We enter this phase of life with family stories and the input from the culture at large. In Western cultures the average age at which a woman stops ovulating is 50.8 years. Because today many women go into hormonal therapy, menopause is delayed, deferred, and in many respects rendered impotent. We are beset with stories from our grandmother's era of women facing intense depression and women "going crazy" when they go through menopause. According to Gail Sheehey who wrote *The Silent Passage*, the severity of symptoms a woman experiences is in part based on the value given to older women in the culture:

> Where status or role was improved, the signs of menopause were not perceived as negative. Indian women of the royal Rajput caste do not complain of depression or psychological symptoms at menopause, since they are freed from veiled invisibility and are at last able to sit and joke with the men . . . In China, where age is venerated, menopausal symptoms are also rarely reported.[9]

She claims that one reason depression is more common in America is because we are not a culture, for the most part, that respects women of age, but rather we venerate youth and beauty and have a "phobia about aging." Therefore we do not have so much an issue of biology as we do of meaning.

For some women going through menopause will plunge them into a winter season if they have not grown through previous winters. Those who view aging and the latter half of their lives as an open door for meaning and productivity will weather this transition well.

The woman who has many roles—parent, volunteer, career woman— has developed a strong sense of personal identity. In these roles she develops a sense of meaning and worth. For her the menopausal symptoms aren't so much an issue of an end, but the beginning of a new stage of her life cycle.

There are other challenges to the fifty and sixty decades besides coming to terms with how we will face menopause. Women on the average live into their late seventies and eighties. The fifties woman has the potential of living for thirty years-vibrantly or in despair. How will we then live? Some women find simplifying their lives in their fifties and sixties gives them opportunity to do things they never took time for in earlier years. For others, they pour themselves into new projects that give back to the community in which they live after asking themselves, "Where can I contribute?" and "What's needed?" Women who have not worked until their children are out of the nest, may return to a career and are in full swing in their fifties and sixties just as their husbands are winding down and returning to the nest. This phenomenon in turn poses new challenges for a marriage in the retirement years.

For the most part, when a woman chooses to grow and change, she gives herself a gift of life and vibrancy in her autumn years. She has developed a maturity that age and experience provides. If she has prepared well, fifty can be nifty, rich, peaceful, and full of meaning.

The Age Seasons

The age seasons of a woman's life do have specific and unique qualities to them that define her as a spring, summer, autumn, or winter woman of years. However, we must remember that many qualities of crises and transition, of growth and change occur not in lock step stages and phases, but rather in unexpected upheavals and crashing blows. It is not so much if we will have a mid-life crisis in our twenties, thirties or forties, but rather when we are faced with the struggles life presents, how will we go through them. And, regardless of the age season we are in, it is the meanings we give to the events in our lives, the stability of our relationships and the degree of control we have over our finances, health, mobility and meaningful work that determines our stability and our ability to cope with the changes and challenges in our lives.

Reflection

1. Take a moment to reflect on the decade you are currently in. Then record the words that best describe you at this time.

2. Have you faced a "mid-life" transition? Can you "draw" a word picture (a metaphor) that best describes your experience?

Chapter Fifteen

Be Still and Know

❧

*T*he Monterey Bay Peninsula is noted for its beauty. Slightly inland from the tip of the peninsula is a massive grove of trees that is the late-winter home of the Monarch butterfly. On the tall Monterey pines they mass together, hanging in cascading clumps in a profusion of orange and black.

The autumn woman resembles the butterfly. She knows that time spent deep in a place of quiet and solitude yields beauty and strength for her tasks. In autumn she is energized and focused to give back to her community, to her family, to life in a way she has not envisioned before. But in order to do that she must learn the message of the cocoon: In silence and solitude we develop the strength to fly.

Like the caterpillar, we view life first in simple dimensions. We are earthbound, rooting around in the common places, growing strong, learning, digesting, doing life. One day there is an urgency to begin spinning new dreams. Anxiety replaces calm and slowly, like the caterpillar spinning its cocoon, we withdraw to a protected place that shields our growth from external forces and attacks. The caterpillar attaches itself solidly to a tree branch so that while it goes through its metamorphosis, it will not be destroyed. We in turn must also withdraw to respond to the inner call to understand the meaning of our own existence. In due season the creature within the cocoon beats its wings swiftly, breaking down the now useless protective covering. Soon a magnificent creature flies free

Like the caterpillar the autumn woman has been changing and growing in a secret place deep within her spirit. Unlike the transformation from caterpillar to butterfly which occurs only once, we need to return to the cocoon repeatedly. We must learn the discipline of solitude and silence in order to have the wisdom, strength, and creativity to be authentic givers in our culture, in order to fly free to become all that our Creator intended us to be.

As a summer women we learned to discover our unique voices. Having a voice is akin to having a self. And when we have a clear sense of self, we are more able to be at peace internally, to balance our lives, and to seek ways to give out of ourselves to others.

The autumn woman can discern more fully where her skills and abilities benefit the broader community. She learns to go outside her comfort zone. As she navigates her seasons, she learns to develop her relationship with her Creator and seeks in autumn a partnership with him in all that she does. The more able she is to speak, the more appreciative she is of silence and solitude. This apparent paradox leads us into the second task of the autumn woman. The autumn woman renews her personal spirit in solitude.

As I drive up and over the coastal range to the ocean, I am always surprised at the change in pressure I experience. As I approach the summit, I pass beyond the magnetic grip of the hectic-paced, noise-filled valley below. My breathing slows, my shoulders relax and my racing, obsessive thoughts explode in shattered bits as a burst of fireworks. The fragments of thought and tension glow for a moment and then are gone. The clatter of sound pollution is almost as clearly visible as the air pollution.

Our world bangs and clangs in a cacophony of electronic and me-chanical sound. Our ears are bombarded by talk shows, music, and commercials. We can know more about the intimate details of strangers than we take the energy or time to know about our neighbors and friends. We retreat into the impersonal world of television and music to retreat and relax. The new information highway promises us three hundred stations of words at the press of a button.

One of the most difficult tasks in our hurried Western culture is to indulge in solitude. We may profess to desire to know God and to seek the fulfillment of a life integrated with the Divine. For most of us, however, it is a discipline we have not cultivated, nor is it valued in the culture at large. Is it possible that the lack of finding a place of solitude in our lives has made us more stressed as a culture, more violent, more at odds with ourselves, even within religious communities where one would expect a measure of intimacy and freedom from strife? Anne Morrow Lindbergh speaks of the importance of alone times when she says:

> Actually these are among the most important times in one's life—when one is alone. Certain springs are tapped only when we are alone. The artist knows he must be alone to create; the writer, to work out his thought; the musician, to compose; the saint, to pray. But women need solitude in order to find again the true essence of themselves: that firm stand which will be the indispensable center of a whole web of human relationships. She must find that inner stillness which Charles Morgan describes as "the stilling of the soul within the activities of the mind and body so that it might be still as the axis of a revolving wheel is still."[1]

The challenge for our autumn woman is to be the still axis in the middle of the revolving wheel. How do we do that? How do we find that place of solitude out of which our activity is empowered? We find that place of solitude by

- learning the lessons of the cocoon.
- learning the discipline of silence.
- actively listening.

The Lesson of the Cocoon

Nature provides us a beautiful lesson about transformation. The caterpillar becomes a vibrant multi-hued butterfly. Coal under intense pressure becomes a diamond. Household garbage and garden refuse, when exposed to heat, become nutrient-rich fertilizer. Likewise, when we sit quietly before the transforming presence of the Godhead, we are changed from one sort of creation to another. We are not just forgiven human beings, but we are changed from earth-bound creatures, to creatures that see the unseen and know what's unspoken as we tune our ears to listen deeply to the voice of God.

Throughout biblical history, the saints modeled the importance of a life that grew strong and vibrant through times in the wilderness, apart from the hectic pace of their culture. In the wilderness, the distractions of life are minimized and the soul renews. Elijah and John the Baptist were wilderness dwellers and powerful prophets. David learned the incredible intertwining of the natural with the personal presence of God while tending sheep on the Judean hillside.

Jesus often left the crowds and went to a mountain or into an uninhabited place to commune with His Father. After His baptism, He went into the wilderness for forty days to be tempted by the enemy and ministered to by angels. When He returned to the world of men, He could say, "I and my Father are one. If you have seen Me you have seen the Father." In solitude and silence, He nurtured a relationship with His Father and listened to know what He was to say and do to give to the people who followed Him.

In solitude we learn to listen to the voice of our Father, and in solitude, we are transformed into a new creation. This transformation is difficult to possess when what we ingest from our world is stress, struggle, sorrow and conflict—whether our own or vicariously ingested through the media. Henri Nouwen claims the spiritual life, the life of the inner person which strengthens and enriches us, is polluted by the compulsions of striving for more work, more money, more friends in the hope of being accepted and seen positively by our own world. He says,

> These very compulsions are at the basis of the two main enemies of the spiritual life: anger and greed. They are the inner side of a secular life, the sour fruits of our worldly dependencies. What else is anger than the impulsive response to the experience of being deprived? When my sense of self depends on what others say of me, anger is a quite natural reaction to a critical word. And when my sense of self depends on what I can acquire, greed flares up when my desires are frustrated. Thus greed and anger are the brother and sister of a false self fabricated by the social compulsions of an unredeemed world.[2]

However, we cannot isolate ourselves from the vicissitudes of life, but rather we are challenged in autumn to renew in solitude in order to live a life that is directed from the inside rather than from the outside. The goal is to reenter the world with a renewed sensitivity. The accomplishment of such a task takes personal discipline.

Strength in Discipline

When I speak of discipline in autumn, I am not speaking of it as a punishment for having done something wrong for which we are being corrected. Rather I use the term "discipline" in the sense of acquiring a skill, a focused attention on, a letting go of randomness in order to focus on something that strengthens. Paul the apostle says, "For the moment all discipline seems painful rather than pleasant; later it yields the peaceful fruit of righteousness to those who have been trained by it" (Heb. 12:11). No matter what season we are in, discipline is painful and most of us fight against the restrictions and sometimes physical pain of implementing a new discipline. In time the new becomes second nature, a part of us. And, if we've been trained by it, we will harvest the peaceful fruit of knowing we are living in a way that promotes life, not death.

A model for the autumn woman who understands discipline is Esther, a spring woman in years, who was the Jewish queen to King Ahasuerus during the Babylonian captivity of the Jewish nation. She is a picture of a woman with ego strength who, through discipline, learns to actively wait in order to act in wisdom.

The context for the story of Esther is important to understand her courage and faith. Esther's parents died when she was young and she was raised by her uncle, Mordecai, who treated her as his own. Throughout the course of the Diaspora, the dispersion of the Jews under King Nebuchadnezzar, the Jewish people became part of the cultures to which they were scattered. Esther and Mordecai were part of the community that had been brought seventy years before to Babylon.

During the early years of King Ahasuerus's reign, the king became displeased with Queen Vashti when she refused to be ogled and paraded around as one of the King's possessions during a drunken festival. In his anger, King Ahasuerus removed her from her position and ordered the most beautiful young virgins to be brought to his harem so he could select a new queen. For a year they were trained and prepared with special foods and ointments to make them even more beautiful. Esther was selected as one of these virgins. At the end of the year of preparation, Esther was chosen to be queen instead of Vashti.

In the course of time, the King's number one advisor, Haman, became enraged that Mordecai would not bow down to him as he passed by. In his rage, he wanted him destroyed. In order to do that he convinced the king the Jews were his enemy. He has the king sign an edict that on a certain day, in all of the king's provinces, the local people were to kill all of the Jewish people who resided there and take their possessions. Mordecai discovered the plot and ordered Esther to act on behalf of her people. He speaks to all autumn women when he says: "For if you keep silence at such a time as this, relief and deliverance will rise for the Jews from another quarter but you and your father's house will perish. *And*

who knows whether you have not come to the kingdom for such a time as this?"
(Esth.4:14, emphasis added)

Esther, as an autumn woman, knows how to actively wait by withdrawing into quiet and discipline. She appropriates a discipline common in Judeo-Christian tradition; that of fasting along with her solitude. She tells Mordecai to call the Jewish people of Susa, the capital, to fast (and, we assume to pray) while she and her maids did the same. For three days they were to neither drink nor eat, but to concentrate on the cry for deliverance.

Given the incredible power we give food, I find it interesting that the discipline of fasting challenges us in an area where our culture is often the most undisciplined. One of the great obsessions of Western culture is eating. Whether for the pure sensuous pleasure of the task or as a replacement for the emotional nurture we do not receive, overeating or starving are struggles many women and men face. Fasting challenges us to be disciplined in a second area, that of our eating and drinking.[3] Thomas Merton claims freedom comes when we are disciplined in the area of our appetites: "No person is free if he is a slave to his/her appetites. Compulsions reduce us to the shadow of a genuine person."[4] Above all else, the autumn woman seeks to be a genuine person.

Traditionally, in addition to a discipline to seek God and His favor, the fast was implemented to elicit God's support, to change His mind concerning judgment, to understand what is confusing in one's personal circumstances, and to gain wisdom for making decisions. The fast also is used to petition God regarding resolutions for the problems of society and for ways to overcome our own weaknesses. The fast is also adopted to seek forgiveness on behalf of a group or for a nation's behavior. Finally, and probably one of the most important for our discussion, fasting is to honor and glorify God. It is designed to draw us into knowing God more fully, to learn His ways rather than only petitioning to gain our own way. Esther seeks wisdom through active waiting while she fasts and withdraws into solitude. After three days, she comes up with a plan which demonstrates qualities of the third task of the autumn woman, which is giving for the common good. We will wait to explore the last of her story in the next chapter.

Renewal in the Discipline of Solitude

The gift of solitude is one most of us women do not give to ourselves. For one reason or another we have a bundle of very rationale reasons for not withdrawing and finding time to renew our personal spirits. Some of you may say, "Oh, my husband wouldn't approve." Others would say, "The demands of my job (children, tasks, obligations) prevent me from carving out time for myself. 'It's such a selfish thing to do,' another would add. Personally I would say, "I would feel too guilty and not enjoy or be nurtured by the time. I'd be too worried about what I had left to do."

The above says to me, "I don't really believe pulling away will benefit me in the long run." In the short term creating a new discipline takes energy even if it benefits us in the long term. Earlier I have mentioned a few ways we can find time to renew our personal spirits. We can find ways to make our heart sing: We can focus on beautiful art, take a walk, exercise, carve out a few moments a day to read a book and focus our eyes on what is pleasurable. Whatever draws us into a place of personal rest, slows our breathing, and gives us joy are ways to begin to understand the journey into silence. Another way a woman can renew her personal spirit is through expending time in the creative arts. A woman in a former generation was able to combine her domestic (work) responsibilities with creative endeavors which renewed her personal spirit.

But at the deepest level, the entering into solitude and silence is a discipline of the spirit. It is the drawing away of ourselves into a place for reading God's Word and communing with Him. The Quaker term is called *centering down;* the early church fathers called it *entering into the wilderness.* Another word for the process of entering into solitude is *contemplation.* Lucy Shaw in her book on journaling describes this succinctly:

> "The Latin word *templari,* from which 'contemplation' is derived, means 'space'; it's also the root of the word *temple,* which we could describe as 'a space prepared for the presence of God.' Contemplation could be paraphrased as *spending time in inner space.* And if you are a Christian, your inner space is already inhabited by God's Holy Spirit, so that your contemplation really does take place in His presence and with His help."[5]

When we renew through contemplation, we fulfill the meditations of the Psalmist when he said, "But I have calmed and quieted my soul, like a child quieted at its mother's breast; like a child that is quieted is my soul" (Ps.131:2, RSV).

It is in essence prayer which "consists of humble waiting—in childlike openness and expectation and listening. To pray means to make ourselves present and available to God so that we are truly ready to open the door when Jesus comes and knocks."[6] Therefore, practicing the discipline of contemplation centers us in the presence of God where we can learn to calm our spirit in order to fill the longing our hearts have for Him.

It is hard to imagine a place without sentences and paragraphs of thought and without an outer focus. During our waking hours, we may not speak out loud constantly, but we chatter on in our heads about the tasks before us, our upsets, and upheavals. Our minds are rarely at rest. In contemplation we learn to put thought and sound outside the room in order to sit quietly and be renewed in silence. That is the nature of contemplation.

The Benefits of Contemplation

Within all of human creation there is a yearning to be loved, to be cherished, to be known, to be the beloved. Entering into a form of prayer that disciplines the mind in silence and allows the heart to respond to God's heart is one of the benefits of contemplative prayer. The metaphorical heart (as opposed to our biological heart) is the place of our personal spirit, the center of our will: "The prayer of the heart is a prayer that directs itself to God from the center of the person and thus affects the whole of our humanness."[7]

Contemplative prayer changes us. We cannot sit in God's presence, experience His love and not be changed. While we sit quietly we may struggle with sleepiness and mental distractions and we might say, "This is a waste of time; I'm not getting anything out of it." But afterwards, we discover we are more patient with our family, less hostile to the guy who cuts us off on the freeway, more aware that our heart is quieter in the midst of life's stressors. We experience His peace, we are more able to cope and we become more honest with ourselves.

Learning the Discipline of Silence

Although we may all have a variety of ways of entering into God's presence and seeking to make contact, some helpful suggestions from those who have practiced contemplative prayer might be of assistance in implementing this attentive, listening prayer. They are as follows:

- Create a place of silence.

- Let go of inner turmoil.
- Invite God's Presence.
- Release rocks in the heart: forgiveness and repentance.
- Awaken to God.
- Receive His blessing.

Creating a Place of Silence

When we fall in love, we create a time and a place to meet the one we are interested in. No matter what else is on our schedule, no matter how tired we are, we are always able to carve out time for the new love. Over time we take the other for granted and the vibrancy of new love dims, and with the dimming we return to our self focus and busyness that excludes love.

As we search for the deeper filling of the well within us, we must carve out both time and a space for entering into solitude, for kindling the love with the perfect Love of the universe. Finding a place of solitude is vital. Scripture says, "But when you pray, go into your inner room, and when you have shut your door, pray to your Father who is in secret, and your Father who sees in secret will pay you" (Matt. 6:6). When we choose to, we can all discover solitude. John Wesley's mother had twelve children in an age when modern conveniences did not ease a woman's domestic burdens. When she needed distance from the clamor or needed to commune in silence, she would stand quietly and throw her apron over her head. At that signal her children quieted down and left their mother alone. Noted author on the value of the contemplative life, Thomas Merton, says this about space:

> There should be at least a room, or some corner where no one will find you and disturb you or notice you. You should be able to untether yourself from the world and set yourself free, loosing all the fine strings and strands of tension that bind you, by sight, by sound, by thought, to the presence of other men. . . .once you have found such a place, be content with it, and do not be disturbed if a good reason takes you out of it. Love it, and return to it as soon as you can, and do not be too quick to change it for another.[8]

What are some possible "rooms"? You can find a time of day when others are not around and consistent with your biological time clock. You can retreat into whatever room or portion of room appeals to you. You can establish one corner of a room where you look out on beauty or where you create a peaceful place to which you are drawn for prayer.

Until you become convinced of the power of this discipline, you may need to ease into the idea of stillness. You may choose a long commute or change a habit. Instead of watching television while ironing or folding clothes, you can practice calming your spirit before the Lord. Or you can substitute hand washing the dishes instead of using the dishwasher, or hanging up clothes for the dryer. Both pursuits, when done in silence, can lead our minds and hearts into quiet channels.

Letting Go of Inner Turmoil

Once you have selected a room into which you retreat, sit in a comfortable place where your breathing can be unobstructed. I have a difficult time spending time in "inner space" with the world tromping through my mind. Whether I journal my thoughts out loud to the Lord or I dump the load I'm carrying into my journal, I find it essential to unload the baggage in order to prepare my heart for silence. Once I've put these concerns on paper, I can always return to them. I have to give myself permission to stop thinking about what lies beyond the door of my inner room for a short time.

When we sit quietly before the Lord, we learn to be focused on only a few words. Silence teaches us to focus our thoughts and our feelings. The silence of listening, centered prayer is "not the human silence of embarrassment, shame, guilt, but the divine silence in which love rests secure."[9]

When we practice the discipline of contemplation, we sit quietly in an anticipatory frame of mind. When we spoke of managing our stress, we discovered the intimate functioning between mind, emotion and body. One technique used in reducing stress is also implemented in contemplative silence. As we slow our thoughts down, we begin to breathe more deeply. As we breathe more deeply, our adrenalin reduces sending messages to our muscles that the crisis is past. As a result there is more blood and oxygen available for higher level functioning.

How we breathe also impacts our ability to be still and quiet. Physiologists teach us to breathe from our diaphragm, from our stomach area rather than from our chests. If we breathe rapidly and shallowly, we are putting more carbon dioxide into our system and reduce the amount of oxygen available for the body's healthy functioning. High levels of carbon dioxide are necessary to put the fight or flight mechanism to work. But to renew our bodies and minds, and to be able to sit quietly, we need to reduce the adrenalin flow that accompanies the carbon increase. As we breathe more deeply, our system functions more efficiently. More oxygen flows in and to our brains and less to our muscles.

Inviting God's Presence

If our purpose is to know God, then we need to find our voice with the Father. Remember, in this form of communion with God, we need not speak an abundance of words. Unlike Eastern meditation which divests the mind of thought, contemplative prayer focuses the mind on the presence of the Father and seeks to know Him. We invoke the Lord's presence in several ways.

First, we sit quietly and relax the muscles in our body. We may want to wiggle our toes and fingers, circle our ankles and wrists and tense and release the muscles in our shoulders and neck. A slow circling of our neck to release the tension is helpful.

Second, we focus on our breathing in order to slow it down. We may want to breathe in all that we might envision God to be and breathe out all of the tension, the stress, the evil, the pain that we hold inside of us. We don't have to analyze it, meditate with our minds on it, figure it out, we just release it.

Third, the contemplatives remind us that focused prayer draws our minds and hearts to the one we choose to worship. We may want a few words said mentally with our focused breathing such as saying "be" as we inhale and "still" as we exhale. Or, "abba". . ."Father." Or, "shep. . . herd", or, "Je. . . sus", with the intent of picturing God manifested in the images of scripture.

You may want to picture a scene from scripture that is a picture of comfort: the Shepherd with the wounded lamb, Jesus holding and blessing the little children, Jesus talking intimately with His disciples, Jesus looking down lovingly from the cross at Peter and His mother, touching the leper or the woman at the well, or Jesus embracing Martha at the death of Lazarus.

Releasing Rocks in the Heart: Forgiveness and Repentance

Have you ever come to someone ready to give them a warm hug and you are rebuffed with a stiffened body. Or have you ever had someone greet you warmly and you feel a harshness within your heart, a coldness and a resistance to draw close to him or her? Sometimes to approach may be dangerous and a distancing is appropriate. But sometimes your heart or another's is hardened with resentment, or anger, or frustration with which you have been unwilling to deal.

When we come into this form of active prayer, we may consciously feel as though there is a hard, granite, impenetrable rock lodged in our hearts. One of the first things we may experience is the Spirit's voice saying "what is *that* doing here?" In His presence the honesty gushes forth and He begins, without words of blame or correction, to massage with His strong, loving hands the hard rock in your heart and mine until it becomes soft and pliant.

As we invite God's presence into our inner being, the Holy Spirit brings to mind grudges, hostilities, areas of unforgiveness, deep wounding, and areas of bitterness. Jim Borst said in *Coming to God:*

> Few things close our hearts to God's grace and to his loving presence as much as resentments, lack of forgiveness and hurt feelings. Our hearts have been created for loving, from deep within ourselves to be channels of His love. Resentment and lack of forgiveness block and poison our hearts. Yet God says through the Psalmist: "Harden not your hearts . . ."[10]

The total process of forgiveness of a lifetime cannot take place in the few moments of silence we set aside each day. However, during that time of quiet, the Lord will reveal slowly and quietly areas that need to be dealt with in order to drain the leaking toxic storage vessel of your heart.

We have already spoken about the season of forgiveness. However, as we go through each day, throughout our lives we will be subject to the disappointments, hurts, and pain of living. Daily the Father will make us aware of the hard places that separate us from Him. After the season of forgiveness, we are more able to keep short accounts and free ourselves of the effects of unresolved resentments.

Awakening to God

As we prepare our hearts by being forgiven and forgiving others, we are ready to receive what God chooses to give to us in the silence. Sometimes we have to rush away before the work is completed. At other times, we may feel a rush of His love in the quiet and we are moved to tears as He speaks quietly: "My child, I love you. In you I am well pleased." We are touched in a way that melts the rocks of protection and speaks to our heart's need to belong.

Receiving His Peace

A third experience, and a very common result, is to feel nothing. We go through the motions, but do not "feel" any differently as we sit quietly. When this occurs, I must remind myself that it is for discipline and the obedience to His call—"be still and know that I am God"—that I am doing this. I even cry out on occasion, "Lord, let this time count even though I'm not feeling Your presence."

But with great relief, I notice a calm in my spirit as I reenter my world. The tension within me has left and I'm able to solve whatever nagging problem I had left at the door. We might call this a delayed reaction. Whatever we call it, we must remember that we are not dictating to God what He can or cannot do, how He will or will not reveal Himself. Seeking to be in His presence is an act of pressing in, of hanging on, of wrestling as Jacob did with the Divine presence, until He blesses us.

In time we can learn how to inhabit that inner sanctuary, the temple of our soul, wherever we are. Henri Nowen said: "Silence is above all a quality of the heart that can stay with us even in our conversation with others. It is a portable cell [inner room] that we carry with us wherever we go."[11] We can take the words we have focused on earlier into our gardening, our business meetings, our domestic chores, while standing in the grocery store line or sitting in traffic. If we are the lamb, the disciple, the child or the healed woman, we can experience anew the restorative power of being in His presence as we go through our daily routine.

Giving Praise

One of the direct results of living a more peaceful life is an awareness of how blessed we are. We have eyes for the blessings and not the woundings. Our mind becomes disciplined to focus on the abundance, and, as we do so, we are nurtured by all that we have received. Scripture says God "inhabits the praises of His people." Interestingly enough, when our thoughts are focused on pleasant thoughts and positive images, there is a corresponding biological, chemical response that allows our stress levels to reduce. We can think more clearly and become more authentic in our personal relationships; we no longer have to hide in fear that we will be found out as being deficient. Rather we will feel settled and calmed knowing we are the beloved of the Father.

The Strength for the Challenge

The autumn woman is challenged to let go of control and to learn to listen in the silence. By drawing away out of the fray of noise and demands, she knows she will continue to be strengthened for the challenges that lie ahead of her. She knows deeply that the more care she takes of herself and the more she nurtures her personal spirit, the more able she will be to go beyond herself, out of her comfort zone to those in need.

Reflection

1. When you think of being disciplined, what does that expression evoke in your mind?

2. Explore your feelings about finding a place of solitude and knowing God.

Chapter Sixteen

A Season of Harvest

❧

The last task of the autumn woman is to move out beyond the safety of her own walls and to participate in giving to the broader community. She appropriates wisdom as she yields to discipline. She understands the paradoxes of faith: we give to receive, let go to get back, die to live, be last in order to be first, be a servant in order to rule. In autumn she is nurtured primarily by the intangibles of a job well done. She accomplishes a task that no one else can or is willing to accomplish. She is satisfied with how effective she is in changing the well being of others rather than by what she acquires or by the attention she receives. Autumn is a season of altruism.

Although we may find more autumn women in the chronological season of autumn than spring women, we discover women of all ages giving of themselves to others-to their family, friends, and co-workers. Giving in a personal dimension is a vibrant and vital part of being female. On a deeper level the autumn woman is a woman who moves out from her own comfort zone of safe living and chooses to go beyond her own boundaries in ways that benefit the broader community. She is not haphazard in her giving, but is wise in where and how she expends her energy. We might say she has found her passion.

When Rosa Parks was in her late thirties she plunged unexpectedly into an autumn season of commitment and passion. She was an exhausted seamstress whose main intent was to sit and rest on her bus ride home on December 5, 1955, in Montgomery, Alabama. The only seat available was a seat designated for whites only. During that ride, a white business man demanded her seat. She refused to yield it. As a result, the bus driver had her arrested. With her arrest, the blacks and some whites boycotted the buses for 381 days. She said in a recent interview, "We were hoping it wouldn't last as long as it did. But we were not willing to go back to the buses (as long as) the same kind of treatment continued . . . We didn't go back until we could ride the buses without segregation."[1] This powerful community action today is recognized as the beginning of the Civil Rights Movement which ended official segregation in the United States. Mrs. Parks action, though uncalculated, propelled her into a current of unexpected change, challenge, and commitment.

Esther, we discovered, was also plunged into a season of committed action when her people were threatened with extinction. While she and all of the Jewish residents of Suza fasted, she planned to enter the king's presence to petition him for a reprieve. By so doing, she put her own life in jeopardy. She knew if she entered the king's presence unbidden and he did not welcome her, she would die. However, he looked on her with favor.

Her plan was to reveal the evil of Haman's heart and to request the king countermand his own order. In the course of days, Haman's evil was revealed and he was put to death. With godly irony and timing, Haman's enemy, the wise Mordecai, is elevated to chief advisor to the king. As a result, new orders are sent out. The Jewish people are given permission to fight back in order to protect themselves. As an autumn woman, Esther goes beyond what is comfortable and convenient in order to save her people. She acts for the common good, not in selfish self-interest.

As autumn women, we may not be credited with starting a successful movement that liberates a race or for saving an entire people from extinction, but we each can develop the qualities that make life meaningful. The commitment to giving away from ourselves comes with a promise from Jesus when He says "Give and it will be given to you. A good measure, pressed down, shaken together and running over, will be poured into your lap. For with the measure you use, it will be measured to you" (Luke 6:38, NIV). Giving is exponential. We give and we receive more abundantly than we can imagine. As we explore the process of giving back, we will look at the following:

- Finding meaning in life-loving and giving.
- Developing empathy: a pre-requisite to giving.
- The reasons we give.

216

- How we can give.
- A strategy for giving—dreaming an autumn dream.

Finding Meaning in Life

I've encountered a number of women of a wide variety of ages who ask the profound questions "What is the meaning of life? What's my purpose here?" In the winters of our lives we may wonder, "What is the meaning of this suffering?" Although no one can answer these questions for another, we can focus our eye's lens on what others have discovered. When we enter into an autumn season we discover the meaning in our losses.

Autumn is the season of harvest, a time to fill the barns and to then give out of the full storage centers of our hearts. For most women this is a constant part of their lives. The meaning of life comes for a woman in part through the quality of relationships and the degree of intimacy she is able to achieve with those she loves. On another level, her meaning emerges out of what she does especially if her work is meaningful. The value and meaning a woman gains from her work is in great measure based on the quality and significance of her work relationships.

Her ability to care for others leads to a very different leadership style in the business world. She has a high desire to work as part of a team and demonstrates a high degree of nurturing skills toward the members of her group. Karen Walden, editor of the magazine *New Woman,* said:

> The qualities that women bring to the office- tolerance, compassion, understanding, generosity of spirit, cooperation, and nurturing- are beginning to have an impact on both genders. One of the biggest changes is that the leadership approach of women is increasingly thought of as desirable in the mainstream workplace. People get to participate in a way they never could before. In my experience, women are very generous and successful in bringing people together, working within committees, negotiating issues in a whole different way. It's not about fighting for power; it's about sharing power. This shift to a more nurturing, loving environment is better for everybody.[2]

Some women lead out of anger, believing they must adopt a tough model or lose respect and credibility. When we abandon the feminine strengths, we abandon the gift women bring to the work force.

However, the most profound encounter that gives our life meaning is the encounter with the living God. When we discover His voice, we learn that knowing Him and His ways gives life its meaning. In that knowing we understand that nothing in our lives is ever wasted. Our failures and sins as well as our successes and joys have equally powerful meaning. Tournier observed, "The day comes when we understand that (the failures) have been more fruitful perhaps than the successes. For it is they which force us to revise our system of values."[3] And in that revision, we move from being "I" centered to "God" centered. In so doing, we move with compassion and empathy into a hurting world. The only comfort my mother could receive after my brother's death was the hope that her suffering would not be wasted, that she would be able to comfort someone else.

When we experience pain and become aware of our own short comings, we are no longer able to stand in judgment of those who are unlike us. This transformation that leads to compassionate giving is illustrated in the encounter Peter has with Jesus at the Last Supper. Peter loudly protests that he would never betray his Lord. He was above that sort of thing. His identity rested in his sense of loyalty and personal power. We can almost see Jesus stare straight into that powerful fisherman's eyes and quietly say, "Peter, I know you better than you know yourself. Once you come face to face with your sin, your weakness, your humanity, your raw self, and turn around, help your brother."[4] He knows our struggles and our weaknesses, but does not judge us for them. But rather He urges us, as he did Peter, to help someone else once we stop denying our weaknesses and face into reality.

We are to make love our aim. As we experience love in our encounter with God and others, we are mandated to pass on in loving God, ourselves, and our neighbor. John Powell summarizes well for us this section on finding meaning in life when he says:

> Love is your calling and destiny. It is the perfection of your human nature. Love is also a gift of God, the highest gift of God's spirit. It is necessary that you recognize the importance of loving yourself. . . You must acknowledge and affirm all that is good in you. You must gently try to understand all that is weak and limited. . . Your success in loving will be proportionate to your openness in accepting the love and affirmation of God. . . In the end, the success of your life will be judged by how sensitively and delicately you have loved.[5]

As in every season, we have the choice to grow in the tasks of the season or to stagnate. We have the choice to be part of the mighty rivers that flow and gush from the high mountain terrain to the sea providing water for crops and spawning ground for fish. Or, we can be like the Dead Sea into which the waters of the Jordan flow and stop. When we do not give out of ourselves we clog up and become filled with sediment, excessively salty, unrefreshing, and without meaning.

Developing Empathy—A Prerequisite to Giving

Whether by nurture or nature, women develop early the ability to give back to their environment, caring for the feelings and well being of others. Although relationships have given us definition in many areas of our lives, the autumn woman knows that she cannot always please others nor is she responsible for making them happy. If she is faced with tough moral, ethical, or spiritual choices that are not popular with those she loves, she chooses to do what is correct for her.

For most women the ability to care for and move close into relationships is an asset. But often the boundaries that give her definition become blurred. She is left emotionally exhausted, discouraged and overwhelmed in doing well. In most cases her giving emerges out of a genuine concern and empathy for others. It emerges out of a life plan of meaning and mission. In other cases, she gives to avoid conflict, to deflect criticism and to gain approval when other arenas of accomplishment are closed to her.

What contributes to this empathic core in women?

In the unique early interaction and attachment between mother and daughter, a daughter learns to show compassion and care for others by identifying with the other and develops the ability to be emotionally close. These are both qualities of the ability to empathize. In showing empathy there is a moving into the feelings of another person as if we were walking in her shoes.

The mother's deep feelings for her infant moves her to care for, protect, and sense the child's needs. In time the ability to sense the other's feelings becomes mutual, where it becomes as important to understand as it is to be understood. Women report the need for this in their primary relationships throughout their lives. This ability to understand and be understood is essential for self identity and for the feeling of connection with those she loves. However, what is difficult for women to do is to show the same degree of empathy for themselves as they show to others.

The ability to empathize connects women to others. It provides the essential ingredient to working in tandem, in their need for being a self in relationship with others rather than being independent and autonomous in their pursuits. It is her capacity to empathize that pulls a woman into the churning surf of change when the lives of others change. It is one reason why women become more depressed than men when they are isolated from those they love, feel silenced, and feel incapable of connecting in a meaningful way with those around them.

Men also develop in a nurturing environment the seeds of compassion and empathy. But for the most part, when men are called into the world of men, the necessity to connect on a deep emotional level is not part of their training. Men are very capable of empathy, but in many cases they must be reminded to incorporate empathy with the masculine qualities of strength, leadership and objectivity.

A woman's challenge is to remain true to her own needs and at the same time have compassion for another. This ability to empathize is what allows us to be the nurturers of young children, allows us to bring compassion and understanding to the work place and neighborhood, and allows us to be passionate in fighting social injustice whether privately or publicly. When coupled with a woman's sensitivity to the moving of the Holy Spirit, strong results follow.

A Woman and Boundaries

Lydia is a newly married woman in her thirties. She is depressed and overwhelmed because she says "no one listens to me or cares about the burdens I carry. I want to listen to my husband's work concerns and I need to support my mother whose husband just died. But I want equal time. However, my husband just doesn't get it. He can't or won't discuss our problems with me." I asked her what specifically she wanted from him that would ease her burden. She looked surprised and honestly said "I don't know. I guess I never thought about it that specifically." Lydia's challenge will be to pull back inside her own body instead of constantly giving out to others. and to ask herself what she needs specifically. It is our responsibility as women to know what matters and work toward our own solutions rather than blaming others who we expect to read our minds and solve our problems for us.

On the one hand we need to have a fluidity of the distance between you and me in order for us to have a deep sense of care and empathy. But I need to learn how to feel genuine compassion without loosing myself in you. We call this definition of where I end and you begin a boundary.

Women have been devalued for their ability to move into the emotional space of another (empathy) and are seen as weak willed when they opt for mercy over justice. These qualities add a vital component to a society. However, there are also times when we need to pull our personal spirit back inside our own bodies and stand firm for an issue.

The most difficult task for women is when someone genuinely needs her, and she must say, "I'm sorry, but I can't do what you request." What are some of these situations where to hold a firm boundary is crucial? One is where our personal integrity or values would be compromised. Another is when our child, or spouse, or friend is acting in a harmful way to himself/herself or toward others. The alcoholic son who wants to return home, but chooses to continue to drink and get drunk must be told, "No, you may not live with me until you choose to stop drinking destructively and get into a treatment program. I want to stay connected to you, but you choose whether you can live here with this condition."

Another situation involves a young woman who wants desperately to move out on her own, but is told by her mother that she is uncaring, selfish and thoughtless to leave home. "Mother," she might say, "I am old enough to be on my own. I love you very much, but I'm going." We can think of many others: Parents make sure a child pays restitution for property he/she willfully damages. A wife expects a spouse to be faithful in marriage. If he is not, she sets a boundary that says "you choose; you can't have it both ways." Finding the balance in each situation can create a personal crisis for women. The autumn woman continues to learn when to be empathic and yield and when to hold firm boundaries. She is a woman of discernment.

Why Do We Give?

In learning theory terms we give to get. As harsh as that may sound, we rarely continue doing something that does not in some way bring a reward. If we are engaged in an activity we say we don't want (for example an addiction), the reward is in the habit. The habit covers over a fear we are unwilling to face. Therefore it benefits us by "protecting" us even though it may not be healthy. On the other hand Jesus acknowledges the power of the reward in giving when he says "give and it will be given to you." Is it possible we can reverse this statement to read "If I choose not to give, hoard my resources, and refuse to show compassion and love to those in need, I will not ultimately receive?

If we are honest, much of our giving may not be totally because it's the right thing to do. Our giving may come out of a need to satisfy an emptiness within us. We may give out of compulsion. The "shoulds" of life are powerful. "I should help out on this committee or that one." "I should visit my parents or call them." "I should go meet that new neighbor." The second half of a "should" sentence is often, "because what will others think of me if I don't." Or, "Someone is going to punish me if I don't." If we give out of compulsion, we are trying to satisfy some inner voice that is telling us "good people do thus and so" and "I will be loved and cherished if I do this." The question to be honestly asked and answered is "what do I want to do?" The woman who gives out of compulsion may find she can quiet that voice inside by *choosing* how she wants to give and where rather than by feeling compelled to. Choosing removes resentment and improves our chances of giving in a way that we will receive back the love we desire.

What are some of the other self focused reasons we give? We may have a deep desire to be valued, needed, and recognized as special. In order to please, we have a hard time saying "no" when we are asked to give or to do something for someone. But the fragmentation leaves us weary and unsatisfied. In order to avoid shame and a feeling of rejection, we may find ways to give that are socially acceptable for the social group we are part of . . . volunteering at the local hospital, participating in the PTA of our local school, being chairperson of a committee for a local club or group. On the other hand, we may choose not to give because we don't feel we have the time, interest and may say "no one has given to me, so why should I help?" When we are honest with ourselves about our motives, we discover what need we have that is fulfilled in our giving or in our resistance to giving.

In autumn we understand that much good is accomplished with questionable motives. But we strive to be authentic givers. We find our giving more and more emerges out of a heart of love and compassion. In fact our giving becomes more focused and authentic as we understand our attitude of heart and remember we have choice. In fact we are more likely to give in areas where we have been wounded and healed.

We give because what we do matters in our culture. In addition to giving back in areas where we have a special interest, we begin to see we are part of a whole and our actions, or our inaction, has an impact culturally as well as personally. We count. In the Old Testament Book of Leviticus (19:9), God commands the Jewish people in that agrarian society to have compassion on the poor. They were to leave a portion of the harvest in the field and to leave the corners unharvested. What remained was for the poor and the transient. It wasn't a handout as they had to do their own gleaning. The command does not take away the dignity of the poor. The book of Proverbs stresses the connection between giving and our own well being: "He who closes his ear to the cry of the poor will himself cry out and not be heard" (Prov. 19:17, RSV). God builds into the ethical code of His people the responsibility of living in community. And in that responsibility the culture at large is blessed.

The autumn woman understands that her giving has spiritual importance. We literally become God's hands and feet when we give. Matthew records Jesus' startling words, "Truly, I say to you, as you did it (as you gave) to one of the least of these (the person in prison, the hungry and thirsty, the naked, the stranger, the sick) . . . you did it (gave) to me." Our faith must be acted out in a lifestyle of compassionate giving not only for those with whom we live, but for the least among us.

The autumn woman sees needs and acts. The passage doesn't say, "End starvation in Africa" or "solve the homeless dilemma in America." But it does challenge us to ask, "When I see the needy, what is my compassionate response?"

Of importance is treating those we pass with respect and dignity. One homeless man who resided at our corner shopping center had purchased paper towels and Windex. He asked if I would like my windows washed. I said "no," but I determined to give him a "handout" as I left the store. "You're denying him his dignity," a voice gently chided as I walked on. I walked back to my car and told him I had changed my mind. When I returned, I had the option to pay him more than he had asked, and he retained his self respect. Giving, we must remember, is an active response to a spiritual commitment. We give in love because we are loved.

When we give out of our surplus or our lack, we break the poverty spirit. I have always been amazed and in awe of the giving spirit in poor communities. What little they have, they share with neighbors in need. Many with larger bank accounts are reluctant to give. They live in fear of loss, of not having enough for retirement, or for their own needs and wants. By giving as a response to God's call to the greater community, we begin to trust that God is in charge of our finances and of our future. It is really an act of faith, that says, "If I give responsibly, in response to a divine directive, I may not live luxuriously, but I will not be abandoned. I will be blessed."

When we speak of giving we are not only speaking of financial resources, but of breaking the poverty mentality that says, "I don't have time," or "I'm afraid." Three years ago a local poor community was designated the murder capitol of America. One night a young man was shot to death in a bungled drug deal on the front lawn of a seventy year old woman's home. She was so outraged by the change in her community that she became a one woman crusader to board up the empty buildings where drug sales occurred and tried to stop the on street sales. She stood on her front lawn and wrote down car licenses, went up to kids on the street who were dealing drugs and confronted them and rallied her frightened neighbors to help her.

But no one was willing to move out of their comfort zone to help until her home was bombed. Then the neighbors rallied to her aid and the police increased their action. Two years later, with a new police chief who creatively added more police assisted by a more active and united community, this community has reduced its homicide rate by sixty-nine percent in just one year. The neighboring communities donated extra police services to the project. What happens to others impacts all of us. We do not live in isolation. In addition, the community developed a new pride and a renewed sense of belonging as they assisted in the project

Where Do Women Give?

Women do not wait until they have accomplished their life purpose before giving into the broader community. They find meaning in their lives, and they discover more about their value as they give of themselves to others. This giving process can be done privately or publicly. The woman who is the chief support of her own children, her grandchildren and her elderly parents may not have the time or energy to give into the community, but she develops a sense of her value as she launches other generations and helps them mature.

Neighborhood Angels

Some women give in ways that often go unnoticed, but their quiet giving enriches the lives they touch. Glenda has been a friend for many years. If she wasn't helping out a teacher in a classroom, she was a doing what was needed for the bands her children marched in. She sewed; she organized; she logged hundreds of miles to be at the band competitions. Although she is not a woman of means, she shares a casserole, or bread, or other thoughtful gesture for those she knows who are in need. My father-in-law, who had Alzheimers disease, lived with us for awhile. When I needed an early morning caretaker to ensure he was dressed and ready for his ride to the senior day care center, Glenda volunteered.

Other women who are vital for the success of organizations are the volunteers who log countless hours in civic and philanthropic organizations. As more and more of the women of our culture return to the work force by choice and out of necessity, non-profit organizations register concern that time and interest in volunteering will wane. Women have been the backbone of cultural structures in education and the arts that would not have existed if not for their volunteer support.

Another area of giving may be connected to a job you do in the work place. Often organizations plan holiday giving opportunities or have an ongoing project they support in the community through financial donations and by hands on assistance. We can find ways of contributing in this way. One woman I know was challenged to come out of her religious and ethnic ghetto when she headed a program for her work that distributed food and gifts to families in lower socio-economic communities at Christmas time. She had to coordinate with representatives of these communities in obtaining names and in coordinating distribution plans.

As economic conditions have changed, the structure of the family has also shifted and changed. More women are in the work force and more adult children are returning home. Some return home after college to save money. Their intention is to move out as soon as financially possible. Others return to stabilize their lives after a divorce, or a daughter returns with a child when there is no father to help support her. In other cases an adult child with spouse and children descend on parents when they face financial reversals. Just as parents expect to have a few years to regain a couple focus and a new vision, they have a house full.

Parents, especially mothers, who are more likely to have their own schedules and lives disrupted, become autumn angels to their adult

225

children as they assist them in stabilizing their lives and launching them with more stability into the adult world.

A Model of Autumn Giving

In spring we tried to figure out what made our heart sing and moved in relationship with our Creator to plan a dream. We implemented and re-evaluated that dream in our Summer season. The dream of our autumn woman may not be a different dream, but it may be a broader dream, with a broader vision. Or, it may be an entirely new dream that emerges in this season of authenticity when our hearts respond in compassion to the needs around us. We first feel the pain of another's suffering. Then we seek solutions to alleviate the pain. Finally we ask others to dream with us.

You may know of neighborhood autumn angels who have recognized a need locally and have acted to alleviate it. Dodie Alexander, with the support of her husband Dick, is one of those angels. When her children were in high school, she became alarmed at the increase of drug and alcohol use in her community. Dodie has an incredible ability to say tough things in gentle ways, of being unrelenting in the pursuit of what is right and of making those who disagree with her, lifelong friends.

In the late seventies she gathered a group of doctors, counselors, educators and students together first to find out what others felt the problem was. Out of these discussions a dream emerged. Alone she could do nothing. But she knew as a community there was hope of stemming the tide. Out of many hours of discussion and planning she formed what is today called the Community Health Awareness Council.[6] This community based organization provides informational services to the community and counseling services for families and children in a tri-city area for prevention and after care where drugs and alcohol have impacted children and their families.

The model bears description. The counseling center, centrally located in a downtown area of our town, is supported financially by a joint powers agreement between three adjacent towns and the elementary, high school, and junior college districts that service these towns. In addition the clients donate what they can for the services. It has become a model of what a community can do to strengthen itself and open its arms to those in need. The center's services have been used by the very wealthiest and by the transient farm worker. Dodie could have complained to herself and isolated by saying, "Oh the problem's too big. What can one person do?" But she didn't. As a result several thousand individuals and families have been helped in its fifteeen year history because one woman dared to act on her dream.

In order to discover your own autumn dream, you must be willing to

- be awakened in your personal spirit to the needs of the world around you. You may ask yourself initially, "What are the needs that touch my heart?" or "What concerns continue to knock on the door of my heart?"

- ask, "What do I need to know about myself and this fledgling idea?" You may say at this point, "I'm not the dreaming type. I don't think there's a particular call on my life or dream for me. I am a better support person of other people's dreams." We can certainly support others in their dreaming process. However, we must remember that there is a call on each of our lives, a purpose that we alone can fulfill. The challenge is to discover it.

- ask, "Who will support my dream?" We were not created to live in isolation, but corporately. The autumn woman asks friends to share her dream and asks them to make her accountable. She asks for honest feedback and for honest evaluation of where she is going.

- ask, "What does God wish to reveal to me?" When we want to know whether we are dreaming our own dream or whether we are responding to the moving of the Holy Spirit, we must set time aside to pray. Praying with the group of women, or a mixed group of men and women on a regular basis until the vision is clear, is crucial to implementing an autumn dream. In the time of praying new ideas emerge, or come after a time of sitting and quiet contemplation.

- recognize the emerging pattern of plans and ideas. The autumn dream takes time to unfold. Unlike the predictable birth of a baby after nine months, the gestation for an autumn dream varies. Esther actively waited for the details of a plan to thwart evil, but she had to act quickly. Other dreams may take longer. But as patterns emerge and plans unfold, the timetable becomes obvious.

- be willing to act. After a period of dreaming, Dodie and her colleagues had to take the courageous step of saying, "Let's make this happen." At this juncture the group searched for resources in order to become a non-profit organization and sought out professionals who could make the dream a reality. It was almost a relief to begin taking the tangible, practical steps that moved the dream from ethereal idea, to substance and form.

- take on only what we can handle at any given moment in time. Any time along the way we can become discouraged.
- let go of discouragement when we hit opposition. Discipline teaches us to center in, return to the Source of our call and the purpose for our action. We might ask, "Do I need to recalibrate and re-evaluate, or is this a natural resistance to the discomfort of change?" Or, "Is the enemy of what's 'good' creating this discouragement?"
- discern between closed doors and our impatience to move on. We must remind ourselves that the dream is a partnership with our Creator and with others who share our dream whether we are starting a counseling agency, or assisting serving lunch at a soup kitchen. The challenge continually is to let go of control and how we want things to go.

Preparation for Today

In autumn we prepare diligently for the season to follow by understanding we have purpose in this life. All of our yesterdays are preparation for the activities of today. In autumn we

- understand the process of personal growth.
- learn power and peace through personal discipline.
- give out of our storehouse for the benefit of others.
- We understand we are in partnership with our Creator to be His hands, feet, voice and arms of love to a needy world. In autumn we learn to let love be our aim.

Reflection

1. Have you ever asked yourself, "What gives my life meaning?"

2. As you look over the examples given of Autumn women, can you identify autumn qualities in your life? Are you aware of the needs in your own community? You may want to list a few and ask yourself, "Where can I make a difference? What's my personal response to problems I see in my community or in my church?"

Epilogue

❦

"*For everything there is a season* and a time for every purpose under heaven" the author of Ecclesiastes reminds us. As autumn days turn chill and winter storms burst into tranquil lives, the seasons come full circle. We are reminded once again that life is ever changing in a predictable sort of way. As women we have learned that growth comes out of sorrow, wisdom comes from knowing pain is a tutor and meaning comes with giving out of our own well of experience.

Nature reminds us of this paradox. Ocean waves relentlessly role and crash with mighty force against rock and shore season after season. With each wave the shoreline and rock shift and change. Over time caverns are carved by the pounding surf into rock. Similarly the creeping caterpillar crawls onto limb and branch and is miraculously transformed, with no effort on its part, into a beautiful butterfly. But in order to fly it must beat its wings and struggle to escape its cocoon. Green leaves change in autumn with one last burst of vibrant color. It is the nature of life to change, to be transformed from one state to another. If we, resist change and hide from life, we do not stay still. Ultimately the other choice is to die-emotionally, spiritually, and in some ways physically. Unlike the force of nature, we have a choice. We can choose to be transformed in our personal spirit, to become all that God has written in our genes and experience to be, or we can resist, stagnate and miss the meaning of the winter, spring, summer and autumn seasons of our lives.

Helen is a woman for all seasons. Her story beautifully describes a woman who has chosen to be a woman in all seasons.

"When my daughter Candice was sixteen she chose to run with a wild crowd. She and her sister attended Christian schools, entering a public high school in grade 9. We had devoted our lives to family events and had incredibly high hopes for both of our girls. When her sister went off to college, I was sad, but very excited for the challenges and experiences she would have. It was a predictable and normal transition of an emerging adult child leaving home.

"But shortly thereafter, Candice became pregnant and moved out of the house. She moved into the ghetto and married the father of her son. I hated this man and every part of what he represented for enticing my little girl away. The following three years became a nightmare that I felt would never end. I withdrew from all of my friends in shame and humiliation. My pride could not handle the well meaning and not so well meaning questions from those I knew. I didn't want to talk to anyone or see anyone. I was convinced God had abandoned me. I discovered that my perfect plan for my daughter was *not* God's perfect plan for *my* life.

"When I became a Christian, I wanted to do it perfectly. So I followed all the rules exactly and never thought about what I was doing. I did what everyone else told me to do. I had no integrity. I showed up as everyone else wanted me to be. But I never experienced the love of Christ for myself. When I hit bottom, I cried out to Him and said, "I need to know you as my friend, but I don't know what that means."

"Over the course of months Jesus dealt with me ever so gently. I had been afraid to relinquish my personal control over life. When I was a child, my alcoholic father abused me and, as the oldest daughter, I took on the role of protector to my mother and sister. In order to survive I numbed out. I totally shut down my feelings of pain, of loss, of terror, of anger and of love. I could feel other people's feelings, but never my own. During this time, I had no other choice than to let go of my daughter. I had no control over her lifestyle, her choices or her happiness. I had to relinquish all of my expectations of how things "should" be. This time was the most significant time of awakening for me. I experienced an incredible inner peace while on the surface I experienced trauma and despair.

"After an escalation of trauma in my daughter's life, she left her husband and filed for divorce. At this time, she returned to our home. Although I had visited her weekly and helped her where I could, my husband had never met his grandson who was two when they returned. I was terrified he would not welcome them. Andrew walked in the door, walked up to Bill, and looked up at him with his big brown eyes. Then he put his little hand in Bill's big one. With one look, the bond of love was sealed between them. The miracle of restoration was beginning.

"As time has passed and she has returned home, I've had to face how wrong I had been for my prejudice and judgment of an entire people based on one person. In my work I was chosen to head up a Christmas program called "Adopt a Family" where families with means buy presents and food for families without resources. I had to spend hours in the very community I hated coordinating the project. How ironic that I was picked to head this program that would benefit and bless the very community I had come to hate. My healing occurred in the exact community I blamed for my wounding. As I gave out of a deep appreciation for the love I felt from God, I was freed from my own bitterness and hatred.

"Unlike many mothers, I have been given a second chance with my daughter. Candice is still very much her own person, but as I have let go and let go and let go and have learned to feel my own feelings, Candice is free to move out and grow up too. We've had to redefine the roles of adult daughter and mother. In addition I have had to learn to look at my own history and what impact it has had on my life and the lives of my children. In many ways Candice gave me a second chance at life where I can begin to experience the richness of emotion. I am incredibly grateful for the furnace of fire."

The major task for us as women is to meet the challenge of living: to show up to life, to embrace pain and joy, to deepen our roots so that we become women growing beside streams of living water where our leaf does not wither so that in all that we do we will prosper (Psalm 1). In winter we must remember that spring will come. When we learn to embrace the lessons learned in the dark night of our souls, we will have a vibrant summer and autumn. Moses learned to wait on God's timing on the back side of the mountain before he was prepared to lead his people out of slavery into freedom. Jesus struggled with His enemy, the devil, for forty days before being prepared for a powerful ministry of giving life to others, and the apostle Paul retreated to Arabia where he learned to let go of his reliance on his personal accomplishments and personal reputation to gain a new identity and power fueled by the Holy Spirit.

Likewise, we will find the power and meaning of the seasons of our lives when we yield to the seasons of withdrawal, embrace the darkness and direct our eyes on one point of light. . . .the power of the personal, living divine light of God that eagerly and personally waits to embrace us in love: "My child," we can hear His gentle voice speak, "I love you. I will never leave you nor forsake you. I have called you out of darkness to live in the transforming light of my presence. I yearn to embrace you, to give you peace, to give you joy, to envelope you with my love. Come home, my child, and know that you have a treasured place in my heart. I have indeed written your name on the palm of my hand where I am constantly reminded of you. Test me! Ask me those tough questions you are afraid to ask: 'do you really exist? Is your nature really love and not judgment or cold indifference? How do I learn to experience your love?' I will answer you. I will comfort you. I will give you peace in all the seasons of your life."

Notes

Chapter 1: For Everything There Is a Season

1. Anne Morrow Lindbergh, *The Gift from the Sea* (New York: Vintage Books, 1965), 96.

2. Joni Eareckson Tada, *A Step Further* (Grand Rapids: Zondervan, 1980), 74.

Chapter 2: A Season of Growth

1. Erik Erikson, *Identity, Youth and Crisis* (New York: W.W. Norton & Co., Inc., 1968).

2. Iris Sanguiliano, *In Her Time* (New York: William Morrow & Co., 1978), 20–21.

3. Duane Hinders, *An Explanation of Sex Differences* (Ph.D. diss., Stanford University School of Education, 1976), 4.

4. Jean Baker Miller, *Toward a New Psychology of Women* (Boston: Beacon Press, 1976), 83.

5. Paul Tournier, *The Seasons of Life* (Atlanta: John Knox Press, 1961), 10.

Chapter 5: A Season of Loss

1. Georgia Witkin, *The Female Stress Syndrome*, 2nd ed. (New York: Newmarket Press, 1991), 88–89.

2. Thomas H. Holmes, and Richard H. Rahe, "The Social Readjustment Rating Scale," *Journal of Psychosomatic Research* 2 (1967): 213–18.

3. Herbert Freudenberger and Gail North, *Women's Burnout* (New York: Doubleday & Company, Inc., 1985), 9.

Chapter 6: A Season of Grief

1. Institute of Medicine, Marian Osterweis, Frederic Solomon, and Morris Green, eds., *Bereavement: Reactions, Consequences, and Care* (Washington, D.C.: National Academy Press, 1984), 39–40.

2. Camille Worman and Roxane Silver Cohen, *Journal of Clinical and Consulting Psychology*, July 1988.

Chapter 7: The Winter of Life

1. Cited in Morris Chalfant, "Retiring the Myths of Aging," *Evangel*, (February 1993), 24–25.

2. Paul Tournier, *The Seasons of Life*, 41.

3. Morris Chalfant, "Retiring the Myths of Aging," 24–25.

4. Imelda Madden, "The Joys of Aging." Source unknown.

5. Dornia Swanson, "Minnie Remembers," first printed in the *The Good Shepherd Trumpet*, reprinted in *The Bible Friend*, 1992.

Chapter 8: The Nature of New Beginnings

1. See chapter 6, "Humpty Dumpty's Fall: The Grief Cycle."

Chapter 9: The Freedom of Forgiveness

1. Colleen K. Benson, "Forgiveness and the Psychotherapeutic Process," a professional paper presented CAPS West Convention (June 21-24, 1990), 3.

2. Catherine Marshall, *Something More* (New York: McGraw-Hill Book Company, 1974), 42–43.

3. John and Paula Sandford, *The Transformation of the Inner Man* (Oklahoma: Victory House, Inc., 1962), 240.

Notes

Chapter 10: A Season of Awakenings

1. For further exploration of scripture on this issue see Hebrews 11, John 15: 7,16.

2. Catherine Marshall, "Prayer That Helps Dreams Come True," *Charisma* (February 1980)

3. Catherine Marshall, *Adventures in Prayer* (Virginia: Chosen Books, 1975), 3—37.

Chapter 11: A Season of Balance

1. John Powell, *Fully Human Fully Alive* (Illinois: Argus Communications, 1976), 22.

2. Dianne Hales and Jennifer Cook, "The Newest 'Disease' of American Women: Exhaustion," *Self* (June 1988), 124.

3. The reader is directed to Jean Lush's book, *Emotional Phases of a Woman's Life* for a comprehensive and clear discussion of the impact of our hormonal system on our lives.

4. Henri Nouwen, *Life of the Beloved* (New York: Crossroad, 1992), 27.

Chapter 12: A Season of Expression

1. Mary Field Belenky, Blythe McVicker Clinchy, Nancy Rule Goldberger, Jill Mattuck Tarule, *Women's Ways of Knowing: the Development of Self, Voice, and Mind* (New York: Basic Books, Inc, Publishers), 167.

2. The label for the "silent women" and the descriptions are based on research by Belenky, McVicker, Goldberger, Rule and Tarule. The names of the other levels and the illustrations are mine.

Chapter 13: Reflections of Worth

1. Ferguson and Johnson, *Trusting Ourselves, The Sourcebook on Psychology for Women* (New York: The Atlantic Monthly Press, 1990), 236.

2. Sally Conway, *Women in Midlife Crisis*, (Illinois: Tyndale House Publishers, Inc., 1983), 89.

3. Judy Foreman, "Mother-Daughter relationship may be life's longest, experts say," *Boston Globe*, 1990.

4. Harriet Goldhor Lerner, *The Dance of Anger* (New York: Harper & Row, 1985) 16, 102.

5. Susan Forward, *Toxic Parents* (New York: Bantam Books, 1989)

Chapter 14: As the Years Turn

1. Erik Erikson, *Identity ,Youth and Crisis,*

2. Mary Field Belenky, Blythe McVicker Clinchy, Nancy Rule Goldberger, Jill Mattuck Tarule, *Women's Ways of Knowing*, 155ff.

3. Laura Schlesinger, KFI talk radio, taken from the program on Friday, March 4, 1994.

4. Peter Koestenbaum, *The Vitality of Death* (Connecticut: Greenwood Press, 1971), 150.

5. Carol Tavris, "Don't Act Your Age!" *American Health Magazine,* July/August , 1989, 53.

6. Sara Nelson, "On Your Own," *Glamour*, March 1993, 154.

7. Anita Spencer, *Seasons-Women's Search for Self Through Life's Stages,* (New York: Paulist Press, 1982), 65.

8. Willard Harley, *His Needs, Her Needs*, (New Jersey: Fleming H. Revell Co., 1986) 10.

9. Gail Sheehey, "The Silent Passage-Menopause," *Vanity Fair,* October 1991, 228.

Chapter 15: Be Still and Know

1. Anne Morrow Lindberg, *The Gift from the Sea,* 50–51.

2. Henri J. M. Nouwen, *The Way of the Heart* (San Francisco: Harper, 1981), 23.

3. It is important to note that an individual who struggles with the eating disorder anorexia nervosa, where abstaining from food is a serious symptom of disease, fasting as a discipline is not recommended. The person whose body weight is severely lowered, who sees herself fat when she is skin and bone, who has lost her period, and where the obsession with food overshadows all other concerns, is encouraged to seek professional assistance from her medical doctor and an experienced counselor to correct this potentially life-threatening disorder.

4. Thomas Merton, *New Seeds of Contemplation* (A New Directions Book, 1961), 85–86.

5. Lucy Shaw, *Life Path: Personal and Spiritual Growth through Journal Writing* (Oregon: Multnomah, 1991), 58.

6. Jack Wintz, *Pathways of Prayer* (Cincinnati: St. Anthony Messenger Press, 1981), 2.

7. Nouwen, *The Way of the Heart,* 77.

8. Merton, *New Seeds of Contemplation,* 81–82.

9. Nouwen, *The Way of the Heart*, 56.

10. Jim Borst, *Coming to God In the Stillness* (Surrey, England: Eagle, Inter-Publishing Services Ltd., Guildford, 1979), 32.

11. Nowen, *The Way of the Heart,* 65.

Chapter 16: A Season of Harvest

1. 1.David Montero, "Parks reminisces about boycott nearly 40 years ago," *Orange County Register*, (February 27, 1994)

2. 2.Lynne Joy McFarland, Larry E. Senn, and John R. Childress "Leading Ladies," *New Woman,*(January 1994), 77.

3. 3.Tournier, *The Seasons of Life*, 44.

4. " . . . and when you have turned again, strengthen your brethren."
Luke 22:32(RSV)

5. Powell, *Fully Human Fully Alive,* 181–82.

6. If you are interested in information regarding the model used by The Community Health Awareness Council (CHAC)for your own community, the address is 711 Church Street, Mountain View CA 94040 or call (415) 965-2020.